Financial Innovation
and the Money Supply

Financial Innovation and the Money Supply

T. M. Podolski

Basil Blackwell

© T. M. Podolski, 1986

First published 1986

Basil Blackwell Ltd
108 Cowley Road, Oxford OX4 1JF, UK

Basil Blackwell Inc.
432 Park Avenue South, Suite 1505,
New York, NY 10016, USA

British Library Cataloguing in Publication Data
Podolski, T. M.
 Financial innovation and the money supply.
 1. Money supply
 I. Title
 332.4'14 HG226.3

 ISBN 0–631–14316–5

Library of Congress Cataloging in Publication Data
Podolski, T. M.
 Financial innovation and the money supply.
 Bibliography: p.
 Includes index.
 1. Finance. 2. Money. I. Title.
 HG173.P63 1986 332.4 85–18637
 ISBN 0–631–14316–5

Typeset by Photo·Graphics
Printed in Great Britain by T J Press Ltd, Padstow

Contents

Preface

Financial innovation has been an acknowledged, but virtually unexplored, area of economics. The monetarist counter-revolution focused attention on the salubrious effects of the control of the money supply in free market economies. It inspired the targeting of the growth rate of the money supply, which has become a feature of economic policies since the 1970s. Yet perhaps the most remarkable development has been the pace, variety and ingenuity of financial change, leaving in its wake increasing confusion about what constitutes the money supply in sophisticated, changing economies.

While claiming that its demand function was stable and its control easily achievable, monetarists presented money as an enduring asset, possessing certain unique attributes. 'Monetary' assets, however, can be created in the course of business interaction by private economic agents motivated by self-interest. Monetary restrictions induce a creative response as a consequence of which the economy can monetize other assets and alter its financial procedures and structure. It is in this context that financial innovation is presented as an under-researched topic worthy of further investigation. The book offers a perspective on existing knowledge in this field and identifies areas where new enquiries are needed.

Financial innovation, as portrayed by current literature, may give the impression that it is a phenomenon of the 1970s, coinciding with a 'breakdown' of the standard demand-for-money functions. Here it is presented as a fundamental constituent of a complex process of financial evolution, and not merely as an isolated episode in modern financial history. Indeed, it is the ancient art of overcoming constraints by creative reaction that reshapes financial markets, making them more perfect. But it is on modern innovations that attention is focused.

The impact of computer and information technology, together with competition, deregulation and financial integration at an international level, have made modern financial markets highly interdependent, flexible, contestable and conductive; but, above all, they have infused into present-day open economies a high potential for circumventive innovation, capable of altering unpredictably the relationships between variables upon whose stability the effectiveness of monetary control depends. Modern economies are thus post-money societies, where traditional distinctions between 'monetary' and 'financial' assets are too fuzzy or ephemeral to be meaningful and where observed 'monetary' regularities are likely to disintegrate once the pressure of policy is put upon them.

Part I is essentially introductory, outlining the theoretical foundations of current monetary policy design, viewing these against a broad historical background, examining the circumstances in which the modern stress on money emerged, and presenting the financial system as an evolving, flexible and increasingly interdependent mechanism generating 'financial' and 'monetary' assets and services.

Definition, identification and measurement of money in developed and changing financial systems are discussed in Part II. Intractable difficulties emerge in the search for a 'money' for purposes of macroeconomic control. Some of them are reflected in the proliferation of 'definitions' of money and in incessant adjustments to monetary aggregates and targets.

Financial innovation receives extensive treatment. Refrences to it are made throughout the text, but in Part III it becomes the principal strand. Selected financial innovations in the USA and the UK are discussed, but the importance of 'swarms' of innovations embodied in the Eurocurrency system, liability and cash management are especially accentuated. Tentative hypotheses about innovation-inducing conditions, diffusion processes and implications to traditional monetary theory and policy are explored.

The book raises a number of neglected yet important questions which challenge the accepted monetary orthodoxy and the wisdom of targeting the money supply. These issues, hitherto overshadowed by the inertia of concentration on the money supply–demand paradigm, deserve wider expo-sure and debate by academics and those engaged in banking and finance.

The text avoids technical detail and concentrates on broad issues, mainly using basic monetary theory; it avoids institutional detail, while stressing institutional change, its causes and its consequences; it avoids, as much as possible, duplicating existing texts. With such an approach, a certain threshold understanding of modern monetary economics is assumed. Thus, the book is likely to be most accessible to readers who have completed at least the first year of a standard undergraduate course in economics, essentially because certain theoretical and institutional knowledge is taken for granted.

It is hoped that the book will also interest those with more advanced economic training by drawing their attention to topics that are frequently overlooked, and that its basic message will be understood by those with a more modest training in economics. Careful documentation has been built into the text to enhance this flexibility, enabling the reader to seek introduc-tory as well as more advanced references.

This book has been completed in a short space of time, when pressures of dwindling resources generally discouraged academic achievement. Inevitably, in such circumstances it owes its existence not solely to my own efforts, but also to the indulgence and understanding of colleagues and those close to me. To them and to an anonymous reader, whose comments proved to be most valuable, I am very grateful. Naturally, I alone am responsible for any shortcomings.

Special tribute must be reserved for my wife, Lesley, and for Barbara Watson, who had to decipher my hieroglyphic script. Lesley, in addition, valiantly overcame a spiteful word processor which insisted that every other file of the book should be regularly wiped out! Sue Corbett, the publisher's economics editor, proved to be most understanding and encouraging.

— Part I —

Introduction: Money and the Financial System

—1—

Setting the Scene on Money

1.1 Money supply targets: a theoretical background

This book focuses on the nexus between the money supply and financial change, and in particular on the interrelation between monetary restraint and financial innovation. The subject is topical, since current economic policies in the West embody a strong emphasis on the control of the money stock. The theoretical inspiration of such policies, widely introduced in the mid-1970s, is the version of the quantity theory associated with Milton Friedman. The theoretical macroeconomic role of money proposed by the theory, together with its policy prescription, are sketched below. A critical evaluation and the usual contrasts with 'Keynesian' theories are omitted, for they can be found in profusion elsewhere.

The control of the money supply as an economic strategy is a recurrent theme in monetary economics. In this chapter, a broad historical perspective is given (section 1.2). This is followed by an interpretation of the evolution of the current emphasis on money as a key macroeconomic variable. Discussion is slanted towards difficulties encountered in defining money when the financial system is undergoing change, which is a principal theme developed in the rest of the book. Readers are assumed to be familiar with the basic monetary macroeconomics currently in vogue; for this reason treatment is highly concentrated and, at times, mechanical. Some theoretical concepts used here are utilized frequently in the remainder of the book.

1.1.1 *Basic monetarist theory*

Basic macroeconomic analysis today stresses that output (Y) and the price level (P) are determined by the forces of aggregate supply (AS) and aggregate demand (AD).[1] Readers should be aware that these concepts are complex and controversial, and it should be reiterated that the quantity theory interpretation is outlined mainly as a theoretical background to the current policy design.

In the monetarist economic scheme, the AS incorporating the assumption of perfectly competitive factor markets is usually portrayed as a perpendicular function in the P–Y space (figure 1.1), with real factors determining the 'natural' rate of output (corresponding to a 'natural' rate of employment).

AD reflects desired expenditure at various combinations of price levels and output. It can be derived from the IS–LM analysis (incorporating flexible prices) with which most students of economics are familiar and which is briefly summarized in the appendix to this chapter. At a given price level, AD is a locus of points at which the money market and the real sector are in equilibrium at various interest rates and corresponding income levels (see appendix). Monetarists believe that it is changes in the monetary demand (viz. in nominal money supply M – see (A1.18) and (A1.18a) in the appendix) that exert the decisive influence on the aggregate demand. At a given price level, AD would rise (shift to the right) mainly following a rise in M and fall (shift to the left) following a fall in M.

In a market economy where markets operate freely and flexibly, the equilibrium level of prices and of income (output) would be determined by the interaction of AD and AS. With reference to figure 1.1, given AS_0 and AD_0, in equilibrium, the price level P_0 and output Y_n would result. In such a scheme, changes (shifts) in AD would lead to price changes without altering output. Thus, a rise from AD_0 to AD_1 would result in the price increase to P_2 without affecting Y.

However, in real life, which brings with it price and wage inflexibilities, changing expectations, various 'frictions' in exchange and production (such as contractual stickiness) and adjustment delays, responses to changes in AD may not simply be traced out along AS. The essential features of these may be captured by including in the analysis a short-run aggregate supply curve (SAS in figure 1.1) which conveys market imperfections or a state of expectations of prices. The flatter the SAS schedule, the greater are assumed to be market frictions or expectational discrepancies. Thus, a rise in AD from AD_0 to AD_1, would, if SAS_0 were the effective aggregate supply relationship, result in output increase to Y_1 and price increase to P_1.

Schools of thought that find their root in classical free market theories regard all deviations of output and prices from equilibria depicted by the equality (intersection) of AS and AD in the model in figure 1.1 as transient or temporary, requiring no external remedial intervention or guidance from the state (by demand management). Thus, point Z_1 in figure 1.1 represents a state of full (multi-market) equilibrium, but a rise in AD_0 to AD_1 may involve some *temporary* stickiness on the supply side of the economy and a movement along the SAS_0 schedule to Z_2, during which both prices and output rise to P_1 and Y_1, respectively. However, 'catching-up' adjustment processes will develop, and SAS will drift upwards (along Z_2Z_3), raising prices and

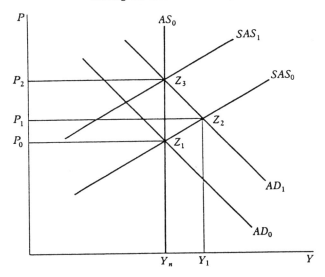

Figure 1.1 Determination of income and price level.

reducing output until final equilibrium is established at Z_3, resulting in a higher price level at P_2 but with output at the original, 'natural' level.

This is a simplified version of an economic mechanism associated with the followers of Friedman, who claim that a rise in the nominal supply of money would lead to a temporary output (and employment) rise, but that in the long run adjustment would be solely in the price level. Thus, *money is neutral in the long run, but not in the short-run.* 'I regard the description of our position as "money is all that matters for changes in nominal income and for short run changes in real income" as an exaggeration but one that gives the right flavour to our conclusions' (M. Friedman, 1970, p. 217).

The long-run neutrality of money is highlighted: 'We shall regard long-run equilibrium as determined by Walrasian equations of general equilibrium, which determine real variables, plus the quantity theory, which, for given real variables, determines the price level' (Friedman and Schwartz (hereafter F–S), 1982, p. 60). Money supply changes always affect the price level, and 'inflation is always and everywhere a monetary phenomenon' and can be counteracted only by monetary means.

The adherents of the 'new classical macroeconomics' (NCM), which links the principles of general equilibrium with rational expectations hypothesis, claim that, provided a change of monetary policy is properly announced and thus anticipated by economic agents, it would lead to a change in the price level without disturbing real variables. This is the so-called 'policy impossibility theorem', implying that a rise in the nominal quantity of money would result in an immediate shift of AD from AD_0 to AD_1 in figure 1.1 along Z_1Z_3, leading directly to the price increase from P_0 to P_2. However, a shock or 'surprise' monetary rise, not anticipated by economic agents, would lead to movements of output and prices initially along SAS_0, before final adjustment at Z_3.

1.1.2 *Control of the money stock: objectives*

Currently pursued monetary policies in the West have their origin in the Friedman version of monetarism, and references to monetarists in the remainder of the book are essentially to the Friedmanite variety. NCM, which may be considered to be, in a theoretical sense, as much contrary to Friedmanite monetarism as it is to varieties of 'Keynesianism', is still regarded by politicians and central bankers as an academic research programme. Friedman and Schwartz (1982, p. 65) consider that 'the theory of rational expectations has been extremely fruitful on an analytic level but as yet is in a preliminary stage as a source of empirically testable hypotheses about the formation of expectations.'

The money neutrality theory links monetarists with their classical predecessors. 'Money is a "veil." The "real" forces are the capacities of the people, their industry and ingenuity, the resources they command, their mode of economic and political organisation and the like.' Nevertheless, 'there is hardly a contrivance man possesses which can do more damage to a society when it goes amiss' (F–S, 1963a, pp. 696–7). In another context, Friedman (1968b, p. 371) agreed with J. S. Mill that money was an 'extraordinarily efficient machine' facilitating exchange. 'Because it is so pervasive, when it gets out of order, it throws a monkey wrench into the operation of all other machines.'

The principal aim of a monetarist policy is thus to stop money going amiss. Monetarists claim that there is only one safe way of doing this. Although the theoretically postulated relation between money and variables such as nominal income is stable and reliable, especially over long runs, empirically it is not precise and is subject to variable time lags. Over very short periods it is indeed 'loose'. Furthermore, information about the state of the economy and the lags involved in political decision-making all militate against policies of discretionary, anticyclical changes in the quantity of money. 'Too late and too much has been the general practice' (Friedman, 1968a, p. 373).

Indeed, activist policies are considered to be a major independent source of economic instability. Friedman's famous prescription for achieving stability in the economy is for monetary authorities to adopt 'publicly the policy of achieving a steady rate of growth in a specified monetary total' (1968b, p. 373).

In spite of methodological and theoretical differences between NCM and other schools of thought, NCM's policy prescriptions, at this stage of the school's development, coincide with those of the followers of Friedman (see Lucas, 1981, pp. 249–60; Minford and Peel, 1983, pp. 79–92). An adherence to rules of behaviour, such as a long-run k per cent growth rate of the money supply, is advocated. Such a prescription is not considered to be optimal, but in the 'present state of knowledge' and 'with the currently available expertise' in policy-making, simple rules are preferred to activist policy (see, e.g., Lucas, 1981, esp. pp. 248–61; Minford and Peel, 1983, esp. ch. 5). It would provide the economy with a stable monetary environment in which agents could undertake their decisions knowing what they could expect money and price levels to be in the future. This policy congruence provides a justification for not giving considerably more attention to NCM throughout the book.

To conclude, for monetarists and NCM, the quantity of money is a critical variable for controlling the level of prices, being, certainly in the long-run, unable to influence the real economy. Monetary policy, in the context of traditional demand management, is superfluous and potentially harmful, for increases in AD might bring about some unnecessary transient disturbances, ultimately and inevitably resulting in inflation. Monetary policy should thus be passive, designed to control the *growth of the money stock at a steady rate*. No other role is envisaged for state intervention except perhaps measures to free the price mechanism from unnecessary frictions by various ways which today are often labelled 'supply-side economics' (e.g., lower income taxes as a way of improving incentives, trade union legislation as a way of counteracting monopolistic power in labour markets, privatization as a way of increasing competition).

1.1.3 *Monetary targets: 'practical monetarism'*

High rates of inflation, accompanied by heavy unemployment in the 1970s, created a climate conducive to the abandonment of the orthodox remedies of demand management and made the simple monetarist prescriptions appealing as a political and economic alternative. The same high rates of inflation also made it difficult to adopt the steady k per cent rule. It was felt that 'practical monetarism', in the form of policies of steadily falling intermediate monetary targets, was necessary in the first instance to bring down gradually the rate of inflation to a more acceptable level. Thus, short- or medium-term monetary targets became a feature of monetary policies introduced in the 1970s (OECD, 1979; Foot, 1981).

There are also some additional arguments advanced in support of intermediate monetary targeting. Monetary policy is likely to be more effective in a system of floating exchange rates than in a situation of pegged rates. However, under the fixed exchange rate regime governments were forced to exercise some degree of discipline over their domestic expenditure in order to maintain the external value of their currency. Monetary targets are seen as an alternative way of enforcing the maintenance of financial discipline in the absence of the fixed exchange rate constraint, which was widely abandoned during the 1970s.

Money is often regarded as an information variable. One implication of the hypothesis of a stable relation (but subject to lags) between money and nominal income is that changes in the supply of money contain reliable information about future changes in nominal income or inflation.[2] Particular emphasis is thus placed on the value of money targeting in influencing expectations. It is claimed that, if money targets were clearly announced and firmly pursued, they would affect expectations of wage and price changes on the part of decision-taking units and would reduce uncertainty. Thus, monetary targets have been introduced in the belief that they would dampen inflationary expectations, and in this context they were compared to an aspect of the old-fashioned 'moral suasion' (Sumner, 1980, p. 109).

The importance of the announcement effect is stressed particularly by the NCM. It should, however, be remembered that the strength of this psychological effect depends on credibility; frequent changes in targets, overshot targets and observed failures to achieve expected ultimate results would substantially weaken its impact.[3] Little evidence is available on the strength of the announcement effect. Nevertheless, it is often prominent among arguments in favour of targeting the money supply (see, e.g., Bank of England (hereafter BE), 1978, p. 34); to some, it is a *sine qua non* of successful targeting (e.g., Sargent, 1981, p. 101).

Monetary targets are also said to set a clear aim for monetary authorities and a more precise and objective measure of success of central bank control procedures than the traditional policies designed directly to influence nominal income or the price level. Thus, by observing the marksmanship of monetary authorities, their technical competence can be assessed more objectively (Sumner, 1980).

Targeting is a two-stage procedure involving questions of controllability and causality (Courakis, 1981, pp. 286–93; Bryant, 1983, ch. 8). First, monetary authorities, by manipulating monetary instruments such as interest rates (used by the authorities in the UK) or monetary base (advocated by monetarists), attempt to hit the monetary target previously announced by the authorities. Second, the adjustment of nominal income to the targeted money rests on the proposition that a stable and predictable relationship does exist between the money supply and nominal income. This scheme is consistent with the economics of the demand for money outlined in section 1.4.

The quantity theory indicates that only one 'money' should be targeted. For a long time, Friedman held a strong and unwavering view on the selection of the 'money' supply for purposes of control based on money targets. In his seminal work on monetary policy (1968b) he stated that 'monetary total is the best currently available immediate guide or criterion for monetary policy – and I believe that it matters much less which particular total is chosen than that one be chosen.' Viewed against the background of the 1960s, when it seemed that the 'definition' of money did not matter (see section 1.4.2), this statement is not, perhaps, astonishing, and appears to stress the need for monetary discipline in economic policy. What is astonishing is that, after considerable accumulation of experience suggesting that the growth of various monetary aggregates can vary in opposite directions, Friedman's view has not altered. He reiterated recently: 'It matters far less whether that aggregate is M1-A or M1-B, M2 or M-n than that a single aggregate be chosen' (1981b, p. 6). Among other procedures, he urged that a long-term target path be set 'for a single aggregate – for example M2 or the base. It is less important which aggregate is chosen than that a single aggregate be designated as the target' (1982, p. 117).

The selection of a 'money' as a target variable is not central to the main theme of this book. It emphasizes, however, the need to investigate carefully the nature and problems of defining and measuring money, which, as we shall see, is not easy in our changing financial environment.

1.2   The meaning of money: a historical perspective

Modern monetary theory has developed as if no serious problems with the meaning and definition of money existed, or as if these problems were, at worst, rather semantic, or a matter of selecting an appropriate M from officially published 'money' series. The Governor of the Bank of England (BE, 1973, p. 193), having observed that there might be many different definitions and computations of the money supply, suspected that 'a number of people who make confident pronouncements about the money supply have never stopped to ask themselves which version they have in mind and why. Yet it does make a difference.'

When economists do focus on the question of what constitutes money in an economy, serious disagreement emerges. This is by no means a new phenomenon. Macroeconomic thought has been dominated by a search for a variable called 'money' which is definable, quantifiable, controllable, and linked in a stable and predictable way with other macroeconomic variables such as nominal income or the price level. Yet it has been one of the more curious characteristics of monetary debate that controversies concerning the role of money in the economy proceeded without a clarification of the underlying concept of money, and certainly without a clear indication of what constituted the money stock of the theoretical discourse. Nevertheless, in major polemics in monetary history, the view taken, often implicitly, on the meaning of money was connected with the broader vision of monetary macroeconomics (Johnson, 1962, pp. 351–5).

At the turn of the century, A. P. Andrew (1899) observed that

It is a singular and, indeed, a significant fact that, although money was the first economic subject to attract men's thoughtful attention, and has been the focal centre of economic investigation ever since, there is at the present day not even an approximate aggreement as to what ought to be designated by the word. [Andrew, 1899, p. 219]

Some economists confined money to mean legal tender; others broadened it to include a variety of financial instruments and even further, so that 'in the end all goods are of the nature of money in so far as they possess a value in exchange ... such is the bewildering confusion of language which confronts the student of monetary problems on the very threshold of his investigations' (p. 224).

The situation today is no different. 'While economists have probably spilled more printers' ink over the topic of money than any other, and while monetary theory impinges on almost every other conceivable branch of economic analysis, confusion over the meaning and nature of money continues to plague the economics profession' (Davidson, 1978, p. 140). Though the fluidity of concepts is not unusual in social sciences, the terminological confusion and the lack of a generally accepted notion of money make it difficult, if not impossible, to carry out a systematic investigation of the role of money in the economy.

1.2.1 *Currency theories of money*

Indulging in very broad generalizations, we can identify two principal strands of thought concerning the meaning attached to money in monetary controversies. Some economists tended to regard money as a clearly identifiable and homogeneous asset. We shall label such views 'currency theories' of money, whose antecedents are to be found in the well-known nineteenth-century bullionist and currency school propositions.[4] Such theories were predominantly catallactic, with a strong emphasis on the importance of a medium of exchange to the effective development of the economy. They overshadowed state or chartalist theories of money, which also looked for a specific definition but stressed money as a creature of the law (Knapp, 1924), and the pervading influence of government sovereignty and legislative force in settlements of trade contracts.[5]

Currency theories tend to define money narrowly, often in terms of a commodity or quasi-commodity standard, and also to stress the enduring and robust character of money thus defined. In their scheme, money remains essentially the same institution as that which has overcome the inefficiencies of primitive barter. Its source is somehow largely independent of the activity within the economy (that is, money is exogenous), and it retains the same basic features regardless of the changing commercial and technological complexities of economic processes as the economy advances. The development of credit in various forms and of new financial institutions are variously regarded as devices for increasing safety and convenience in handling money, for increasing the efficiency of the use of money, as forms of finance essentially redistributing saving to deficit units, or as alternatives to tangible wealth; but somehow they are not regarded as usurping the qualities of money, which remains a unique asset.

Where, in the considerations of currency theorists, money is not thought to have unambiguous qualities not possessed by other financial assets, the issue of substitutability between money and other assets, if debated at all, tends to be confined to a narrow alternative: over a period of history, to bank notes for bullion, demand deposits for bank notes and time deposits for demand deposits. The quantity of money is often quite mechanically and, regardless of how it comes about, *causally and directly* linked to prices, certainly in the long run. In an early version of the quantity theory, money was likened to a liquid whose level when poured into a bottle identified the price level (Scitovsky, 1969, p. 66). Though, in the more recent versions, complexities of the economy are not denied, somehow these are contained in a 'black box' housing very stable mechanisms which translate monetary impulses into predictable nominal income or price level outcomes.

Related to this is the stress on the stability of the velocity of circulation of money. Though often regarded as a measure of efficiency in the use of money, it is nevertheless presented as a constant or institutional datum which changes very slowly, if at all, and is unaffected by variables such as the value of transactions or the price level.

The policy implications and prescriptions of currency theories involve a strict control over the creation of money, preferably automatically through a set of rules such as ingot plans, gold standard or constant monetary growth rate. The money supply 'is selected as that part of the whole debit–credit system which is essentially capable of being controlled. Control the money supply, said Quantity theorists, and the rest of the debit–credit system must fall into line' (Hicks, 1965, pp. 282–3). The financial system in this paradigm was compared to a concertina – a pressure on the monetary end would leave the whole thing squeezed (Cramp, 1962, p. 5). Thus, a monetary restriction (usually on an arbitrarily defined 'banking' sector) would not be offset by the action of other financial agents, which are looked at essentially as intermediaries in saving and investment processes and not as the creators of alternative 'money'.

1.2.2 *Financial theories of money*

One is tempted to use the traditional label of 'banking' to describe those propositions that deny the validity of currency theories. However, that label was used to categorize the nineteenth-century views which highlighted the role of the banking system as the prime supplier of fiduciary and flexible 'money' and as the dominant financial intermediary. To emphasize a further evolution from that structure, we shall call them 'financial theories'. It is urged in this text that the exclusion of considerations of broader financial markets is liable to give us an incomplete, if not distorted, view of 'monetary' matters.

A search for the origin of financial theories of money need not detain us. It was evident to the classical economists in the Industrial Revolution that the emergence of the credit system (essentially, bank credit system) altered the meaning of money (currency) as a medium of payment and a macroeconomic variable. New financial assets appeared, and their genesis was not independent of the business situation; the more complex credit relationships that developed cast doubt upon the existence of a direct mechanical dependence between the orthodox money and prices.

In *A Treatise on Money* (1971), Keynes, though he remained essentially in the framework of the currency theories, urged that the relationship of the quantity of money, the velocity of circulation and the price level 'is not of that direct character which the old-fashioned quantity equations, however carefully guarded, might lead one to suppose' (vol. 1, p. 132). The banking and credit system and the rate of interest played a vital part in his transmission process of monetary changes. Such developments later crystallized into theories that considered monetary influence operating on macroeconomic variables through complex channels. *The General Theory* (Keynes, 1973) and the Radcliffe Report (1959) were in this mould.

As the financial system developed, it became increasingly difficult to distinguish between 'money' and other means of settlement of debts. Economists thus often referred to 'circulating media',[6] which usually included coins, bank notes and deposits and sometimes other instruments, such as bills of exchange and promissory notes. Differentiated circulating media signified a dispersion of the function of the means of payment over a variety of instruments.

What constituted circulating media was rarely precisely defined. Sometimes the media included 'all we pay with' (Schumpeter, 1963, p. 699), and became a broadly understood 'money' appropriate for a financial structure more complex than that of a more primitive metallic standard. Which circulating media functioned as money emerged from the *general financial practice and custom*, which evolved as a result of a number of economic and technological pressures. The media preserved the status of 'money' for as long as confidence of the users was maintained.

In contrast to currency theories, the financial approach considered that the stock of circulating media held by the public at any time was not determined exogenously, but was related to the preferences of the public itself. 'The money quality of assets is something imposed by the business habits of people; it is attached in varying degree to various assets; and the attachment can be and is varied over time in a completely unpredictable manner' (Sayers,

1957, p. 5). The pressure of real demand as a factor in the generation of circulating media was often stressed. In this connection the 'real bills' or 'commercial bills' theory of banking received support. It claimed that the media developed from the interaction between economic agents and were essentially a response to business needs or the needs of trade.[7] This implied the absence of an effective barrier to the expansion of circulating media for as long as real demand existed. Provided loans were issued against a good self-liquidating security, ensuring a future inflow of goods on to the market, they were not thought to be inflationary.

Some adherents of financial theories do not necessarily reject the concept of narrowly defined 'money' (essentially, coin and notes), but its unique position in the set of other means of exchange is denied, and such money is considered to be only *one of the financial variables relevant to macroeconomic analysis*. The state may decide what legally serves as money, but the market chooses the 'money' of economic transactions in general. Indeed, narrow 'money' might well play a significant role in the financial system. Schumpeter (1963) expressed it for economies much less sophisticated than today's Western economies:

> The huge system of credits and debits, of claims and debts, by which capitalist society carries on its daily business of production and consumption is then built up step by step by introducing claims to money or credit instruments that act as substitutes for legal tender and are allowed indeed to affect its functioning in many ways but do not oust it from its fundamental role in the theoretical picture of the financial structure. [Schumpeter, 1963, p. 717]

In this evolutionary view, the case for money is constructed from the inefficiencies of barter, and the case for the banking and financial system is constructed from money (narrowly specified). Thus, on the base of such money, we have superimposed a complex system of liquid assets. It is the financial system that monetizes the assets, giving them the quality of encashability with acceptable transactions costs and little risk of capital loss. The fact that such assets are convertible into the 'money' supplied by the monetary authorities is an important factor in maintaining confidence in the financial system.

In this paradigm, if the velocity of circulation of money is utilized in economic analysis, then, in contrast with currency theories, it is regarded as unstable and as being related to changes in the quantity of circulating media. If money remains only narrowly defined and its quantity becomes restricted, then real demand can be accommodated through an increased use of money substitutes or the emergence of new substitute instruments, resulting in a rise in the velocity. Late in the nineteenth century, Wicksell (1936, pp. 54–100) argued that new forms of credit reduce the need to hold money (cash) and that there is no theoretical limit to the velocity of circulation. Such views were echoed, in defiance of the quantity theory tradition, by Keynes (1973, p. 299), the Radcliffe Committee and others to be mentioned later.

The financial system, in the context of financial theories, has been likened to a balloon – squeezing the monetary part would effect a compensating bulge elsewhere (Cramp, 1962, p. 5). Such a vision of the behaviour of the financial economy implies the futility of controlling the narrow money supply and the need, if control is required, to subject the whole financial sector to the same kind of control or influence so as to internalize asset substitutions which would otherwise take place.

R. S. Sayers (1960), for instance, developed a theory which was a logical descendant of earlier propositions going as far back as Thornton, who saw no possibility of drawing a line between circulating media and various devices facilitating exchange (bills, book debts) and regarded any control of the money supply as neither possible nor desirable (Reisman, 1971). Sayers rejected the paradigm of a distinct and identifiable category of money and the velocity of circulation as its analytical satellite. Viewing monetary management from the standpoint of a policy to influence economic activity, he stressed the futility of controlling money defined in terms of any subset of financial claims, because of an inevitable frustrating effect of new money substitutes and portfolio adjustments which would eventually make the controlled quantity a 'small change' of the payments system.

The important thing to note from the above sketch is the impact of financial evolution and the developing financial structure on the changing perceptions of money and its role. With the evolution of a more complex financial structure, it became more difficult to define money clearly, either as a means of payment or as a macroeconomic variable capable of influencing nominal income or prices. Furthermore, the independence of the money supply from real developments in the economy was questioned as fiat money replaced traditional commodity-based money.

1.2.3 *Chronic ambiguities*

Monetary theory and the relevance of its policy propositions have suffered from our neglect of definitional issues. Referring to the great monetary debates of the eighteenth and nineteenth centuries, Schumpeter (1963) commented:

> There is indeed a flavour of primitivity, not to say crudity, about the conceptualisation of those economists which at the time or later led to various misunderstandings and futile controversies. This is no mere matter of terminology. In the case before us, hazy terminology was the result of haziness of thought about what money is and what money does. [Schumpeter, 1963, p. 698]

Though in the late nineteenth and early twentieth centuries economists continued to debate the nature and functions of money, discussions 'did not excite much interest and without exception did not produce very interesting results' (ibid., p. 1086). Essentially, economists thought that 'money is what money does' (Viner, 1955, p. 247), and not very much attention was paid to precise definitions during the debates on Fisher's exchange equation. Many economists, such as W. C. Mitchell (1927, e.g. pp. 117–122) and even H. C. Simons (1936, e.g. p. 5), who foreshadowed current monetarism, preferred to use the term 'circulating media' rather than money. The term faded out of use with the Keynesian emphasis on the money stock in the liquidity preference theory of interest rates; the money stock thus became a key variable of modern monetary macroeconomics.

The participants of the latest monetary debates do not seem to have learned from past misdemeanours. Theoretical polemics on the role of money have taken place with little or no consensus as to what money is and what constitutes its components in a financially complex economy. 'Lately there has been much talk about money and even less agreement than heretofore about what it is' (Mason, 1976, p. 525). In the 1960s (as will be seen later) little attention was given to the definition of money – with rather unfortunate consequences in the 1970s, when specific measures of money became necessary for purposes of monetary policies based on monetary targets.

The meaning of money, as in the past, has remained ambiguous.

> The ambiguity arises from the use of the same concept – money – to denote an asset that is important for explaining changes in the price level and an asset that renders a variety of 'services', usually summarized by some indefinable phrase. These phrases include, but are not limited to, 'medium of exchange', 'liquidity', 'synchronisation of receipts and payments' and 'a temporary abode of purchasing power'. [Meltzer, 1969b, p. 30]

Such ambiguities, together with further ambiguities arising from the concept of money of macroeconomics, will be discussed in later sections.

If only the ambiguities were of a semantic nature, the problem would not be serious. One could perhaps simply suggest different names for different monies (Bryant, 1980, p. 44). However, as mentioned earlier, different concepts of money, often held only implicitly, are an integral part of wider controversies concerning the working of the economy. Definitional issues become inextricably entangled with substantive propositions and imply different approaches to measurement. Not infrequently, definition and measurement, which are logically distinct, though related, processes, are confused in economic literature.

> [Economists] have not paid sufficient attention to the conceptual, analytical, and technical issues involved in defining and measuring the money stock and

other monetary aggregates. Many treat definition and measurement as identical issues and as an easily solvable technical problem (best left to the Fed), while others seem to imply that the whole matter is not crucial for their analytical or empirical work – any one of the M's will do. [Lombra, 1980, pp. 274–5]

It is thus useful to distinguish between 'money' as a concept employed in analytical and theoretical analysis and 'money' as a measured or more tangible counterpart of it. We shall refer to the latter as an *indicative definition* which 'describes money by its observable characteristics, for example notes and coin, bank deposits and so on' (Casson, 1981, p. 54).

1.3 Focusing on the money stock

1.3.1 *The Keynesian influence*

The introduction of money into the macroecnomic system was an important element of Keynesian economics. In the liquidity preference theory, Keynes insisted that it was the supply of money and the demand for speculative balances that determined the rate of interest. Lengthy debates with Robertson and Ohlin, who asserted that the interest rate was the price not of money, but of credit or loanable funds, ended rather inconclusively. However, it was the Keynesian position which became the accepted orthodoxy, challenged now mainly by some monetarists, who assert that 'The "price" of money is not the interest rate, which is the "price" of credit' (Friedman and Schwartz, 1982, p. 26).[8]

Thus, the stock of money in the Keynesian theory became an important variable in the formation of national income (formalized in the *IS-LM* model – see appendix to this chapter) and not just, as in the crude quantity theory, in the determination of the general price level. Generations of students of economics accepted this situation almost for granted.

The Keynesian model, presented in the *General Theory*, incorporates a developed financial system in which 'money' is bank money. Yet Keynes's money supply, and certainly the money supply as used in most textbook interpretations, is exogenous and does not fundamentally differ from commodity-based money in a primitive financial system usually portrayed in early versions of the quantity theory.[9] In that sense, it is indistinguishable from the 'money' of monetarists.

Economists traditionally associated metallic standards with 'sound money', which promoted price stability. The desire for such stability is common to all economists, but the question of what constitutes 'sound money' in a modern, financially sophisticated economy is, as already observed, a source of bitter divisions between them.

Yet not all economists accepted the clear perception that M was some specifically defined stock of money. Hicks, the principal creator of the

IS-LM model, did not necessarily interpret M as a *single asset, money*. Though the initial construction of *LM* (called *LL* then) was based on M being the given quantity of money, when the construction was completed, Hicks generalized the schedule:

> Instead of assuming, as before, that the supply of money is given, we can assume that there is a given monetary system – that up to a point, but only up to a point, monetary authorities will prefer to create new money rather than allow interest to rise. Such a generalised LL curve will slope upwards only gradually – the elasticity of the curve depending on the elasticity of the monetary system (in the ordinary monetary sense). [Hicks, 1937, p. 140]

The important stress in our context is not on the operation of the monetary authorities, but on the fact that Hicks looked at *LM* as representing the *monetary system* rather than just the equilibrium of the money demand and supply at various combinations of interest rates and income. He used this extended concept of *LM* in other contexts, such as the trade cycle theory, where he again conceptualized *LM* as 'a relation holding with a given monetary system rather than with a given supply of money in the sense of bank credit' (Hicks, 1950, p. 146). Revisiting the subject recently, he observed that such an interpretation makes it 'unnecessary to raise those puzzling questions of the definition of money, which in these monetarist days have become so pressing' (1980–1, p. 226).

Attempts to widen the attention of economists to embrace not just 'money', but the activities of the whole financial sector, and to link these with aggregate expenditure, were made in the 1950s and early 1960s by J. G. Gurley and E. S. Shaw in the USA and R. S. Sayers and the Radcliffe Report in the UK. After a limited success, they were overshadowed by the writings of monetarists, who, in the 1960s and 1970s, refocused study and research on the money supply. Using the terminology of the previous section, emphasis shifted from financial theories of money to the currency view. Thus, the topic of financial change and innovation was relegated from its mainstream position to the water's edge, while empirical associations between money ('somehow' or 'however' defined) and other macroeconomic variables became the fashionable preoccupation.

Meltzer (1969b, p. 28) commented that 'much of the active empirical work on the financial institutions, that six years ago seemed to promise a richer analysis of financial markets ... has been relegated to the policy literature where activity waxes and wanes with decisions of regulators to favour one sort of financial instruments or another.' Undergraduate curricula began to focus increasingly on money, to the *neglect of the financial system from which all modern 'money' emanates* and which has been playing a progressively important part in the economy.[10] Though today interest in broader financial matters is returning, 'students of economics often reach the end of their courses with only the most basic knowledge of the financial system' (Bain, 1981, p. viii).

1.3.2   *The monetarist influence*

Of all monetarists, Friedman was particularly responsible for selecting money, to the exclusion of other financial variables, as the *dramatis persona* of macroeconomic processes. Described by one of his academic opponents as 'a man of unusual ingenuity and powers of persuasion, but also an impish character of whom one can never be sure whether he is serious or just kidding ...' (Kaldor, 1981, p. 452), he produced, in collaboration with A. J. Schwartz (hereafter F–S), a massive and scholarly trilogy (1963a; 1970; 1982) devoted primarily to the money supply.

The first part of the trilogy, probably the most influential, opens its 860-page exposition with a typically clear announcement that 'This book is about the stock of money in the United States' (F–S, 1963a, p. 3). The concept of money portrayed is quite static and is consistent with that of currency themes outlined earlier. It is imbued with the characteristics more of a commodity money than a fiat money in a continuously changing financial system. Indeed, F–S stress their preference for a monetary system whose operations would not be far removed from a commodity money system. Any arrangement whereby monetary authorities would deliberately respond to events by adjusting the supply of money in the interest of stabilization was decidedly rejected.

> The blind, undesigned, and quasi-automatic working of the gold standard turned out to produce a greater measure of predictability and regularity – perhaps because its discipline was impersonal and inescapable – than did deliberate and conscious control exercised within institutional arrangements intended to promote monetary stability. [F–S, 1963a, p. 10]

The institutional arrangement necessary to enforce a fixed monetary growth rate advocated by the authors is essentially a device which would make modern 'money' behave like a more primitive, metallic money. (Hicks, 1967, pp. 166–8).

In the course of a detailed study of nearly a century (1867–1960) of American monetary history, during which many institutional and structural changes took place, the money stock in F–S (1963a) retains the same definition (currency and all bank deposits) and seems to transcend all changes in the structure of the economy. Indeed, the authors' basic conclusion is that, in spite of changes in both external and internal arrangements, the impact of changes in the stock of money on the rest of the economy appeared highly stable. The close and stable association between money and economic activity, nominal income and prices, is interpreted in terms of a causal relation triggered by money. Macroeconomic variables such as nominal income and prices are, in general, 'dancing to the tune called by independently originating monetary changes' (1963a, p. 686).

The independent source of monetary changes is highlighted – money does not, in general, appear to reflect changes in the underlying economic activity. F–S do not deny that business conditions can influence the creation of money, but predominantly the money stock changes are not derived from them; money is 'clearly the senior partner', especially over longer periods.[11]

> The existence of an important independent influence running from money to income explains the contrast we have noted between the variability in monetary arrangements during the near-century we have studied and the stability of the relation between changes in money and in other economic variables. [F–S, 1963a, p. 694]

The development of the financial system, together with new intermediaries and financial instruments, were interpreted as secular phenomena attributed to the growth of wealth and to structural changes in the economy brought about by factors such as industrialization, corporate economy, and a switch from direct ownership to the holding of claims. Thus, new financial assets were seen more as substitutes for real assets than as substitutes for money. They could exert an influence on the velocity of circulation of money, but the dominant influences on velocity were expectations concerning the future stability (F–S, 1963a, pp. 644–72). Even the post-1945 rapid rise of savings and loans associations in the USA (building societies in the UK) is interpreted in this way and was not deemed to have had the effect of diminishing the demand for money.

F–S reasserted this view recently (1982, pp. 34–6). Though admitting that theoretically the money supply function depends on the financial structure, they claimed that it was not possible to judge whether the impact of institutional change had major or minor effects on the function. They thus accept that the nominal quantity of money is independent of the variables entering the demand function and can therefore 'be treated as an exogenous variable entering into the determination of such endogenous variables as nominal income, prices, interest rates, and real income'.

However, the changing 'financial sophistication' was acknowledged to have an influence on the behaviour of the velocity of circulation of money, and 'indeed it affects what items we designate as money' (F–S, 1982, p. 216). Regrettably, this issue receives comparatively little attention, and the financial sophistication is dealt with in statistical estimates by using a dummy variable.

The view of Freidman and his associates on the robustness of money in conditions where the developing financial structure generated new financial instruments contrasts with the perception of his renowned predecessor,

H. C. Simons, who considered that 'private initiative has been allowed too much freedom in determining the character of our financial structure and in directing changes in the quantity of money and money-substitutes' (1936, p. 3). In advocating a policy of a fixed quantity of circulating media, Simons was well aware of the lessons of monetary history:

> The fixing of the quantity of circulating media might merely serve to increase the perverse variability in the amounts of 'near-moneys' and in the degree of their general acceptability, just as the restrictions on the issue of bank notes presumably served to hasten the development of deposit (checking-account) banking. [Simons, 1936, p. 5]

He thus looked for ways of reforming the financial system, in order 'to minimize the opportunities for the creation of effective money-substitutes' by the private sector as a *sine qua non* of maintaining an effective fixed monetary rule; but he could not see a realistic solution. Thus, in reassessing the practicability of establishing 'a simple, mechanical rule of monetary policy', he thought that *the conditions for it did not exist*.

> Its limitations, however, have to do mainly with the unfortunate character of our financial structure – with the abundance of what we may call 'near-moneys' – *with the difficulty of defining money in such a manner as to give practical significance to the conception of quantity*. [Simons, 1936, p. 16; my italics]

Young Friedman (1948) was strongly influenced by Simons and supported his idea of a reform of the financial system so as to 'eliminate both the private creation and destruction of money'. He echoed Simons's 100 per cent reserve ratio proposal as a way of separating 'the depository from the lending function of the banking system'. Clearly, by the 1960s the view held by the Chicago school of the economics of the relationship between money and the financial system was reassessed.[12]

The monetarist prescription of the passive control of money, as noted already, effectively attempts to make modern money behave like some more primitive metallic money. Indeed, if one were to assume that gold supplies could expand steadily, the k per cent money growth rule would be indistinguishable from the rules of the gold standard, which operated in the nineteenth and early twentieth centuries. It should be remembered that the perception of sound money embodying some important characteristics of metallic money is not confined to monetarists. However, the need for some automaticity in the control of money arrangements, the need to isolate the stock of money as the target of control, and the need to confine economic policy only to the control of money, letting the market forces do the rest, are propositions specifically connected with the Friedmanite brand of monetarism.

Furthermore, it is persistently stressed that 'what matters is the quantity of money', not interest rates, money market conditions, credit conditions and the like (Friedman, 1973, p. 4; also 1982, pp. 100–17). The nominal money supply is believed to be the only monetary magnitude that the authorities can control. All other monetary variables (such as interest rates) were considered to be unreliable as policy targets (Friedman, 1968b, pp. 372–3; 1980a).

The whole field of monetary economics has been limited by Friedman and his followers to the study 'concerned with discovering how a variation in the supply of money affects real output, prices, interest rates, investment and saving' (Walters, 1973, p. 19). Such exclusive emphasis on the money supply was not a feature of early quantity theorists, who, in their search for monetary explanations of the trade cycle or changing price levels, often referred to *money and credit*, and to the operations of the *financial system*. To modern monetarists, the distinction between credit conditions and money is of key importance. Money is the 'star performer'; credit conditions, if at all relevant, are cast in the role of 'supporting players' (F–S, 1963b, p. 105).

1.4 The demand for money: a new research theme

1.4.1 The stable function of a small number of variables

In the theoretical structure of monetarism developed by Friedman and his disciples, and hailed in the 1960s and 1970s as the 'monetarist counter-revolution', it was the demand side of money that was highlighted – 'The quantity theory is in the first instance *a theory of the demand for money*' (Friedman, 1956, p. 147).

It was postulated that the demand for money was to be interpreted as the demand for real balances, whose function was stable and played a crucial role in explaining macroeconomic relationships. The stability of the function made it possible for us to trace out the effects of changes in the nominal money supply. To Friedman's followers, the money demand became of crucial significance, analogous to that of the consumption function during the developing years of the 'Keynesian revolution'. Its statistical relationship was simple to understand theoretically and not too hard to estimate statistically, but promised to contribute to the resolution of some central issues in macroeconomic theory and policy (Johnson, 1971, p. 9).

The main disagreement between monetarists and their opponents, usually referred to as 'Keynesians', centred around the demand for money and related to issues such as the transmission process of monetary action, the range of assets included in the wealth portfolio and, above all, the stability of the function. The 'Keynesian' demand function for money, presented in most textbooks as part of the *IS–LM* structure, is also stable and well behaved. However, it is considered to misrepresent Keynes, who suspected that the function, owing mainly to expectational factors and uncertainty, was unstable and unreliable for policy purposes.[13]

Another pillar of the monetarist counter-revolution was the faith in the *methodology of positive economics*, which rejected the 'descriptive realism' of the then prevailing Keynesian economics and its concomitant tendency to rely on increasingly large macroeconomic models. The essence of the positive approach was to isolate the crucial economic regularities in small, predominantly single-equation, models in order to predict something large from something small, often neglecting to make explicit the causal chain linking the two. Comparing the prediction derived from such models with experience became the only acceptable test of the validity of hypotheses and a key feature of monetarist methodology. 'This methodology obviously offered liberation to the small-scale intellectual, since it freed his mind from dependence on the large-scale research team and the large and expensive computer program' (Johnson, 1971, p. 9).[14] The appeal to empirical evidence was presented as indicative of the use of scientific methods in monetary investigations as opposed to 'Keynesian' conjectures. Looking back on this aspect of the 'counter-revolution', McCloskey (1983, p. 498) observed that by the 1960s the positive methodology had become so powerful in the minds of economists, especially monetarists, that 'most of the explicit debate took place in its terms. Yet in truth crude experiments and big books won the day, by their very crudeness and bigness.'

As ardent adherents of the methodology of positive economics, monetarists embarked on numerous 'small-scale' empirical studies of relationships between money and other macroeconomic variables. Indeed, Friedman (1968a, p. 39) defined the quantity theory as '*the empirical generalization* that changes in desired real-money balances tend to proceed slowly and gradually or to be the result of events set in train by prior changes in supply, whereas, in contrast, substantial changes in the supply of nominal balances can and frequently do occur independently of any changes in demand. The conclusion is that substantial changes in prices or nominal income are almost invariably the result of changes in the nominal supply of money' (my italics).

Monetary economics from the 1960s onwards has been dominated by considerations of the demand-for-money function. This function received more attention than the more traditional, and more awkward, concept of the velocity of circulation, though the latter continued to be used. A vast concentration of academic effort, coupled with a large input of computer time, resulted in a massive output of studies devoted essentially to the question of the money demand. Throughout this work it will be assumed that readers are familiar with the basic theory of the demand for money and are aware of the main developments in the empirical studies of the subject.[15]

The key hypothesis which economists were testing was that there existed a demand for money which was a stable function of a small number of arguments, invariably including income or wealth and interest rates. The demand functions estimated were predominantly aggregate or macroeconomic functions (only occasionally estimated separately for households and firms). *Their links with microeconomic foundations were rather tenuous.* Such factors as transactions costs, which were stressed in the behaviour of individual cost-minimizing economic agents (as in the transactions demand for money) or the uncertainty of portfolio-maximizing agents regarding the future movement of asset prices (as in the asset demand for money), were not explicitly incorporated in the macroeconomic demand functions, essentially because of measurement difficulties (Goodhart, 1975, pp. 43–7).

> Faced with the problem of trying to provide some empirical, factual clothing to
> the corpus of theory, the tendency has been to use observable, objective, *ex post*
> data as proxies for subjective, *ex ante* expectations, wherever possible, and to
> dispatch those variables which have no obvious *ex post* quantitative counterpart,
> such as transactions costs and uncertainty, to that statistical limbo of being
> represented by a constant, a trend term or some other 'dummy' variable in the
> usual regression analysis. [Goodhart, 1975, p. 45]

Thus, as a result of measurement difficulties, elements thought to be of vital importance in the theory of the money demand were left out of the empirical investigations (Coghlan, 1980, pp. 113–14) and theoretical literature on the demand for money showed a greater diversity of approach than can be found in empirical applications (Feige and Pearce, 1977, p. 441).[16]

A key reason for which estimates of macroeconomic demand functions are needed is to provide a guide or a basis for policy incorporating monetary targets (Parkin, 1978, esp. pp. 252–3; Freedman, 1983, pp. 103–4). This view, consistent with the methodology of positive economics, was touched upon earlier. The omission of complex relationships (as in a transmission mechanism of monetary action in an economy with a highly developed monetary system) or of expectational variables does not much matter, so long as the statistical relationship between the observable dependent variable and few explanatory variables is stable and predictable (Meyer, 1975, pp. 41–5). 'The chief goal in empirical work is to find a way of organizing experience so that it yields "simple" yet highly dependable relationships' (F–S, 1970, p. 199). As long as the demand for money remained stable, changes in the supply of money would yield predictable results useful for policy purposes.

In general, the substantive results obtained from the econometric studies of the demand for money before the mid-1970s were interpreted as indicating strong support for monetarist propositions. Time-series studies for the USA appeared to show that the demand for money was stable over long periods of time, 'despite major institutional, social and political changes' (Meltzer, 1963, p. 227), and despite a substantial change in the sophistication of the financial system. 'The evidence in favour of the existence of a stable relationship between the aggregate demand for real balances and a few variables is overwhelming' (Laidler, 1971, p. 91). Most evidence came from the USA but was corroborated by growing evidence from the UK, although the UK demand functions were, in contrast to those in the USA, sensitive to small changes in specification (Laidler, 1971, pp. 95–6).

In a survey of the US evidence, however, Laidler observed signs that 'there has been a slow shift over time of the demand-for-money function, a shift that has yet to be explained, but which may well be the result of the increasing financial sophistication of the American economy'. Empirical evidence showing that structural shifts in the demand for money and changes in the pattern of substitution between 'money' and 'near monies' occurred in the 1960s (Slovin and Sushka, 1975), tended to be eclipsed by the general belief in the stable demand function.

A study by Cagan and Schwartz (1975) revealed that, as the interest elasticity of the demand for money appeared to be decreasing over the time during which financial intermediaries expanded, financial sophistication might be enhancing the effects of monetary policy. In the light of such conclusions, the increasing pace of financial innovation in the early 1970s was often dismissed as being not quite relevant to money management, on the grounds that the evidence (much of it accumulated in earlier years) concerning the stability of the demand for money indicated *no necessity to review the conventional monetary analysis* (Meigs, 1975).

The issue of the changing financial structure will be explored in Part III of this book. We may, however, observe that the monetarist 'counter-revolution' introduced a strong presumption that the demand-for-money function, a lynch-pin of macroeconomic relationships, was inherently stable and explainable by a small number of variables. It was indeed becoming *a substitute for knowledge of the complexities of economic life* and, in particular, for the growing intricacies of the financial system. An understanding of the details of the allocative mechanism of the system was not considered vital in aggregate analysis along the lines of positive economics.

1.4.2 *Neglecting the definition of money*

Another generally accepted conclusion which emerged before the mid-1970s was that the demand-for-money function was stable, *no matter how money was 'defined'*. It was already pointed out that general macroeconomic theory devotes comparatively little attention to the concept and the indicative definition of money. Definitional difficulties are invariably admitted, but rarely developed.

Monetarists themselves, though they readily acknowledged the controversial nature of the definition of money, and the difficulty of arriving at a 'correct definition', devoted little attention to the definitional issue, certainly in comparison with the effort invested in the study of the demand for money and the broader role of money in economic activity. As the famous, or infamous, reference to money being dropped from a helicopter indicates, the precise indicative definition was not initially seen as essential to the central arguments of monetarists.

In the debate following the publication of their 1963 work, Friedman and Meiselman (1965, pp. 753–4) suggested that neither they nor their critics experienced much difficulty with selecting a useful empirical counterpart of the theoretical concept of money, and that they were concerned lest the ease with which these were found might discourage experimental work on the measurement of money. In 1970, after devoting, for the first time, considerable space to the concept and definition of money, F–S observed (1970, p. 1) that the problem of the indicative definition of money received more attention than it deserved, and they applauded Keynes for suggesting that the dividing line between money and non-money should be put 'at whatever point is most convenient for handling a particular problem' (Keynes, 1973, p. 167).[17]

Until the 1970s, the definitional debate was largely confined to the choice in the USA between 'narrow money', meaning currency and demand deposits, and 'broad money', meaning currency plus demand and time deposits. Both were considered to reflect 'temporary abodes of purchasing power', but the choice of the latter by F–S (1963b, p. 130) was admitted to be for statistical convenience; 'that enables us to use a single concept for the whole of our period'. This aspect will be further discussed in Part II.

The problem of the definition of the money supply was most frequently raised in the context of estimating the demand functions for money. Agreement on the stability of the demand for money, and the imperviousness of the stability of the demand for money function to the 'definition' of money, was quite general despite some disagreement on other matters. For instance, Laidler's (1971) results suggested greatest stability where short-term interest rates and permanent income were included as explanatory variables; in Khan (1974) this occurred when long-term interest rates were used; in Laumas and Mehra (1977), a stable demand function was compatible with short- or long-term rates and with current or permanent income.

Meltzer found that 'the demand function developed here is stable for several alternative definitions of money. These results seem to hold for both nominal and real cash balances and for a number of short and long periods' (1963, p. 244; see also Laidler, 1969, p. 518). Thus, for monetarists, for whom the test of the choice of an aggregate was 'in the usefulness of the definitions selected in uncovering dependable and reproducible empirical regularities' (F–S, 1970, pp. 197–8), there was no pressing need to search for the 'right' measure of money (Meltzer, 1969a, p. 18). The neglect of definitional issues was not confined to the USA. 'Little systematic work has been done in the UK on the question how to define the money stock' (Duck and Sheppard, 1978, p. 3).

It is interesting to observe that those who opposed monetarism tended to concentrate their criticism predominantly in the areas of the transmission mechanism, demand for money specifications and stability, exogeneity of money, and technical econometric issues. This is reflected, for instance, in M. Desai (1981), where expressions of scepticism about definitional matters and the measurability of money, though clearly made (e.g. pp. 164, 201-3), are submerged by the weight given to the other aspects.

Occasionally, however, the definitional problems were highlighted. J. Tobin (1965, p. 4), a persistent critic of monetarism, found the lack of clarity concerning the choice of 'money' by F–S (1963a) to be a principal weakness. 'Sometimes Friedman and his followers seem to be saying: "We don't know what money is, but whatever it is, its stock should grow steadily at 3% to 4% per year."' D. Gowland (1978) too thought the definitional problem to be serious and intractable:

> Money is used by monetarist authors such as Milton Friedman as a theoretical concept which may or may not exist in the real world. Certainly it does not correspond to any easily measurable definition. Like beauty, money lies in the eye of the beholder – that is, the definition must depend on how people regard an asset rather than upon the nature of the asset itself. [Gowland, 1978, pp. 19–20]

1.4.3   The 'breakdown' of the demand for money

Confidence in the stability of the demand-for-money function was shaken when, in the 1970s, it became clear that single-equation models of the demand functions of the 1960s and early 1970s were not stable when estimated with the data for the 1970s (Goldfeld, 1976). The 'breakdown' of the demand-for-money function in the USA in the period 1974-6 became known as the 'missing money' episode because the traditional functions seriously overpredicted the demand for money. At about the same time, in the UK the traditional equations underpredicted the demand for money (Artis and Lewis, 1976; 1981, ch. 2). More specifically, in the USA the demand function for M1 overpredicted monetary growth in 1974-6 and 1979-80, was roughly 'on track' in 1977-8, and began to underpredict from 1980. In the UK, serious underpredictions were noted with M3, but a respecified demand function for M1 was found to have been reasonably stable (Coghlan, 1978) until 1980, when it began to wander away from the predicted path (Allen, 1983, pp. 99–102).

The overprediction in the USA was only a general manifestation of the 'breakdown' problem. Some estimated income and interest elasticities became implausible; the size of the coefficient of lagged dependent variable also indicated an implausibly long adjustment period (Goldfeld, 1976; Judd and Scadding, 1982, pp. 995–6).

Hypotheses to explain the breakdown included the occurrence of some structural shift in the economy, a mis-specification of the function, and contentions that the breakdown indicated an inherently unstable demand relationship. Methodology and econometric methods relevant to the demand-for-money investigations too received considerably more attention than hithertofore. This will be developed in section 3.2.2.

The debates about the demand for money continue, but gone is the cocksureness about the stability of the function which characterized the 1960s even on the part of economists who entertained a strong presumption that there was a stable demand for money and who believed that it was only a matter of time before research resulted in its identification. It is, however, clear that the demand function, in the form in which it was estimated before the early 1970s, failed to reveal stability in the 1970s, that is, at the time when policies based on money targets were being introduced.

For our purposes, the following points should be stressed. First, suspicions of a mis-specification of the demand-for-money functions were not confined to the right-hand side of the equation, but involved the dependent variable too. One of the symptoms of the breakdown became the sensitivity of statistical results to the 'definition' of money employed. It became clear that 'there is no theory of the demand for money which is applicable regardless of the definition of money employed' (Coghlan, 1980, p. 135; also Foot, 1981, pp. 23–5). Even so, the definition of money is frequently discussed not so much as a topic in its own right, but as *an irritating difficulty in the search for a stable demand function* for money. We return to the problems of definition and measurement of money in Part II.

Second, institutional changes and financial innovation began to emerge as factors relevant to the explanation of the instability in monetary relationships. For some economists these were indeed the prime culprits of the breakdown. A valuable and interesting byproduct of the problems with the demand for money function was a greater concentration of effort to bring back into monetary economics a broader perspective which includes the impact of the complexities of modern financial systems. Though studies of financial change and innovation multiply, they are still in an exploratory stage and are only beginning to link financial change with the main structure of macroeconomics (Hadjimichalakis, 1982). Readers will be introduced to the nature and character of financial developments in Part III.

Appendix

The *IS–LM*, which continues to form the basis of most introductory and intermediate macroeconomics texts, is a generally used structural macro-economic framework (Friedman, 1970), containing money as an argument. Readers are assumed to be familiar with the rationale of the analysis, and thus the exposition here is brief and rather mechanical. More systematic explanations may be found in most macroeconomic textbooks.[18]

The model elaborated here is assumed to contain functions which are typically considered in intermediate macroeconomics. It is later adapted to illustrate the 'monetarist' case. To keep matters simple, we assume linear analysis in a closed economy and make the usual initial assumption that the level of prices remains fixed.

The real sector consists of:

$$C = C_o + c(Y - T) \quad \text{(consumption function)} \quad \text{(A1.1)}$$
$$T = T_o + tY \quad \text{(income tax function)} \quad \text{(A1.2)}$$
$$I = I_o - vR \quad \text{(investment function)} \quad \text{(A1.3)}$$
$$G = G_o \quad \text{(government expenditure function)} \quad \text{(A1.4)}$$
$$Y = C + I + G \quad \text{(equilibrium condition)} \quad \text{(A1.5)}$$

where C is consumption expenditure; C_o autonomous consumption; c marginal propensity to consume; Y national income; T tax revenue; T_o tax not related to income; t marginal rate of tax; I investment expenditure; I_o autonomous investment; v coefficient of interest rate R (measuring interest sensitivity of investment); G_o autonomous government expenditure.

By first substituting (A1.2) in (A1.1) and then substituting in (A1.5) together with the respective functions for C, I, G we obtain:

$$Y = C_o + cY - cT_o - ctY + I_o - vR + G_o . \quad \text{(A1.6)}$$

Solving for R in terms of Y, we have

$$R = [(C_o - cT_o + I_o + G_o)/v] - [Y(1 - c + ct)/v] . \quad \text{(A1.7)}$$

This is the equation of the *IS* function.

The monetary sector is represented by:

$$M_d = M_o + kY - qR \quad \text{(demand-for-money function)} \quad \text{(A1.8)}$$
$$M_s = M \quad \text{(supply-of-money function)} \quad \text{(A1.9)}$$
$$M_s = M_d \quad \text{(equilibrium condition)} \quad \text{(A1.10)}$$

where M_o is the demand for money independent of income Y and interest rate R; M_s is the exogenous money supply, equal to M; and k and q are coefficients of Y and R, measuring income and interest sensitivity of the demand for money, respectively.

Substituting (A1.8) and (A1.9) in (A1.10), we have

$$M = M_o + kY - qR . \quad \text{(A1.11)}$$

Solving for R in terms of Y, the equation for LM is:

$$R = [(M_o - M)/q] + (kY/q) .$$ (A1.12)

The equilibrium condition of the system is:

$$IS = LM$$ (A1.13)

Substituting (A1.7) and (A1.12) in (A1.13),

$$[(C_o - cT_o + I_o + G_o)/v] - [Y(1-c+ct)/v] = [(M_o - M)/q] + (kY/q) .$$ (A1.14)

Solving for equilibrium Y, and by various rearrangements, we can obtain the equation of Y:

$$Y = \{(C_o - cT_o + I_o + G_o)/[(vk/q) + (1-c+ct)]\} + \{(M-M_o)/[k+(1-c+ct)q/v]\} .$$ (A1.15)

By simple differentiation, multipliers for Y with respect to each of the variables in the numerators of the right-hand side of (A1.15) can be derived. The expenditure multiplier a_1 for changes in G_o or I_o and 'monetary' multiplier a_2 for changes in M are:

$$dY/dG_o = 1/[(vk/q + (1-c+ct)] = a_1$$ (A1.16)
$$dY/dM = 1/[k+(1-c+ct)q/v] = a_2 .$$ (A1.17)

a_1 and a_2 are parametrically stable as long as all the coefficients (denoted by lower-case letters in (A1.16) and (A1.17)) remain the same. They enable us to predict the change in Y following a disturbance in government expenditure ($dY = a_1 dG_o$) or a change in the supply of money ($dY = a_2 dM$). They both contain 'monetary parameters' (k,q) as well as 'real parameters' (c,t,v), reflecting an essential aspect of the interdependence between real and monetary forces which was highlighted by Keynes in his references to the 'monetary economy'.

If, with reference to (A1.15), we can express the sum of autonomous items in the numerator of the first component on the right-hand side as A (viz. $C_o - cT_o + I_o + G_o = A$), and if in the numerator of the other component we assume that M_o is zero (that is, that the demand for money (A1.8) would depend only on Y and R) and thus represent the numerator simply as M standing for the money supply, then (A1.15) can be rewritten simply as:

$$Y = a_1 A + a_2 M .$$ (A1.18)

This expression summarizes aggregate demand at a given price level, suggesting that Y may be disturbed either by changes in A incorporating changes in components of IS (e.g. fiscal changes in G_o or I_o) or by a change in M. Figure 1.2 shows the usual graphical IS–LM where changes in A (shift of IS) or M (shift of LM) would have an impact on economic activity (viz. Y).

Much of the recent debate in monetary economics referred to the magnitude and stability of the multipliers. Stability is also an issue (to be developed later) in the context of the demand function for money, where the interest sensitivity of the demand for money q has an important bearing on the effectiveness of monetary policy.

The lower the q, the higher is the slope of LM. By examining (A1.16) and (A1.17), it can also be seen that the lower the q, the less is the expenditure multiplier a_1 and the higher is the money multiplier a_2; that is, the less interest-sensitive the demand for money is, the less effective will be fiscal policy (or a change in expenditure such as investment) and the more effective monetary policy. In the extreme 'monetarist' case where q is zero, a_1 would become zero (as (vk/q) in (A1.16) would become infinitely large), and a_2 would reach its maximum value $1/k$ (see (A1.17)). Only monetary policy would have any influence on economic activity. Equation (A1.18) would become:

$$Y = a_2 M . \tag{A1.18a}$$

Figure 1.3 illustrates this situation when only a shift in LM would affect Y; changes in IS would only disturb interest rates. Though such a situation would be an 'extreme monetarist' case, monetarists usually stress that 'monetary demand' is of overriding importance.

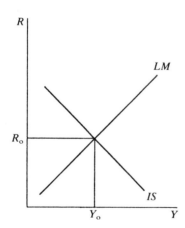

Figure 1.2 *IS–LM* model: a general case.

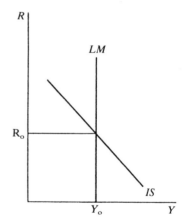

Figure 1.3 *IS–LM* model: an 'extreme monetarist' case.

Equation (A1.18a) can be expressed with prices P explicitly included, giving:

$$Y = a_2(M/P) .$$ (A1.19)

Thus, with a given a_2 and nominal monetary demand M, income would vary inversely with the price level P. This explains the shape of AD in the text.

Notes

1 Elaboration of propositions made in this section can be found in most intermediate macroeconomics texts. For instance, for a very succinct treatment see Chrystal (1983, esp. chs. 2–4 and 10). For more extended discussions see Dornbusch and Fischer (1981, esp. chs. 11–13); and Parkin and Bade (1982, esp. chs. 9–12 and 27–32).
2 A distinction between targeting and forecasting is pertinent in this context (see e.g. Sumner, 1980, p. 112).
3 House of Commons (1981, sections 5.9–5.10); Foot (1981, esp. pp. 34–5). The Treasury and Civil Service Committee concluded, however, that there was no evidence to suggest that declarations of targets exerted a quick effect on wage and price expectations (House of Commons, 1981, ch. 11).
4 See e.g. Mints (1945); Robbins (1958); Fetter (1965).
5 State theories of money have an ancient tradition (Schumpeter, 1963, pp. 392–6). Perhaps the best known exponent of the state theory of money was Knapp (1924), more recently supported by Lerner (1947). Totally opposed to the state theory of money is the Austrian school, which advocates 'free banking' and the shaping of 'monetary' relationships purely by market forces. 'The State Theory is not a bad monetary theory; it is not a monetary theory at all' (Mises, 1953, p. 468). See also Mises (1978); and Hayek (1976).
6 Alternative terms are widely deployed, for instance, 'auxiliary media' (e.g. Robbins, 1958, pp. 105–6); the Austrian school often referred to 'fiduciary media' or 'circulation credit', though a variety of other terms was also used (see e.g. Mises, 1978, esp. pp. 71–120, 136–40; 1953, pp. 261–8).
7 For a brief account of the development of the theory see Podolski (1973, pp. 12–17); for a critical account see Mints (1945). Recent contributions include Sargent and Wallace (1982); Humphrey (1982).
8 The debate on this issue still reverberates; see e.g. Timberlake (1983) and Graziani (1984).
9 For a development see Hicks (1977, pp. 58–60 and 74–80). This narrow view of money (and the consequent interpretation of liquidity preference as a money demand function) can be inferred from the General Theory. There are other contexts where the General Theory is modified (see e.g. Davidson, 1978, chs. 6–8) and the liquidity preference theory is broadened to include even the Radcliffe Report position (Ritter, 1963).
10 While the index number (1980 = 100) of GDP (and in brackets industrial production) rose from 68 (68) in 1961 to 88 (90) in 1971 and 99 (97) in 1982, the respective index of output from banking, finance and insurance rose from 47 in

1961 to 73 in 1971 and 110 in 1982 (National Income and Expenditure, 1983, pp. 18–19). Whereas there was a general decline in total employment between 1971 and 1984 of some 4 per cent, employment in banking, finance and insurance rose by some 40 per cent and its share in total employment rose from 6 per cent in 1971 to 9 per cent in 1984 (*Department of Employment Gazette*, August 1984, table 1.2).

11 The stock of high-powered money (the monetary base) was found to be 'the major factor accounting arithmetically for changes in the stock of money' (F–S, 1963a, p. 684). The F–S treatment of the determinants of money, however, has been criticized as seriously incomplete (Temin, 1976).

12 For a broader perspective on the evolution of Chicago monetary views see Tavlas (1977).

13 These aspects of interpretation are to be found in, e.g., Minsky (1975), Shackle (1972, esp. pp. 150–240), and Davidson (1978). Shackle (1974, p. 2) refers to two faces of Keynes on this issue: one, where the effects of money are amenable to orderly dissection; the other, where 'money is what unbuckles the harness and allows the horses to gallop into the wild'.

14 For a critical evaluation see Clower (1964) and Caldwell (1982, ch. 8). Positive methodology was not universally accepted. Clower (1971, pp. 25–6) commented that the growing influence of monetarists 'is regarded by some as a triumph of scientific truth over Keynesian dogma, by others as a regrettable retreat into orthodoxy, by yet others as the replacement of one fashion in half-truths by another.'

15 Examples of surveys of the demand for money studies include Meltzer (1963), Goldfeld (1973, 1976), Goodhart (1975, ch. 3), Laidler (1977, 1980), Havrilesky and Boorman (1978, chs. 7–8), Coghlan (1978), Dennis (1981, ch. 6) and Judd and Scadding (1982).

16 The general specification of the regression equation for the ('long-run') demand for money was:

$$(M/P)_t = m_t = a_0 + a_1 Y_t + a_2 R$$

or expressed in multiplicative form:

$$m_t = b_0 (Y_t)^{b1} (R_t)^{b2}$$

and usually transformed into logarithmic form:

$$(\ln m_t = \ln b_0 + b_1 \ln Y_t + b_2 \ln R_t) ,$$

where (M/P) is the real money balance m; Y income (or wealth); R interest rate.

The above specifications imply complete adjustment. However, in most specifications it was assumed that there was a gap in the adjustment between the desired ('long-run') real money balances and the balances actually held (Havrilesky and Boorman, ch. 7). This resulted in a commonly used specification with a partial adjustment mechanism incorporating a lagged dependent variable, such as in:

$$m_t = \lambda a_0 + \lambda a_1 Y_t + \lambda a_2 R_t + (1-\lambda)m_{t-1} ; \qquad (0<\lambda<1)$$

where λ represented the adjustment coefficient.

'Empirically', there was considerable support for the use of an adjustment mechanism involving a lagged dependent variable. Indeed, a generally accepted 'empirical' conclusion was that: 'only those demand functions which allow for an "adjustment mechanism" yield stable estimates of the parameters'. (Laumas and Mehra, 1977, p. 915)

However, the theoretical justifications for utilizing mechanisms with a lagged dependent variable (usually based on some 'adjustment costs' or 'buffer-stock' rationale) were not convincing. For development see: Courakis (1978); Hetzel (1984, pp. 185–188); Goodfriend (1985, pp. 208–211); see also section 3.2.2.

17 Keynes's reference to this is in a footnote to a discussion of the determination of the rate of interest as a reward for parting with liquidity in exchange for a 'debt'. It is in no sense a conclusion to any systematic evaluation of the indicative definition of money. In the General Theory Keynes was rather careless in the use of terms: money, cash, 'liquid cash' (pp. 169, 170, 205, 235), 'debt'. He followed the too-common practice of avoiding the complexities of the definition of money while arguing with classical economists about the nature of the rate of interest (see esp. Keynes, 1973, chs. 14–15 and 17).

18 See texts cited in n. 1 above. For a sophisticated treatment of *IS–LM* see Poole (1970); Driscoll and Ford (1980) are also useful.

—2—

The Financial System: Source of Monetary Assets and Services

2.1 Financial evolution

In comparison with the amount of attention given to the association between money and other macroeconomic variables, the relation between financial development in general and real development, and the interaction between financial and non-financial sectors, have been sadly neglected. We do know that in various capitalist economies long-run financial development and real development exhibit interesting similarities and a strong interdependence. But such knowledge has not been integrated with the main corpus of economic theory and has, in particular, been neglected in the recent past by monetary economics which, as mentioned, has concentrated on the unique and robust influence of money.

In a comparative study of the subject, R. Goldsmith concluded that 'In most countries a rough parallelism can be observed between economic and financial development when periods of several decades are considered' (1969, p. 48). In the course of development, 'financial superstructure' tends to grow more rapidly than the infrastructure of national income or wealth.

As economies have grown, a greater concentration and specialization in the financial structure has evolved in step with similar developments in the industrial sector. Such changes have become more pronounced as the separation between savings and investment processes and between ownership and control has become more distinct.

Financial development in the modern sense started everywhere with the banking system. Banks emerged as the dominant intermediaries, although in the process of development other financial institutions appeared and in many cases, after a point, grew at a faster pace than banks. Such processes were accompanied by rising complexities in the financial structure (viz. financial institutions and instruments).

The parallelism in the long-run development of financial and real structures naturally raises the question of a possible causal connection. Goldsmith

(1969, p. 48) was unable to supply a definite answer: 'There is no possibility, however, of establishing with confidence the direction of causal mechanism, i.e. of deciding whether financial factors were responsible for the acceleration of economic development or whether financial development reflected economic growth whose mainsprings must be sought elsewhere.'

The question remained of almost no interest to the mainstream economists, who preferred to focus on the much narrower relation between money and nominal income or money and the price level and inflation. Only economic historians and economists dealing with underdevelopment enquired further into the matter. Obstacles to financial innovation and change were found to hinder industrialization processes (Cameron, 1967). The 'neo-liberal' school of development economics stresses the need to create organized financial markets as a vital ingredient of growth strategy, arguing that financial development is a necessary, but not sufficient, condition for a successful development strategy.[1]

Leaving aside the merits of this proposition, we may note that, for the mainstream economists, focusing mainly on industrial economies, the financial system does not really seem to matter, in spite of the fact that in such economies it represents a key growth sector in terms of the contribution to national income and employment, and generates financial services and instruments from which we select our 'money'. 'The only financial institutions worthy of detailed attention are banks, some of whose liabilities happen to be money, with other institutions considered only in so far as their activities complicate the tasks of monetary authorities' (Bain, 1981, p. ix). Yet, perhaps the mysteries and puzzles of 'money' can be solved only with a better understanding of the complex financial interrelationships and linkages with the real sector.

The income velocity of circulation of money is sometimes used to reflect a relationship between 'money' and the financial system. Monetarists (F–S, 1963a, Friedman and Meiselman, (F–M), 1963) claim that the long-term tendency of the velocity is to fall, claiming that money is a 'luxury', that is, a product with income elasticity of greater than unity (e.g. F–M, 1963, p. 173). This view of a secular decline in velocity has been challenged (e.g. by Tobin, 1965, pp. 472–83), and more recent studies of long-term trends in velocity for broadly defined money indicate a U-shaped relationship (Jonung, 1978; Bordo and Jonung, 1981; Klovland, 1983). Such a pattern can be explained first by a rising banking habit connected with monetization processes, that is, increasing use of bank money for transactions purposes. The rising part of the U is attributed to the growing sophistication of the financial system.[2]

In the initial stages of development, banks were used intensively for the payments services which they provided and also as intermediaries between savers and investors. In the *Treatise*, Keynes (1971, vol. II, p. 191) noted that banks supplied substitutes for 'state money' and money transfer services, and at the same time acted as middlemen for lenders and borrowers. 'This duality of function is the clue to many difficulties in the modern theory of money and credit and the source of some confusion of thought.' Lavington (1934, pp. 5–7) stressed that the money market performed two elementary functions: supplying the stock of money, and 'facilitating the transport of capital'. The functions, however, were simultaneously performed and were totally inter-dependent. It is not clear at what point and for what reason banks were unable to supply all services necessary for further real development.

Financial institutions emerging subsequently appeared to cater for new and more specialized financial requirements of more sophisticated econo-mies. Gurley and Shaw (1955, pp. 520–4) considered banking to have become a relatively declining industry as soon as the institutionalization of saving and investment ceased to be confined to the monetary sector and became a kind of product differentiation in the field of finance.

Looking at banks purely as creators of money, meaning essentially transactions services, one can perhaps understand the subsequent need for intermediary services (Coghlan, 1980, p. 13). Yet it is not clear why banks did not generate the capacity to act as intermediaries and diversify their services.

Modern views on financial evolution stress the process of response to profit opportunities arising out of various frictions found in the financial sector – frictions produced by inadequate information, reflecting (sometimes) market segmentation and excessive transactions costs. Thus, innovation designed to overcome such frictions, as well as obstacles presented by financial regula-tion, is an important element in the evolving structure of the financial sector. Conditions which induce innovation and the process of financial innovation are thus important to the understanding of financial change. Indeed, financial development is increasingly seen as a process of making markets more efficient by overcoming market frictions or imperfections. Intermediaries can derive economies of scale in the acquisition of information and its use to take advantage of profit opportunities revealed by such imperfections (Wood, 1981, esp. pp. 146–52).

One possible explanation for the relative decline of banks might be that, as they supplied services akin to public goods by operating the vital payments and settlement system and became the principal intermediary, they were singled out and subjected to state regulation – some form of original supervision and monetary control – in the public interest. This does raise an important question relevant to the meaning of modern money, namely, Were banks regulated because they were banks, that is some unique 'creators of money', or have they become 'banks' because they had been regulated? Economists increasingly believe that present diversified financial structures can, in large measure, be explained by the influence of state regulatory intervention (to be developed in Part III).

A budding school of thought, predictably labelled 'new monetary economics' (Hall, 1982), has been engaged in a re-investigation of the nature of monetary standards in order to achieve a better understanding of the present monetary developments.[3] Interest has been rekindled in the possibility of economies functioning in a stable way with no traditional money but a system of 'free banking' (Vaubel, 1977; White, 1984b). In principle, banks are not unique financial institutions and do not necessarily play a special role in the determination of the price level.

Monetary regulations (e.g. reserve requirements, interest rate restrictions), however, are of critical importance to the understanding of the nature of money and the financial structure. It is the regulations which create artificially the demand for money conceived in terms of central bank liabilities (Fama, 1980; Wallace, 1983, p. 6). The existence of such a demand is a necessary condition for the sucessful monetary control of the price level (we return to this topic in chapter 7).

In a more recent contribution, Fama (1983) claimed that, provided there is a commitment to control the price level, it would be sufficient for the purpose to control the supply of a fiduciary currency. It seems that no other requirements for such a currency exist than that it should have a reliable demand function. Indeed, fresh-cut beef, steel ingots and spaceships (Fama, 1980, pp. 43, 56), or barrels of oil (Fama, 1983, pp. 8–9), or anything for which a well-defined demand function could be established can serve as a numeraire to control the price level. By definition, such a currency would be an imperfect substitute for bank deposits and other financial claims. In such an economic system, the financial sector (including banks) would remain totally unregulated, concentrating on making funds available to finance real activity. Basically, this represents a different version of the orthodox quantity theory dichotomy in a *laissez-faire* environment. Narrowly defined money (currency) controls prices; real resources are allocated by the interaction of real and financial markets quite independently.

It is not the intention here to elaborate on the issues raised by the above propositions. They are presented principally to indicate a search for an explanation of money and financial evolution and scepticism about the traditional monetary theory and policy. Historical evidence casts doubt on the practicality of some abstract monetary standards. However, the theoretical money or 'free banking' models can serve as a contrast with the current monetary arrangements and provide a useful aid in the assessment of the present financial system (White, 1984a).

Studies of actual financial systems invariably stress change, evolution, responsiveness and flux. It is doubtful whether a financial system ever achieves a stationary state, and, if ever equilibrium is achieved, it is achieved in a dynamic and not a static sense. Thus, representation of financial influences through *IS-LM* (see appendix to chapter 1) can be of value only if one assumes frequent shifts and changes in the slope of the *LM* function (Sheppard, 1971, p. 103). Regarding the money supply, in this state of change, as being 'demand-determined rather than being exogenously proscribed by central authorities is not so heretical either with respect to the history of economic thought or practice' (Sheppard, 1971, p. 105).

Studies by monetarists appear to be the exception in the context of historical investigations of financial systems, in the sense that they portray financial developments as subordinate rather than dominant in the understanding of money and its characteristics and functions. In the next section the functions of the financial system are outlined and in the remainder of the text we shall explore the nature of money and the problems of its measurement in increasingly financially flexible and sophisticated economies. Forces which induce financial sophistication and evolution are of particular interest.

2.2 Functions of a modern financial system

The importance of financial markets is often explained in textbooks with the help of indifference curve analysis. This demonstrates that, with a financial system offering us, at a given rate of interest, the possibility of borrowing (hence, investing without the necessity of having excess of income over expenditure) and of lending (hence, saving in order to provide for future expenditure greater than future income), a greater level of welfare can be achieved (a higher indifference curve combining current and future expenditure can be reached) by savers or investors (see e.g. Coghlan, 1980, ch. 7). This offers a useful introduction to the economics of the financial system. For our purposes, however, we shall resort to a more elaborate descriptive analysis of the main functions performed by a financial system, but without evaluating the efficiency with which such functions are performed.

This is not to indicate the relative unimportance of efficiency aspects. Indeed, the financial system is often stressed as a 'means of collecting surplus funds and of allocating them to the most efficient purposes on the basis of prices and yields' (Revell, 1983b, pp. 148–9). It is simply because the main purpose of the analysis below is to highlight the nature of modern 'money' and the difficulties encountered in defining and measuring it in conditions of financial change.

The financial system has recently been described as 'a complex network embracing payments mechanisms and the borrowing and lending of funds' (Wilson Report, 1980, para. 90). It also performs other functions and supplies other services, but these are considered to be more peripheral. The major functions of the financial system are discussed below under three headings: monetization and the payments mechanism, intermediation, and asset transmutation.

2.2.1 *The payments mechanism*

As already mentioned, economies in early stages of development evolve financial systems which are essentially monetary systems. A prime function of the financial system is to provide a unit of account and a means of payment, in order to replace a less efficient system of barter. The use of a third commodity – money – in transactions reduces the transactions cost (including search and information costs) of barter. The replacement of barter with monetized and more organized markets is associated with a move away from subsistence production to an increasingly commercial production bringing advantages of scale and specialization.

Money, often a commodity money such as gold, is, in the early stages of monetary development, a clearly identifiable asset which is generally acceptable in the ultimate settlement of debts. But, like other aspects of a developing economy, money and the payments system are subject to evolution. 'Money' is, above all, a social institution and does not remain static. New means of exchange and debt-transfer mechanisms, mentioned in chapter 1, develop and become generally acceptable. Fiat money tends to replace commodity money, which is more costly to produce and more costly and inconvenient to hold.

In financially sophisticated economies, it will be argued later, it is exceedingly difficult to identify 'money' which performs the classic functions ascribed to it by economic theory. In the early 1970s such tenuous connections with commodity money as had existed since the end of the Second World War disappeared completely. All 'money' today is fiat money, that is, claims generated by the financial system, predominantly by its private sector. Upon the slender but important base of legal tender there are layers of financial claims possessing, in different degrees, different characteristics such as liquidity, return, convenience and risk. Traditionally, economists attempted to identify some of these as 'money'.

In financially developed economies, 'post-banking' economies, it may well be more rewarding to look not for unique assets serving as means of exchange and payments or stores of value, but for *payments and money transfer services rendered by a variety of financial institutions* catering for differing demands of clients. Such demands may be closely linked with other services such as information or credit. What is, however, clear is that the provison of funds transfer services, debt settlement arrangements and means of final payment is a key function of the financial system, which is not likely to be discharged only through a clearly definable set of financial assets called 'money', or provided exclusively by a narrow set of financial institutions such as banks. In the context of the role of money in economic growth, Clower (1968) observed that

There exists no accepted or acceptable microeconomic foundation of the theory of an economy in which money plays an *essential* role as a means of payment. All we have is a general theory of an economy in which money is one of many alternative means of payment, which is to say that its only obvious function is as a store of value and unit of account. [Clower, 1968, p. 877]

This view is consistent with financial theories of money mentioned earlier.

Banks have traditionally provided and operated the main payments and money transmission services. They were the principal depository institutions where the public held its cash for transactions purposes. Because of the performance of this function, banks generated current account balances described as the 'bedrock of their resources' (Wilson Committee, 1979, vol. 3, para. 37). For a long time, they have represented a stable base on which banking developed. Although the banks' hegemony in the money transmission system still remains, it is, as we shall see later, being increasingly challenged by new financial and technological innovations and by regulatory changes, the effect of which is to lower the barriers to entry and to disperse the money transmission and settlement services between institutions other than banks.

2.2.2   Financial intermediation

The traditional analysis of the function of intermediation stresses that the process of economic growth involves a continuous switch of resources from declining industries to the newly developing, from savers to borrowers. Emphasis is inevitably given to financial institutions as intermediaries between surplus units (whose income exceeds planned expenditure) and deficit units (whose planned expenditure exceeds planned income). Thus, the financial system is said to bring lenders and borrowers together. Indeed, the system does link the two, but the links are complex and potentially of crucial importance to an effective performance of a modern economy.[4] Only some basic points concerning intermediation are stressed below.

Financial intermediaries do not simply passively channel funds from savers to borrowers: they affect resource allocation by changing terms and conditions attaching to saving and financing. In a fully monetized and financially developed economy, saving and investment processes are almost completely divorced. We shall thus discuss first the mobilization of saving and then move to investment finance.

The accumulation of saving entails attracting savings from large sections of the community. Motives for saving are an important consideration of macroeconomic theory and are assumed to be familiar to the reader. In a competitive financial system, intermediaries attract savings by offering various advantages to savers; these increasingly involve packages of services, including payments and debt transfer facilities and availability of credit, in addition to interest return and access to funds. *Distinction is increasingly blurred between savings deposits and balances held for the transactions and precautionary purposes associated with money.*

Arrangements with regard to provision for retirement, house purchase and the education of children are a particularly important aspect of savings mobilization. In their bid to attract savings, financial intermediaries affect attitudes to consumption and saving, so that they not only help to determine the medium of saving, but also affect the propensity to save, that is, raise the savings function. 'We can be confident that these efforts by the financial institutions to market saving will increase the level of saving that actually takes place' (Bain, 1981, p. 42).

Like saving, investment is considered to be an activity crucial to economic reproduction, growth of income and technological progress. There is some debate concerning the determinants of investment. Of financial variables, the most frequent explanatory variable of investment is the rate of interest in relation to the expected profitability of investment. Variables indicating the impact of the availability of external finance on investment decisions are rarely considered. Indeed, the extent to which availability of investment finance encourages entrepreneurial activity is a hotly debated issue. The Wilson Report (1980, para. 81) summed up: 'It has often been argued that business expansion can more easily be thwarted by lack of finance than prompted by its ready availability. In effect, finance is like a string – it is easier to pull than to push.' Readers are reminded that economists more often are concerned with relations between the availability of money and investment than with finance and investment.

Funds are also demanded by the personal sector for consumption purposes, especially the purchase of durable goods. The finance of housing, normally classified as investment, is of key importance.

In a competitive financial system, financial institutions must supply funds in ways attractive to corporate or personal clientele. This involves not only the usual considerations of the method of interest payment, the principal repayment, the duration of the loan and tax considerations, but also *reliability of the financial provision*. Financial institutions increasingly must manage their liabilities to ensure that they can meet prior financial commitments. To do this, they make competitive use of arrangements in the wholesale money market. Financial institutions, including banks, are clearly more than just passively involved in supplying the economy with industrial and consumer finance. The implication of this will be elaborated in Part III.

2.2.3 *Asset transmutation*

The process of financial intermediation refers to activities related to the flow of savings and investment in the economy. Asset transmutation or transformation function stresses the fact that, at any time, there is a stock of assets possessing different characteristics and yielding different services to wealth-holders. Such assets are supplied collectively by the financial system and supplement the stock of real or tangible assets (Moore, 1968, ch. 1). At the same time, deficit units can resort to a variety of methods of borrowing which meet their particular preferences.

There is an organic connection between intermediation and asset transmutation functions. In the course of intermediation, a wide variety of savers are supplied with claims on institutions in which they deposit their funds. It is these claims that we often call 'money' or liquid assets (that is, assets that are comparatively free from default risk, and are easily encashable without a serious danger of capital loss). With the funds deposited by savers, financial institutions acquire investments, including medium- and long-term investments, in the form of loans or claims on other financial institutions or corporations. Thus, financial institutions are involved in maturity transformations.

The importance of banks in maturity transformation is often underlined, for reasons already referred to. Banks generate deposits (viz., 'monetary assets') which are repayable or transferable on demand. In this connection, they have developed efficient payments, money transfer and debt-clearing systems, and until recently enjoyed a near monopoly in this respect. They usually lend for longer periods. In principle, the operations of other financial units are not different, but the characteristics of their assets and liabilities may well be, especially with regard to the liquidity and expected return. Thus, the essential behavioural feature of all financial units is that, in soliciting funds from surplus units, they generate claims on themselves, and with the funds thus realized they acquire other, mainly financial, assets.

All financial assets, however, result from contracts or transactions between economic units. They are essentially debts or claims arising from ordinary business interactions which involve some future settlement or contractual obligation. Such assets can, for instance, be created or destroyed quickly by acts of borrowing or repayment.

In a sophisticated economy, consisting of a variety of financial institutions and financial procedures or instruments, there is a wide choice of arrangements between economic units and financial institutions. There is a possibility of different patterns of intermediation and different patterns of wealth-holding. A given stock of wealth in a primitive economy can be held essentially in real terms, that is, in terms of tangible assets such as land, equipment or commodity money (which might be associated with high costs of storage and security). In an advanced economy, personal wealth is increasingly held in indirect securities such as bank deposits, building society accounts, insurance and superannuation policies, investment and unit trusts. In turn, the financial institutions have claims to ownership of tangible wealth, viz. direct securities such as shares.

Two important points should be highlighted in connection with asset transmutation function. First, in a financially developed economy, financial assets are differentiated not only by the identity of the debtor (state, financial and non-financial companies), but also in terms of attributes such as term to maturity, method of repayment, transferability, rate and mode of interest payment, and tax liability on income from interest. Assets with varying characteristics are continuously generated to meet the preferences of both savers and borrowers. The availability of financial assets, possessing different risk-return characteristics upon which stress is placed in the context of portfolio optimization, permits wealth-holders to exercise wide choice in their portfolio management. Diversification of portfolios enables them to avoid risks associated with the uncertainty of asset price changes. Indeed, there are strongly held views that the evolution of the financial system is best explained in the context of a progressive risk reduction (Moore, 1968, ch. 2; Silber, 1975, p. 56).

Second, some assets are considered to possess unique features of money which distinguish them from other liquid assets. Monetary assets are indeed connected with particular services they yield to *individual units*. However, quite often it is their *macroeconomic role* as determinants of some important macroeconomic variables which is being highlighted. At the same time, the link between the micro- and macroeconomics of money is tenuous (see section 1.4.1). These considerations will be developed later.

2.3 Interdependence and sensitivity

In a sense, in advanced economy most economic units are, at least in a small way, financial intermediaries. They may be surplus or deficit units, but, regardless of this, they may at the same time be borrowers and lenders. Large corporations in particular now attach considerable important to the management of their financial assets and liabilities, and, as will be seen in Part III, such activities collectively can exert an impact on national monetary management.

The essential reason why financial institutions play a special role in the financial system is the size of their operations. They are able to derive economies of scale in gathering information and processing it, in transactions in financial markets, and in portfolio management and risk-bearing. Thus, as already noted above, they reduce market imperfections in the financial system (see also Goodhart, 1975, pp. 102–10; Bain, 1981, p. 11). Such imperfections are related to market segmentation and regulatory activity.

To appreciate the operations of any financial or monetary system, it is necessary to understand the financial functions exercised by the state. In an advanced economy, the state plays a key part through budgetary activity of the public sector and through financial regulation. The state's involvement in the former sense can, in principle, be reduced to that of any other deficit or surplus unit, although in practice the mode of financing its deficits (and on occasions its surpluses) can be complex and can have serious repercussions on the rest of the economy. (This point will be illustrated in chapter 6.) The state's seigniorage in the issue of currency has both fiscal and monetary implications.

The state's involvement as regulator has a profound effect on the currency standards (touched upon earlier), on the structure of the financial system, and on patterns of intermediation and asset transmutation. Regulations on banks (originally the principal intermediaries and, until recently, near monopolists in the payments system), often associated with the banks' role as 'creators of money', are particularly germane to the understanding of the present diversified financial structures and the changing nature of 'money' in modern advanced economies. Further attention is given to this aspect in chapter 7.

The financial system, and not just the monetary sector, which is an integral part of it, links savers, investors, lenders and borrowers, the state as the regulator with all types of financial institutions. *In a given regulatory framework, the decisions of each group interact with those of other groups in a complex web of interdependence*, about which we need to know much more than we do now.

Viewing financial evolution as a process of reacting to opportunities arising from market imperfections, it is often dangerous and misleading to maintain a clear distinction between various financial markets in a competitive situation. The Radcliffe Committee (Radcliffe Report, 1959, ch. 4), in its analysis of the financial sector, even at the time when that sector was relatively shielded from competition by various forms of regulation, warned of the dangers of placing firm dividing lines between the activities of financial institutions, and in particular between 'the market for credit' (nowadays the 'money market') and 'the market for capital'. One of the Report's key conclusions (para. 315) was that, 'while most financial institutions are unwilling to make a large change in the maturity distribution of their assets, nearly all of them are prepared to switch some part of their funds to take advantage of unusually favourable opportunities of short-term or long-term investment. Pressure in one part of the market soon makes itself felt in other parts.' The readiness to shift traditional preferences and to innovate has now become much stronger and involves not only the assets side, but also the liabilities side of operations.

Financial entrepreneurship and innovation create new financial assets and processes, with characteristics designed to satisfy hitherto unfulfilled requirements or to overcome constraints imposed by state regulation or self-regulation which had become excessively restrictive. The existence of all financial assets also depends critically on the attitudes of their holders – on the confidence which they have in the debtor (e.g. bank, building society).

Given the above view of financial processes, doubt exists about the usefulness of the orthodox money multiplier presentation of money creation:

$$M = kB$$

where M is 'money', k is a multiplier derived from some financial relationships reflecting stable preferences of economic agents, and B is a monetary base. Stable k can be tolerated only if one accepts the sacrifice of behavioural processes involved in 'money' creation for the sake of simplification (Goodhart, 1975, pp. 129–36) and if one views banks narrowly as 'money creators' rather than, together with other financial units, as financial intermediaries.[5] It is generally accepted today that the assumptions concerning the monetary system which were necessary for the multiplier exposition of the generation of money in a sophisticated and competitive economy are too heroic for the exposition to be useful, especially for policy purposes.

Monetarists (e.g. Friedman, 1981a, pp. 57–9) nevertheless claim that it is necessary and sufficient to control B, and that the monetary authorities can do so directly, because the base consists of their own liabilities. Often this point is made with an implicit understanding that a change in the monetary base can be achieved painlessly and is but a matter of appropriate monetary procedure of the central bank.

Technically, it is true that the monetary authorities should be in position to control their liabilities, though in a financial economy where all claims, including those of public authorities, are generated as a result of financial interaction between economic agents, desired changes in government liabilities cannot be achieved without some effect on the interrelated financial relationships. Changes in the monetary base in the UK are related to the size of the central government borrowing requirement, outcomes of marketable and non-marketable public debt operations, and external currency flows.[6]

Only if the consequences of the change in the monetary base are known and acceptable can there be any sensible reference to effective control (see e.g. Goodhart, 1975, pp. 153–6; Dennis, 1981, pp. 195–201; Artis and Lewis, 1981, pp. 121–30). Indeed, it has been argued that in a sophisticated economy the monetary base, like all other 'monetary' totals, is entirely endogenously determined (Moore, 1983).

A financial identity, showing the counterparts of £M3, which will be discussed in section 4.3, reflects more realistically than some monetary base, however defined, the complex influences on the generation of assets constituting this monetary aggregate. The extent to which monetary authorities can secure control over such an aggregate, especially when financial innovation occurs, will also be considered later.

2.4 'Money' in a flow-of-funds framework

Many interesting features of a modern financial system are reflected in a flow-of-funds (FF) matrix (see table 2.1). In particular, such a matrix can be used to illustrate financial interdependence and to indicate factors responsible for changes in some monetary aggregates.

The matrix combines capital accounts with financial transactions accounts, thereby relating the outcomes of decisions on the allocation of income with

Table 2.1 Flow of Funds, UK, Annual Matrix, 1983 (£million)

	Row No.	Public Sector	Monetary Sector	Other Financial Institutions	Industrial and Commercial (1)	Personal Sector	Overseas Sector	Residual Error
CAPITAL ACCOUNT								
Saving	(1)	+ 4,756		+6,398	+24,835	+16,977	−2,049	
Taxes on capital and capital transfers	(2)	− 1,188		− 335	+ 475	+ 1,048	—	
less:								
Gross fixed capital formation at home	3	−13,442		−5,704	−15,103	−11,441		
Increase in value of stocks and work in progress	4	− 886		− 85	− 3,528	− 571		
FINANCIAL SURPLUS +/DEFICIT −	5	−10,760		+ 274	+ 6,679	6,013	−2,049	−157

FINANCIAL TRANS-ACTIONS ACCOUNT
Changes in financial assets and liabilities

Assets: increase+/decrease−
Liabilities: increase−/decrease+

cont.

6	Notes and coin	− 822	+ 129	—	+ 117	+ 583	− 7
7	Market Treasury bills	− 32	− 29	+ 75	− 47		+ 33
8	British Government securities	− 9,468	+ 229	+ 6,669	+ 353	+ 1,314	+ 903
9	National savings	− 2,955		+ 11	+ 83	+ 2,861	
10	Other public sector debts	+ 262	− 238	+ 12	− 86	+ 49	+ 1
11	Issue Department's transactions in commercial bills	− 725			+ 725		
12	Government foreign currency and overseas financing	+ 137					− 137
13	Official reserves	− 603					+ 603
	Local Authority debt:						
14.1	Temporary	− 66	+ 83	− 45	− 27	+ 72	− 17
14.2	Foreign currency	− 78	—	—			+ 78
14.3	Sterling securities	+ 233	− 254	+ 4		+ 24	− 7
14.4	Other sterling debt	+ 2,308	− 1,748	− 156	− 37	− 365	− 2

Table 2.1 cont.

	Row No.	Public Sector	Monetary Sector	Other Financial Institutions	Industrial and Commercial (1)	Personal Sector	Overseas Sector	Residual Error
Public Corporation debt:								
Foreign currency	15.1	− 101	+ 115	−			− 14	
Other	15.2	+ 236	− 227	− 4	−	+ 15	− 20	
Deposits with banks:								
Sterling sight	16.1	+ 91	− 4,369	+ 324	+ 1,396	+ 2,138	+ 420	
Sterling time	16.2	+ 16	− 8,590	+ 1,931	+ 2,086	+ 931	+ 3,626	
Foreign currency	16.3	− 4	−22,020	+ 499	+ 1,834	− 167	+19,858	
Deposits with building societies	17		+ 694	−11,928	+ 740	+10,489	+ 5	
Bank lending (excl. public sector)								
Foreign currency	18.1		+20,392	− 790	− 616	+ 73	−19,059	
Sterling	18.2	− 748	+10,829	− 1,498	− 2,086	− 4,992	− 2,253	
Trade credit	19				+ 916	− 349	+ 181	
Loans for house purchase:								
Building societies	20.1			+11,041		−11,041		
Other	20.2	− 75	+ 3,597	+ 153		− 3,675		
Other public sector lending	21	+ 470			− 60	+ 25	− 435	
Other lending by financial institutions	22	−		+ 1,129	− 505	+ 624		
Unit trust units	23			− 608		+ 608		
UK company securities	24	− 481	+ 60	+ 2,371	− 1,095	− 2,335	+ 1,480	
Overseas securities	25	−	+ 2,773	+ 3,310	+ 580	+ 450	− 7,113	

Life assurance and pension funds	26	− 58		−13,945		+14,003		
Miscellaneous domestic instruments	27	—	—	− 101	+ 27	+ 74	—	
Direct and other investment abroad	28		− 282	+ 3	+4,062		− 3,783	
Overseas direct and other investment in United Kingdom	29		− 209	− 143	−3,880		+ 4,232	
Miscellaneous overseas instruments	30	+ 595		− 96	− 698		+ 199	
Accruals adjustment	31	+ 740	+ 4	+ 274	−1,200	+ 182		
TOTAL FINANCIAL TRANSACTIONS	32	−11,128	+ 939	− 1,508	+2,582	+10,343	− 1,228	
Balancing item	33	+ 368	+843		+4,097	− 4,330	− 821	− 157

—nil or less than £½ million
Relationships between rows: 1+2−3−4=5; 6 to 31=32; 32+33=5
(1) Industrial and commercial companies.

Source: *BEQB*, June 1984, p. 217

N.B. This is a somewhat condensed version of the annual matrix published in the source and regularly published for each year in *Financial Statistics* (table S17).

those concerning changes in the distribution of wealth. It thus identifies and measures financial flows connected with the accumulation and disposal of funds in the economy as a whole, and therefore shows the sources and uses of funds by economic sectors.

The columns of the financial transactions matrix represent changes in the holdings of assets and in sources and uses of funds of each surplus or deficit sector, indicating changes in their balance sheets. For instance, the personal sector in 1983 deposited with the monetary sector (viz. increased its monetary assets by) £2.9 billion (under 'Personal sector', the sum of rows (16.1) – (16.3)), but also increased its debts (liabilities) with the monetary sector by £4.9 billion (rows (18.1) and (18.2)), not counting net lending of £3.5 billion for house purchase, which came from the monetary sector too (row (20.2)). The sector sold £2.3 billion of UK company securities (row (24)), but purchased £4.2 billion of government stocks and National Savings (rows (8) and (9)). Changes in preferences of sectors reflected by FF matrices can have an important bearing on monetary control.

Rows represent the distribution of financial claims between the supplying and the demanding sectors. For instance, the suppliers of sterling sight deposits (row (16.1)) are banks; the demanders or holders are all other sectors. Building society deposits (row (17)), though demanded by other sectors in small quantities, are predominantly held by the personal sector. Examining the FF matrix, and in particular the annual matrices for a series of years, can be quite rewarding, and readers interested in monetary and financial matters are strongly encouraged to do so.[7]

From the FF matrix it is possible to identify changes to some monetary aggregates, including sterling M3 (£M3), serving as the key monetary target (to be discussed in section 4.2). If we abbreviate the names of the sectors (columns), we have:

Other financial institutions	ofi
Industrial and commercial companies	ic
Personal sector	ps

and the names of assets (rows)

Notes and coin (row (6))	N
Bank deposits (sight) (row (16.1))	D
Bank deposits (time) (row (16.2))	T
Bank deposits (foreign) (row (16.3))	F

Then, for example, N_{ic} would mean notes and coin of industrial and commerical companies; T_{ps} would mean time deposits of the private sector; and so on.

The change in monetary aggregates can be read from the FF matrix as shown below. Values are for 1983 (in £ billion).

Row (6)   Row (16.1)

$$\Delta M1 = (N_{ic} + N_{ps}) + (D_{ofi} + D_{ic} + D_{ps})$$
$$\Delta M1 = 0.1 + 0.6 \quad + 0.3 \quad + 1.4 + 2.1 = 4.5$$

Row (16.2)

$$\Delta £M3 = \Delta M1 + (T_{ofi} + T_{ic} + T_{ps})$$
$$\Delta £M3 = 4.5 \quad + 1.9 \quad + 2.1 + 0.9 = 9.4$$

Row (16.3)

$$\Delta M3 = \Delta £M3 + (F_{ofi} + F_{ic} + F_{ps})$$
$$\Delta M3 = 9.4 \quad + 0.5 \quad + 1.8 - 0.2 = 11.9$$

Thus, monetary aggregates are extracted from a large interrelated system of financial flows resulting in changes in the holding of assets. The extent to which the results of some asset changes are so clearly distinguishable from other asset changes as to deserve a special label of 'monetary' changes, and the extent to which such changes correspond to changes in money of economic theory, will be further elaborated.

Even the somewhat shortened version of the FF matrix in table 2.1 does clearly convey the complexity of the financial system, the variety of financial assets and liabilities, the international character of finance, and the importance of the link between the outcome of 'real' decisions expressed in the capital account and of financial transactions in the rest of the matrix. It suggests a connection between production, saving and investment decisions in the 'real' sectors, and in the complex world of financial and monetary transactions, both at home and abroad, and both in sterling and in foreign currencies.

It should, however, be stressed that the matrix is an accounting system, an *ex post* expression, based on a set of conventions which may be limiting in a conceptual and statistical sense. Like any accounting system, it supplies us with some vital information, but it does not have the same explanatory or predictive value as behavioural models. On the other hand, the FF matrix yields some identities that are useful in the analysis of changes in monetary aggregates, which can be helpful for monetary control purposes.

Some economists consider that the FF framework provides the basic accounting system underlying any general model of the monetary or financial mechanism (Modigliani and Papademos, 1980, pp. 119–24). Flow-of-funds accounting offers a development in macroeconomic theory which overcomes a number of shortcomings of both conventional supply and demand for money and the *IS-LM* analyses. The Yale school of economics, and the Cowles Commission in the USA in particular, have for some time sought to develop models which integrate decisions on saving and expenditure with portfolio decisions. In the *IS-LM* model, these are undertaken in separate sectors: expenditure decisions in the *IS* 'market' and portfolio decisions in the *LM*, the money market. More specifically, in the *IS-LM* model the savings function explains why households save, but there is no function describing how they wish to hold the increases to wealth. With a given wealth, wealth-holders, in deciding on their portfolio balance (in *LM*), determine asset prices (interest rates). 'The unwelcome implication is that wealth-owners and savers, in formulating their portfolio demands, ignore the fact that they are at the same time saving to augment their wealth. In contrast to the *LM* markets in stocks, the simultaneous *IS* equations are grinding out *flows* of goods and services' (Tobin, 1982, p. 187). In reality, financial markets simultaneously handle flows emanating from saving in various sectors and portfolio readjustments by the sectors. It is difficult to separate intermediating functions and asset transmutation functions broadly interpreted (see section 2.2).

Referring to an FF matrix, Tobin, the best-known protagonist of the Yale school, succinctly summarized the approach:

> [A] column represents a sector's balance sheet (stocks) or sources and uses of funds (flows). A row distributes the stock or flow of an asset over the supplying and demanding sectors. The task of theory and estimation is to bring the columns to life by functions relating sectoral portfolio and saving decisions to relevant variables, and to bring the rows to life as a set of simultaneous market-clearing equations. [Tobin, 1982, p. 175]

Thus, a complex general equilibrium model may be envisaged to convey, more convincingly than the *IS-LM* scheme, the interdependence between the real and financial sectors of the economy. Indeed, this approach is already being utilized in large macroeconomic forecasting models. For instance, there is no directly controllable 'money' in the Treasury or the Bank of England macro-models, and no explicit demand for money function is modelled (H.M. Treasury, 1979, pp. 74–84; Thompson, 1984, pp. 139–43).

From our point of view, the objective is not to elaborate on flow-of-funds models as such, but to draw attention to the possibility of incorporating into a macroeconomic model a disaggregated financial sector in which demand and supply relationships for a number of financial assets are included, allowing us to avoid the difficult problem of having to define and select a unique 'asset' called 'money'. More importantly, a simultaneous equations scheme would allow us to reflect the interdependence characterizing market economies with sophisticated financial systems. Such an approach would provide more information than the orthodox approaches, where money often is the only financial asset relevant to the explanation of income or price changes.

The idea of disaggregation to avoid definitional difficulties surrounding money, and, more fundamentally, to prevent an information loss which, by definition, is involved in using aggregates, is by no means new.[8] Financial modelling on a large scale, however, is difficult, complex, and often hampered by the lack of appropriate data and resources needed to supply team research effort. Sometimes regarded as a 'Keynesian' methodology of 'descriptive realism', it runs counter to the more widely accepted positive economics method of predicting something large from something small (compare section 1.4.1). Nevertheless, it may well be a more appropriate approach to cope with the problems of analysing financial change than the latter (Backus *et al.*, 1980). Macroeconomic models containing 'money' as the only explicit financial variable must continue to beg the question of what kind of 'money' is involved and what information it yields (Tobin, 1983b, p. 516).

In this chapter we have stressed that the explanation of the continuing evolution of the financial sector from which monetary assets are derived is to be found in the response to the changing requirements of the 'real' sector and the provision of financial services which overcome market imperfections and friction. Interdependence and the pressure to adapt emerge time and again as the important features of the financial system. Given a relatively unfettered state of competition in financial markets, the above characteristics suggest that it might well prove singularly difficult to identify 'money' which meets the onerous burden imposed upon it by macroeconomic theory and by policy inspired by monetarism.

Notes

1 See Shaw (1973) and McKinnon (1973) in the USA, and Thirlwall (1974) in the UK.
2 In some studies (Bordo and Jonung, 1981; Klovland, 1983), the ratio of currency to broadly defined money was used as an empirical proxy for secular changes in financial sophistication.
3 Hall (1982) outlines the school's views mentioning some of its disciples. See also the conference contributions in the *Journal of Monetary Economics*, vol. 12, 1983; finally, a survey by White (1984a) is particularly useful.
4 Indeed, the key objective of the Wilson Committe (1980) was to discover whether the British economic ailments were in any way connected with ineffective financial intermediation. See also Carrington and Edwards (1981).
5 Derivation of a simple bank credit multiplier k can be found in most texts (see e.g. Dennis, 1981, ch. 7). Examples of the orthodox multiplier exposition, together with their comparisons with the alternative portfolio adjustment approaches to the generation of money, are to be found in Goodhart (1975, ch. 6).
6 In the UK, change in the wide monetary base M0 (see section 4.2) can be expressed in the following accounting identity:

$$\Delta M0 = CGBR - net\ SGD - net\ OSB + MM$$

where CGBR is the central government borrowing requirement, SCD refers to sales of central government debt to all sectors, OSB is other sterling and foreign currency borrowing and MM, all forms of assistance by the Bank of England (for details see BE, 1984c, pp. 488–9). Though the expression does not imply a behavioural relation, it suggests that the usual statement that monetary authorities should be able to control their own liabilities is an oversimplification.

7 FF matrices are published in *Financial Statistics* (tables S17) and *BEQB* (see e.g. *BEQB*, June 1984, pp. 212–21).

8 Various forms of disaggregation have been utilized in monetary economics. Disaggregation has been attempted in connection, for instance, with demand-for-money studies in terms of sectoral demand functions (for business firms, households, etc.); see e.g. Goldfeld (1973, pp. 626–32; 1976, pp. 709–20). Examples of models incorporating a disaggregated monetary sector, but often including 'money' as an important variable are not uncommon. Some large forecasting models are of such a character (see Thompson, 1984). A variety of structural models with the flow-of-funds as the underlying framework have been developed: see e.g. Hendershott (1977); Modigliani and Papademos (1980); Papademos and Modigliani (1983); Backus *et al.* (1980).

— Part II —
In Search of Money

—3—

Identification and Measurement of Money

3.1 *A priori* approaches to the definition of money

3.1.1 *Money's functions*

'When the student is asked "what is money?" he still has no choice but to give the conventional answer. Money is defined by its functions: anything is money which is used as money: "money is what money does"' (Hicks, 1967, p. 1). The functions are usually specified as: a unit of account, a means of payment and a store of value, and a standard of deferred payment.

The foundation literature to the economics of money traditionally takes a *microeconomic starting-point*: what is money to an individual transactor or wealth-holder and why is it demanded? The answer is usually given in terms of the functions stated above and related to increased utility derived from monetization, that is, from the introduction of money to overcome the constraints characteristic of barter.[1] The discussion is then extended and generalized to indicate the resulting improvement in the welfare or efficiency of an economy with a money system as opposed to a barter system. How such money finds its way to a macroeconomic model approximating an advanced economy is rarely considered.

Apart from the customary functions of money stated above, some economists, following Keynes (1973, p. 294), emphasize the role of money as 'a subtle device for linking the present to the future'. Our expectations of the future affect our present actions; uncertainty about future developments drives us into holding money as a store of value (or temporary abode of purchasing power). This characteristic is strongly related to money being a medium which is always acceptable in all markets.

This aspect of money is often linked with another social device which helps to overcome uncertainty in business transaction, namely contracts, including money wage contracts. 'In a world of uncertainty where production takes time, the existence of money contracts permits the sharing of the burdens of uncertainties between the contracting parties whenever resources are to be committed to produce a flow of goods for a delivery date in the future' (Davidson, 1978, p. 149). The importance of contracts was further empha- sized by Arrow and Hahn, who added that money is also 'a link between the past and the present. If a serious monetary theory comes to be written, the fact that contracts are indeed made in terms of money will be of considerable importance' (1971, p. 357). It is also argued that money plays 'an essential and peculiar role only when contractual obligations span a significant interval of calendar time' (Davidson, 1980, p. 298).

The time dimension and uncertainty pose some difficulty to orthodox economic analysis, founded on the essentially timeless Walrasian framework in which trading is moneyless. The reference above to the lack of a 'serious monetary' theory alludes to difficulties which have been experienced in solving the puzzle of how to introduce money into the general equilibrium system, and thus create a monetary theory which would be a logical extension of the theory of value. The dilemma of 'How to make money appear without making the standard theory disappear' (Ostroy, 1973, p. 608) is approached by visualizing an exchange economy as a sequence of disaggregated bilateral trading arrangements or chains. The case for money is made on the basis of its general acceptability as a means of exchange and the consequent reduction of transactions costs. Research in this field is abstract and mathematical, but the concept of sequential trading and the stress on the transactions costs rationale are widely exploited.

Uncertainty and contracts are closely linked with transactions costs, which include information costs on vital aspects of exchange such as the demand for and supply of goods traded and their pricing. Transfers from one form of wealth to another, and the contracting and recontracting which accompany each disturbance from an equilibrium situation, also involve costs. To individuals or society, the asset which would thus reduce transactions costs and the length of a transactions chain would be money, and thus a part of wealth would be allocated to holding it (Brunner and Meltzer, 1971, p. 799). 'Deferred payments, borrowing, credit and payments system expand when a standardized asset with well known properties becomes available' (p. 800). However, society does not necessarily converge to a single medium of exchange. 'Even in highly developed economies with extensive monetary institutions, transactors can use specialized information to develop transac- tions arrangements that lower transfer costs by avoiding the use of money' (p. 802). We may, however, recall that, in the context of the macroeconomic demand function for money, uncertainty and transactions costs, so strongly highlighted in the microeconomics of money, are usually assumed away because of measurement problems.

3.1.2 *Macroeconomic emphasis*

Before Keynes influenced its course, macroeconomics was concerned essen- tially with the theory of the trade cycle. At that time, monetary and credit theories clashed with real theories of economic fluctuations. Keynes reorientated the thrust of macroeconomics to national income formation. Although, after a period of comparative neglect in the 1960s and early 1970s, we are currently witnessing something of a revival of interest in the trade cycle theory, the dominant concern of modern macroeconomics remains income and price formation. Interest in money in this context has been confined essentially to 'macroeconomic money', a variable which, through the rate of interest or more complex channels, influences nominal income – or, in some versions of the quantity theory, directly affects the price level.

There seems to be a gulf in economics between the microeconomic consideration and the macroeconomics of money, so much so that the two appear to be effectively different subjects. Bronfenbrenner (1980, p. 309), commenting on the four traditional functions of money, added a fifth function, that of 'a "handle" for macroeconomic management, discretionary or otherwise by "monetary authorities"'. He noted that there were other alternative handles, better or worse, such as the budget and exchange rates, but was unable to point out what was the 'money' which can thus be 'handled'.

Brunner and Meltzer (1971) considering this issue in their influential work, suggested that

> The recognition of the central role of a medium of exchange does not imply that the collection of assets that serve as medium of exchange is most appropriate for explaining movements of the general price level. A definition embracing a larger collection of assets is appropriate if there are close substitutes for the medium of exchange on the supply side. [Brunner and Meltzer, 1971, p. 803]

This, once again, reminds us of the ambiguities attaching to the term 'money' (compare section 1.2.3).

It would have been highly convenient if all the functions associated with money pointed to a definite real-world counterpart. The *a priori* functional approach, whether embracing the traditional four functions, or together with the macroeconomic control role, or with its modern emphasis on uncertainty, contracts and transactions costs, does not unambiguously point to an indicative definition, to any single real-life object or collection of assets. Indeed, some of the functions may be performed jointly or separately by a number of counterparts.

To monetarists, the issue of the indicative definition of money has became basically empirical.

> A distinction between 'money' and 'other assets' has been found extremely useful for a long time in many contexts. There is nothing that makes this inevitable. The continuum of assets might be so gradual, and substitution between various types so easy and frequent, that no sub-total would have any particular significance short of, let us say, total non-human wealth. It is an empirical generalization that this is not the case: there is a sub-total, labelled

'money' for convenience, which it is useful to distinguish because it is related
to other economic magnitudes in a fairly regular and stable way, though its
particular content may be different from place to place or time to time. This
empirical generalization underlies the distinction between price theory and
monetary theory – a distinction that has been central in economic analysis for
centuries. [F–S, 1970, p. 90]

This approach is consistent with the methodology of positive economics.
The chief goal of empirical work is 'to find a way of organizing experience so
that it yields "simple" yet highly dependable relationships' (see section 1.4).
Thus, the search for the empirical or experimental 'definition' of money
begins. If economic theory does not show the way, statistics might.

Yet it is by no means obvious how to design statistical investigations which
would yield 'money' appropriate for macroeconomic purposes. The difficulty, of course, is that what is appropriate for macroeconomic purposes
depends on one's perception of macroeconomics. Different macroeconomic
theories would point to different concepts of money (see section 1.2). Herein
lies one of the great difficulties of appraising the identification of money
empirically, discussed below.

3.2 Empirical 'definitions' by 'best' results

The empirical solution accepts that definitional issues should be decided not
as a matter of principle, but as a matter of expediency (F–S, 1963a, p. 650),
on 'the grounds of usefulness of organizing our knowledge of economic
relationships' (F–S, 1970, pp. 104, 137). However, in the absence of a clear
theoretical indication of what constitutes money, there are some serious
methodological difficulties in this approach. Indeed, it is doubtful whether
definitional issues, in general, can be solved empirically or statistically.

An excellent exposition of methodological pitfalls is given by W. E. Mason
(1976), who reminds us that it is too easy in this procedure to confuse the
concept of money with the quantity, viz. the definition with the quantifica-
tion of money. In the absence of the 'right' theoretical definition of the
concept, there cannot be a 'right' empirical definition. Strictly speaking, it is
not the definition, but the identification, which is derived empirically. What
is involved is a selection of liquid assets – of 'various identified species of the
unidentified genus, money' (Mason, 1976, pp. 525–6). The crucial warning is
that 'Conceptualization must precede definition in order to produce a testable
hypothesis capable of empirical verification as a theory' (p. 533).

Bearing this in mind, some attempts to measure the quantity of money or
to identify monetary assets will be outlined briefly. Fundamentally, two
approaches are encountered: one, the identification of a set of assets which
are sufficiently close substitutes to be easily aggregated into 'money', and
which can collectively serve as the 'money' of macroeconomics; the other, a

selection of assets containing qualities of 'moneyness', and the measurement and aggregation of the 'moneyness'.

A range of techniques has been used to identify money, some of which are of considerable technical sophistication. The purpose here is to provide a general exposition avoiding technical and operational detail. Care will be taken to point out the context in which money is being 'defined' empirically.

3.2.1 *Dual criteria of correlation*

We recall that monetarists see the essence of empirical work in the ability to organize experience so as to produce highly dependable relationships.

> One of the successful devices for achieving this has been the use of carefully chosen, 'right' levels of aggregations of different items, as in such a construct as 'money', 'income', 'consumption', etc. . . . This choice . . . is one that cannot be made by any single set of hard and fast rules. It is a question of judgement on the basis of criteria that are inevitably incomplete and often unformulated. The test of the choice is in the results, that is, in the usefulness of the definitions selected in uncovering dependable and reproducible empirical regularities. [F–S, 1970, pp. 197–8]

In a well-known study of the relative performance of a simple Keynesian macroeconomic model with a simple monetarist model, M. Friedman and D. I. Meiselman (F–M) argued that 'the precise empirical definition of variables should be selected so as to put the theory in question in its best light' (1963, p. 181). Accordingly, they sought the help of correlation coefficients in selecting their variables – to 'correlate alternatively defined measures of the independent variable with the dependent variable and then select the concept which yields the highest correlation'. With regard to the aggregation of financial assets in order to arrive at the appropriate money stock measure, two criteria were specified:

1 money was to be that aggregate which had the highest correlation with money income;
2 income must be more highly correlated with the aggregate than with each component of the aggregate.

The authors took into account only three components of the money supply (currency, demand deposits and time deposits) and tried to determine whether time deposits (D_t) should be included in the money aggregate. If the aggregate inclusive of D_t were more highly correlated with income than that excluding it, and if the correlation between D_t alone and income were less than the correlation with the aggregate, then D_t would be considered to be a close substitute for other components and would have to be included in the aggregate selected.

The choice fell on the 'broad aggregate' embodying all the components. It was then used to show that there was a close and consistent relation between the stock of money (viz. the aggregate) and income (or aggregate consumption).

The above-mentioned criteria were modified and utilized by others. G. G. Kaufman (1969) extended the number of financial components of 'money' to embrace some claims of financial institutions other than commercial banks, and provided for time lags of up to four quarters between changes in the aggregates and GNP, and for time leads of one and two quarters. The main conclusions for the 1953–66 period were that only a limited number of 'definitions' satisfied the dual criteria. The 'definition' of money changed depending on whether financial assets were related to income in current, preceding or following periods.

D. T. Hulett (1971) introduced a distributed lag dispersed over several quarters. His results (for the period 1953–68) were essentially similar to Kaufman's, and the application of distributed lags did not alter the conclusions drawn from the discrete-lag experiments. However, whereas Kaufman concluded that his findings for the whole period did not differ greatly from those observed for his two sub-periods, Hulett discovered that many of the correlation coefficients had changed significantly in his sub-periods. 'A developing financial sophistication of the household and business sectors over the recent years may have led to some of the differences between the two sub-periods' (Hulett, 1971, p. 464). The fact that the dual criteria were more often met in the second sub-period was interpreted by the author as indicating that the increasingly competitive nature of US financial markets in the 1960s resulted in a more widespread asset substitution. These aspects will be discussed further in Part III.

The empirical approach suggested by F–M soon attracted criticism, mainly of a methodological nature. The selection of data in this manner resulted in the circularity of argument. 'This practice of using the same data, or roughly similar data, both to choose the definitions of variables (the definition being, of course, really part of the overall hypothesis) and to test the hypothesis is particularly suspect' (DePrano and Mayer, 1965, p. 732). To some it was inadmissible as a scientific procedure (Lombra, 1980, pp. 275–7). W. E. Mason (1976, p. 532) generalized the criticism nicely, stating that 'An empirical definition of money designed to validate a monetary hypothesis precludes empirical invalidation.'

Before departing from the correlation between income and money, the significance attached by Friedman and his associates to the statistical relation between the two variables should be accentuated. With reference to both the USA and the UK, F–S claimed that:

> The level of nominal income parallels with great fidelity the level of the nominal quantity of money, and the rate of change of nominal income parallels the rate

of change of the nominal quantity of money . . . . This parallelism is a manifestation of the stable demand curve for money plus the excellence of the simple quantity theory approximation. [F–S, 1982, p. 7]

3.2.2 *Demand for money stability criteria*

The importance of the demand for money in the monetarist counter-revolution has already been mentioned (section 1.4). Following a lengthy discussion of *a priori* approaches to the definition of money, F–S (1970, p. 137) discouraged the usual practice of placing emphasis on money as the medium of exchange: 'We see no compelling reason to regard the literal medium-of-exchange function as the "essential" function of the items we wish to call "money".' Instead, stress was placed on conditions of demand. Referring to their historical studies (see section 1.3), they claimed that, while conditions of money supply changed drastically, demand conditions remained stable. 'Hence we are led to put primary emphasis on demand and to seek a definition of money that could be regarded as having as nearly as possible the same meaning to the holders of money balances over the entire period of our study' (p. 139).

This point was expressed in more specific terms when it was suggested that the desideratum was a monetary total whose real value bears a relatively stable relation to a small number of variables, such as wealth or income, interest rates, and the rate of change in prices (F–S, 1970, pp. 139–40). Meltzer (1963, p. 222) took the issue a step further, suggesting that: 'The problem is that of defining money so that a stable demand function can be shown to have existed under differing institutional arrangements, changes in social and political environment, and changes in economic conditions, or to explain the effects of such changes on the function.'

The procedure for finding the 'right' definition of the money supply, by discovering the most stable money demand postulated by monetarists, became quite widely accepted in the 1960s and 1970s. Laidler claimed that, in order to influence the behaviour of the economy in a predictable way by manipulating the money supply, the necessary preconditions were that:

> the authorities must be able to control the volume of that set of assets that most closely corresponds to the 'money stock' of standard macroeconomics; at the same time the demand function for this stock of assets must be stable enough for the consequences of changing its volume to be predictable with a high degree of reliability.[2] [Laidler, 1969, p. 509]

Disregarding the difficulty of agreeing on what constitutes the 'standard macroeconomics', it is clear that, if the empirical criterion for the identification of money were the predictable ultimate results of macroeconomic policy, then the *controllability* of money and the *stability* of its demand would be equally important. In practice, these two aspects are rarely considered together, and the stability of the money demand has received considerably more attention in this context.

A frequently encountered procedure has been to select the most statistically efficient aggregate in the process of searching for the specification of a stable demand for money. The 'right' money stock was a byproduct of the demand-for-money studies – 'in determining whether a given function is stable with respect to a number of theoretically appropriate variables, one is able simultaneously to determine the appropriate definition of the money aggregate' (Khan, 1974, p. 1206). The aggregates usually considered were the 'narrow' and 'broad' totals available from official statistical publications.

As already stated, until the episodes of demand-for-money 'breakdown' in the mid-1970s, there was a general consensus that demand-for-money functions were stable and robust, regardless of the 'definition' of money (section 1.4). Thus, resorting to the stability criterion in order to identify the 'right' counterpart of theoretical 'money' was rather inconclusive. 'The question of definition must still remain open' (Khan, 1974, p. 1217). Laumas and Mehra (1977, p. 915) also concluded that, as the demand for M1 and M2 in the USA were both stable, the choice of 'definitions' could not be made 'by appealing to the stability criterion'. Some suggested that the aggregate to be used should therefore be the one which was easier to control (Laidler, 1969, pp. 523–4).

Attempting to define money by the criterion of stability is, just like the dual criteria above, methodologically unsound, as it involves a circular argument. One cannot simultaneously determine the stability of a money-demand function and define 'money'. A further serious difficulty lies in the fact that the concept of stability used in the context of the demand for money has not been uniformly understood and interpreted.[3] In the theoretical literature, Friedman and his associates often refer to the relative stability of the demand function which contains a small number of variables. The stress is on *functional* stability; that is, the function need not be static, but its behaviour must not be erratic or unpredictable. Yet the interpretation of the stability of the function, especially in the context in which it is of interest to us, has been narrower.

The meaning most frequently attached to stability was parametric stability, implying not so much the constancy of coefficients defining a demand relationship, but rather the absence of significant differences between the regression coefficients in various sample periods, signifying that the demand process remained unchanged. There were however other, less restrictive, interpretations of stability, such as those associated with the application of varying parameters models,[4] which assume that parameters may be subject to permanent and transitory changes over time. Such models are said to be stable only if regression parameters are not subject to permanent variations over time.

A variety of statistical tests of stability of demand-for-money functions have been used (Boughton, 1981a, pp. 582–4; Judge, 1983, pp. 7–9). Most commonly, these were applied in the context of testing the specification of the model, and not in the context of investigating whether there has been an institutional or behavioural change in the process being modelled. Thus, there was frequently a prior assumption that there existed a stable relationship between the demand for money and a few explanatory variables, but some uncertainty remained about this relationship's specific form. The search for the most appropriate dependent variable (viz. 'money') was an important aspect of it. Judge (1983, p. 12) concluded that 'stability tests appear to have been used in the demand-for-money context primarily as a means of choosing between specifications rather than in testing for genuine structural change'.

Moreover, because of the variety of tests of stability used, it was not possible in most cases to reach clear conclusions as to whether a given function was stable. 'What is possible is to identify specific cases of instability and to associate them with the economic factors that seem likely to have produced them' (Boughton, 1981a, p. 593). However, in the early 1980s, even those who earlier staunchly advocated defining money by the criterion of stability admitted that the demand for money 'has shifted in an unpredictable way in a number of countries', and that the *definition of money by best results had ceased to be a feasible option* (Laidler, 1981, p. 4).

The relatively poor performance of the traditional demand-for-money functions in the 1970s was associated with growing criticism of the design of econometric experiments in general. Some issues, though not directly relevant to our main concern here, are nevertheless pertinent and are briefly summarized below. Other widely debated subjects (such as causality and exogeneity) are left out in this context.

In the attempt to put his theory in the best light (compare section 3.2.1), the researcher often tended to stray into the practice of pulling 'from the bramble of computer output the one thorn of a model he likes best, the one he chooses to portray as a rose' (Leamer, 1983, p. 37). Thus, specification searches, designed to select the most promising regressions with the most statistically effective data, were unduly influenced by a strong element of advocacy for the theory which was being subjected to empirical tests (Cooley and Le Roy, 1981). Prior beliefs, rather than complete sample information, tended to be reflected in reported results.

Another area of criticism relates to procedures when dealing with multivariate time-series analysis (Hendry and Richard, 1981). In this realm, exemplifications based on the demand for money (short-term, transactions demand) are not infrequent (e.g. Hendry and Mizon, 1978; Hendry, 1979). Standard econometric models were, in the 1970s, tightly specified with prior restrictions (see n. 16 in chapter 1), paying insufficient attention to the time-series characteristics of data. The alternative approach to modelling now advocated underlines the role of stringent evaluation in model-building. Essentially, the recommended method is to begin with a general, deliberately over-parametrized, dynamic model, which is then subjected to a process of data-based simplifications. The process involves the application of some stringent model design criteria (Hendry, 1983, pp. 193–220) and sequential testing, leading to re-parametrization and eventually to the derivation of a simplified specification. The general-to-specific procedures encompass the earlier specifications and enable us, to some extent, to account for the instability and predictive failure of previous, more restricted, models.

The advocates of the new approach to time-series analysis have thus been critical of the older estimated demand-for-money equations and their interpretation. The bold assertions of F–S (1982) concerning the stability of the demand for money, based on the traditional econometric method, proved unjustified after the data used were subjected to the analysis following the more rigorous model evaluation procedures (Hendry and Ericsson, 1983). However, the debate on econometric methodology is continuing, and in this connection the sense in which an economic relationship is stable is not completely settled. It may be noted that the new methodology has had a greater impact in Europe than in the USA, where the standard demand-for-money functions continued to be widely used in the early 1980s.

The above developments, relating to time-series analysis, refer to single-equation models. One of the consequences of the financial developments in the 1970s was the recognition of the possibility of shifts of both the demand and the supply functions for 'money', and also of a disequilibrium between them (Artis and Lewis, 1976; 1981, pp. 17–25).

Traditional demand-for-money studies tended to assume that the economy was 'on the demand curve' – the assumption which was considered to absolve researchers from paying serious attention to the problem of identification. (The term is used here in the specific, statistical sense, and not in the general sense used in the text in connection especially with the indicative definition of money.) However, with the possibility of demand shifts emerging clearly in the 1970s, issues of identification and simultaneity could no longer be ignored. Indeed, specification searches which did so were severely criticized. T. F. Cooley and S. F. Le Roy (1981) judge identification and simultaneity in the context of monetary studies to be intractable issues; even when the demand for money is specified using a simultaneous equation (money supply and demand) model, the identification problem is hard to solve, as both the money stock and the interest rate are considered by the authors to be endogenous. 'Thus we are left with the conclusion that we are unpersuaded by existing attempts to estimate a money demand equation, but we are unable to supply an attractive alternative' (Cooley and Le Roy, 1981, p. 843).

Furthermore, serious questions are now being asked in some quarters about the appropriateness of using the demand-for-money functions, except perhaps for narrow aggregates. Aggregating financial assets by a simple summing assumes implicitly that the assets are perfect substitutes. As components, particularly those of broad aggregates, are not likely to be perfect substitutes, and indeed include some distant substitutes (according to some empirical enquiries), there is 'really no demand equation for the simple sum aggregate at all' (Barnett, 1982, p. 702). This point will be explained in section 3.4. However, demand functions for some narrow aggregates have not been well behaved; consequently, in the USA, M1 as a target became unreliable in 1983, and a similar fate befell the Canadian M1 following the spread of financial innovations (Freedman, 1983). Thus, the identification of money by criteria of demand stability today looks quite hazardous. This point will be further developed in the context of financial innovations.

In all, investigations of the demand for money, defined by monetarists as a stable function of a small number of variables, were assigned an ambitious task in monetary economics. They were intended to indicate the essential elements of a predictable transmission mechanism, to 'define' the money supply, and to distinguish between money and its substitutes (a point to be developed later). It is perhaps not surprising that they have not accomplished these tasks conclusively. It is also possible that, within the framework of positive methodology, economists held overinflated expectations from econometrics; that they utilized statistical procedures too mechanically, and leaned too far towards putting their theories in the best light.

3.3 Measuring the 'moneyness' of assets

As already pointed out, in seeking an indicative definition of money, one set of difficulties emanates from the fact that monetary theory does not yield a clear guide to the identification of 'monetary' assets; the other derives from the considerable complexity, flexibility and adaptability of the financial sector which supplies the economy with claims (assets) from which we endeavour to select combinations which comprise 'money definitions' or 'monetary aggregates'.

A fairly common approach to the selection problem is to look upon the set of financial assets as a spectrum or continuum of assets possessing, in different degrees, the characteristics of 'moneyness'. One procedure used in 'defining' money is to choose assets which are close substitutes and then to combine them to derive a monetary total. It is implicit in this approach that there is a gap, a clear break, in the continuum, which it is necessary to discover empirically, and which offers us a natural dividing line between 'money' and 'near-money', or 'money' and 'non-money' assets.

Another, though related, approach is to measure the degree of 'moneyness' of all financial assets deemed by a prior knowledge to possess monetary characteristics, and to construct a weighted average or index which combines this 'moneyness'. Implicit in this approach is the view that financial assets are composite commodities or joint products containing 'moneyness' separable from the 'non-money' part. Thus, the measures of 'moneyness' serve as weights in deriving an indicative definition of money. Assets with the highest value of 'moneyness' can be assigned weights of one, and those with the lowest degree (non-money assets), weights of zero. A simple aggregation of assets implicitly allocates an equal weight of one to the components of the aggregate and of zero to all other assets. 'Moneyness' is often understood intuitively, as it is rarely clearly defined. Frequently, accent is placed on the transactions characteristics or transactions 'services' of money; sometimes its other qualities, such as 'liquidity', are emphasized.

The substitutability of assets is a controversial issue, related to the clash of the 'currency theories' and 'financial theories' of money (see section 1.2). In the postwar period, the main protagonists of the financial theory of money were Gurley and Shaw (hereafter G–S) (1955, 1960) and the Radcliffe Committee (Radcliffe Report, 1959). Their views, touched upon briefly in section 1.2.2, opposed the quantity theorists in debate that seems to have ebbed and flowed without coming to an end. The central theme of the debate has been the extent to which a restrictive policy operating on a quantity of money (by using interest rates) is likely to be circumvented by the offsetting effect of the growth, in the private financial sector, of liquid assets possessing monetary properties.

G–S and the Radcliffe Report directed attention specifically to the substitutability between money and assets of non-bank financial inter-mediaries. They claimed that a restriction on the supply of money, narrowly defined, would, as part of the transmission process, lead to the substitution of liquid assets (e.g. deposits of savings institutions) for money. Thus, the issue of substitutability between various financial assets became hotly disputed.

3.3.1   *Extension of simple correlation*

In the late 1960s, the proposition of the dual criteria of F–M inspired a somewhat more sophisticated technique of indicating substitutability than the simple correlation mentioned earlier. Proposed by Timberlake and Fortson (1967) and extended by Laumas (1968), it consisted of using multiple regression to measure the 'degree of moneyness' of liquid financial assets.

The original formulation used was:

$$Y = a + bM + cS$$

or

$$Y = a + b[M + (c/b)S]$$

where Y was nominal income, M currency and demand deposits and S a 'savings variable'; a, b, c were coefficients. The 'degree of moneyness' was to be indicated by the regression coefficients of M and S (viz. b and c). If $0 < c/b < 1$, then S would have some degree of moneyness; if $c/b = 1$, then M

and S would have the same degree of moneyness; and if $c/b < 0$, then S would be 'an investment' – the holding of M would have to be lowered to acquire S.

Laumas's results for 1947–66 US data showed that the degree of moneyness (c/b) for time deposits was 0.58; for mutual savings deposits, 0.48; and for savings and loans shares, 0.32.[5] All savngs variables were interpreted as having a significant degree of moneyness, substantiating the G–S position. From the point of view of finding a macroeconomic money equivalent, the degree-of-moneyness measure suggested above has similar methodological shortcomings to the F–M dual criteria.

3.3.2 *Interest cross-elasticity of the demand for money*

The demand for money was mustered to resolve yet another issue – that of substitutability between liquid assets, indicated by the interest cross-elasticity of money demand. The approach is to specify and estimate a demand for an asset considered to be money (usually currency and bank deposits) with explanatory variables including rates of return on one or more assets considered to be substitutes (in addition to income or wealth variables and sometimes other variables). The values of interest cross-elasticity can then be indicated by the estimated regression coefficients. Conventionally, high or rising interest cross-elasticity signifies the existence of good substitutes.

There are some difficulties with this approach. They are related to the more general matters of specification and estimation of the demand-for-money function.[6] The discussion below is confined only to some points of direct relevance in this context. First, the components of the dependent variable, 'money', are implicitly treated as perfect substitutes. In the majority of empirical studies, 'money' is assumed to be an interest-free asset, and thus there is no problem with 'own' interest rate. Some economists now disagree with this approach, claiming that, though explicit interest is not paid on a major component of 'money', that is, demand deposits, there is an implicit interest payment (arising from services associated with the holding of such deposits, which may include reductions of loan rates or the remission of service charges) which can be converted into an estimate of 'own' interest rate on money.[7] The issue of the increasing proportion of deposits bearing explicit interest contained in the narrow measure of money will be discussed in Part III. There is also a problem in choosing the potential substitutes for money and their rates of return. The inclusion of a number of interest rates on the substitutes in the demand specification also leads to serious problems of collinearity among them.[8]

Perhaps the most serious problem is the lack of agreement as to what value of cross-elasticity is to be taken as indicating close substitutability (Feige and Pearce, 1977, pp. 443, 456, 463). F–S (1970, p. 128) noted: 'the same numerical elasticity is described by one author as showing that the assets are "close" substitutes, by another that they are "weak" or "distant" substitutes. This ambiguity reflects the absence of any clear purpose in terms of which to judge the size of the elasticity.' Taking the usual price-theoretic convention of 'elastic' meaning a value of elasticity of more than one, and 'inelastic' less than one, the issue appears quite straightforward. However, such a mechanical acceptance of the convention does not serve as a useful guide in linking empirical results and policy issues.

Even if a value could be agreed, the division between money and other assets based on such a value would be excessively finite. As already stated, assets embodied in the monetary total are assumed to be perfect substitutes. In reality, financial assets share many characteristics, and many of them may indeed be close substitutes for each other. The question is whether some of them would be perfect substitutes, and whether there would be a justification for adopting an approach which appears to separate clearly the money totals from other assets (from near-money, or non-money). Among financial assets it is difficult to find perfect substitutes for, say, cash or demand deposits; on the other hand, few financial assets are unrelated to these. Thus, the all-or-nothing approach in 'defining' money does not appear to be very satisfactory (Chetty, 1969, p. 271).

In spite of some confusion in interpreting results, most studies of the demand for money in the 1960s and 1970s, using both cross-section and time-series data, revealed a low substitutability between narrowly defined aggregates (currency and demand deposits) and other financial assets. A study by Cagan and Schwartz (1975), designed to test the Gurley–Shaw–Radcliffe hypothesis that the demand for money was getting more interest-elastic as a result of an increasing number of money substitutes, found that, on the contrary, it was becoming less interest-elastic (implying a steeper LM, and hence a greater impact of money on economic activity). More recent evidence is, *in general*, not inconsistent with this conclusion.

We shall return to this topic in Part III, in the context of evaluating the impact of financial innovation on the demand for money. Readers should be warned, however, by Feige and Pearce (1977), who, in concluding their excellent survey on the substitutability between money and financial assets, observed that we should not necessarily interpret the above findings in terms of the insignificance of the effects of financial innovations on either the demand for money or monetary policy. Multicollinearity among interest rates, and the incorporation of only the readily available interest rates in demand-for-money equations, might understate the impact of financial changes or factors such as transactions costs, on which there are no readily available data (compare section 1.4.1). 'Future research on the issue of substitutability will therefore require not only the creation of more relevant data bases, but also a growing attention to institutional detail, which will hopefully enable us to take account of qualitative changes in asset characteristics. . . .'

A similar concern was expressed in a later study (Lieberman, 1979), whose substantive conclusions were at odds with the general results summed up by Feige and Pearce. Before discussing these, we may note two innovations introduced by the study concerning the specification of the demand-for-money function, partly to account for the financial changes mentioned above. Lieberman (1977) experimented with a novel scale variable (using a financial transactions variable estimated from bank debits to current accounts adjusted for currency transactions) as an alternative to the traditional income or wealth, and incorporated a time-trend as a proxy for the rate of technological change.[9] Interest rate elasticity of demand was found to increase as the money aggregate was made more inclusive. Liquid assets, including non-bank deposit liabilities, were found to have been demanded in part as narrow money substitutes (viz. for transactions motives) and in part as assets.

In general, these results supported the G–S hypothesis in the sense that near-monies were, at least to some degree, substitutes for money, though evidence on the extent to which 'near-monies' became 'nearer-monies' over time remained unsettled. The author concluded that: 'The mass of contradictory evidence on the money substitution issue suggests the need for additional research. And if near-monies do emerge as close money substitutes, additional research will be needed to re-examine the channels of monetary policy, as well as to review policy instrument and indicator issue (Lieberman, 1979, p. 251).

3.3.3 *Money as a weighted aggregate*

The main difficulty with measuring money as a weighted aggregate has been the derivation of appropriate weights. A weight would need to provide a measure of 'moneyness', or of monetary characteristics contained in each financial asset deemed, on the basis of some prior knowledge, to contain such characteristics.[10]

In a seminal work, V. K. Chetty (1969) suggested a more direct measure of substitution between financial assets than the interest cross-elasticity mentioned earlier. His general approach was to regard money as a weighted average of monetary assets with weights being related to the substitution parameters. The initial step was to include money M (currency and demand deposits) and asset T (time deposit) in a CES (constant elasticity of substitution, borrowed from production theory) utility function subject to a two-period constraint.[11] A regression model was derived from the marginal conditions of the maximized utility function subject to the constraint. Elasticity of substitution between money and time deposits was then obtained and subsequently was used as a weight for aggregation purposes. The model was then generalized[12] and extended to include four financial assets: M, T, shares in savings and loans associations (SL), and deposits in mutual savings banks (MS).

Chetty's substantive conclusions supported the G–S thesis. M and T were near-perfect substitutes (with coefficient equal to one), and SL and MS were close substitutes. His 'adjusted' definition of money, M_a, in the USA (based on 1945–66 data) was:

$$M_a = M + T + 0.880\ MS + 0.615\ SL$$

It includes two perfect substitutes (M and T) and two near-substitutes of money (MS and SL).[13] The velocity of circulation of M_a over the period 1951–66 was shown to have been virtually constant.

More recently, Chetty's results were corroborated by Barth *et al.* (1977) who, using an S-branch utility tree technique, found, as did Lieberman, that time deposits, mutual savings bank deposits and savings and loans deposits in the USA were substitutes for money; thus the authors favoured a 'broad definition' inclusive of these assets.

A number of technical difficulties[14] were discovered with the Chetty procedures, including the specification of his budget constraint, which made it difficult to compare his results with those derived from interest cross-elasticity estimates discussed earlier. Chetty's work nevertheless has inspired considerable debate and research which is still continuing today.

When Chetty's model was estimated using cross-section (rather than time-series) data, the results obtained were quite different (Edwards, 1972). No substitutability was found between money and 'near-moneys' (viz. between money and time deposits and non-bank savings deposits), but there was strong substitutability between time deposits and non-bank savings deposits. Thus, Edwards advocated the narrow money definition, but held that, if the definition were to be broadened, it would have to be broadened to include all 'near-moneys' (viz. T, MS and SL) which were good substitutes for each other.

Another interesting contribution to the debate on the substitutability of money and financial assets was by Moroney and Wilbratte (M–W) (1976), who, like Chetty, set out to estimate the elasticity of substitution between money and assets by households, but during the period 1956–70. Whereas Chetty postulated that money and liquid assets were arguments in a utility function which is maximized subject to an asset budget constraint, M–W assumed that households maximized wealth subject to a 'technological transactions constraint', which includes money,[15] in a model which is much more complex and incorporates the permanent income concept and an explicit dynamic adjustment process. They also extend the range of assets by including short-term government bonds and long-term corporate bonds as potential substitutes for money.

M–W's results suggest that substitutability between money and other interest-bearing assets is similar. Consequently, 'if portfolio substitutability is the salient criterion for choosing "near-monies", short- and long-term bonds qualify on equal footing with the time deposits' (M–W, 1976, p. 194). Thus, if a measure of macroeconomic money were to be a weighted liquidity aggregate or an 'adjusted' definition of money, then 'this aggregate must include short-term and long-term bonds (and probably other assets we have not considered in this paper) on an equal footing with the limited range of assets included. . . .'

The model suggested by Chetty has more recently been subjected to a thorough critique by D. J. Donovan (1978, pp. 678–82) and J. M. Boughton (1981b). The essential criticism is that Chetty's model is excessively restrictive, but can be generalized, essentially by making the utility function homothetic and by relaxing the strong separability restriction which implied that the determinants of utility were completely independent of each other.[16]

By relaxing the assumption that the marginal rate of substitution between financial assets is independent of income, Boughton proposed a model which modified the strong separability assumption and restored homotheticity with respect to income. He was concerned about the 'temporal constance of relationships' over the period 1953–75, which witnessed 'frequent and substantial innovations in the market for financial assets' (1981b, p. 378). Wishing to take these into account, but without modelling them explicitly, he incorporated some modifications such as an implicit interest rate on demand deposit, filtered data to reduce the effects of common trends,[17] and deflated values of assets. To allow for shifts caused by regulations, a dummy variable was employed.

The substantive finding contradicted Chetty's results. Elasticities of substitution between money (narrowly defined) and other liquid assets (T, MS, SL) were lower than those in Chetty, and 'there has been a significant trend away from money in favour of the substitute assets that is not otherwise explained by the hypothesized relations in the model' (p. 385). The conclusion thus corroborates those on p. 70 above, pointing to the empirical definition of money consisting of currency and demand deposits only.

Considerable effort has been exerted to make the approach suggested orginally by Chetty methodologically more consistent. Attempts are being made to apply rigorously methods and techniques of modern consumer demand theory in order to derive liquid asset demand equations from a generalized representation of preferences by utility-maximizing households (Donovan, 1978, pp. 680–91). The literature on this is complex and technically demanding. Two aspects of it deserve mention here: the need to derive the user cost (or rental prices) of monetary services, and the need to define further the concept and techniques of measures of substitutability required for selecting 'admissible assets' for aggregation purposes (Barnett, 1982, pp. 695–7).

Chetty's budget constraint did not incorporate the condition that the sum of expenditures on the service flows yielded by liquid assets be less than or equal to total expenditure on monetary services. To be able to formulate such a budget constraint, the relevant prices of the service flows obtained from liquid assets, that is the rental prices of the assets, had to be found. Donovan (1978), who developed a model of demand for liquid assets utilizing methods of modern applied demand theory, derived the rental price of monetary services which could be used in the budget constraint.[18] The usefulness of this concept will be mentioned again in the next section.

An experimental work by N. A. Ewis and D. Fisher (1984) perservered with the translog (transcendental logarithmic) utility function approach to the study of the demand for money in the USA over the period 1969–79.[19] Their results are of a provisional nature, but are of interest in the context of asset substitutability.

The assets considered were M1 (narrow money), time and savings deposits in savings and loans associations, short-term Treasury securities, and foreign assets. While, with the exception of foreign assets, no *strong* substitutability between monetary assets was found, M1 was a weak substitute for domestic assets except time deposits. Evidence of strong substitution between domestic assets and foreign assets is of interest. Stressing the tentative nature of their results, Ewis and Fisher assert that only the narrow definitions of money would be satisfactory policy targets, and that the low substitutability between domestic financial assets suggests that their simple summation into broader aggregates would be unwise. The last point will be further elaborated in the next section.

Thus, substantive results on substitutability of assets are sensitive to model specification and the use of data. In general, evidence suggests low substitutability between narrow money and liquid assets. There is thus unease about high level simple-sum monetary aggregates which implicitly assign to their component assets equal weights. This is the issue which is explored in section 3.4.

The search continues for a satisfactory utility or production function specification, one that would permit the parameters of the functions to be used in the determination of weights in order to identify the 'moneyness' of assets, or a weighted 'money' total – that is, for a function which could serve as an aggregator function.

3.4 Money as a monetary-quantity index

3.4.1 *Divisia money aggregates*

In 1977 the staff of the Federal Reserve Board began to work intensively to identify the 'definition of money' that is most useful to the implementation of monetary policy. Perhaps the best known outcome of this work, the 'redefined' monetary aggregates, appeared in 1980. A less known research programme is aimed at constructing a monetary measure using a rigorous application of aggregation theory and index-number thoery.

Essentially, 'moneyness', or a measure of monetary transactions services, is expressed as an index number based on the Divisia quantity index. The construction of Divisia monetary aggregates by their principal author, W. A. Barnett, and his associates is a logical outcome of the search for a measure of 'moneyness' along the lines of Chetty (1969) and others, mentioned earlier. The authors of the Divisia aggregates, however, note that the idea of deploying index numbers in this context is considerably older, going back to R. Hawtrey in the 1930s.

The construction of a monetary-quantity index raises many complex and technically difficult problems. The exposition below is designed to introduce the reader to the main contributions in this field and to indicate the principal underlying issues in a non-technical way. It draws on the work of Barnett and his associates.[20]

The traditional money aggregates, as noted earlier, are simple sum totals, which implies that their components receive equal weights (of one) and are thus implicitly considered to be perfect substitutes. The other implicit assumption is that 'goods' or 'assets' not entering a monetary aggregate have zero substitutability with the assets included.

There has been a tendency, in both the USA and the UK, to introduce 'broader' aggregates (discussed in the next section), incorporating an increasingly extended spectrum of liquid and less liquid assets. In the previous sections we observed that, on the whole, empirical studies did not reveal a high degree of substitutability between financial assets which are now part of these aggregates. Doubt must thus exist about the wisdom of the traditional aggregation. Barnett compares simple aggregation to the summation of subway trains and roller skates in an aggregate of transportation vehicles (1982, p. 689).

The basic point is that an aggregation of monetary components, whose object is to try to indentify 'money' in terms of the 'flow of services that constitute the output of the economy's monetary-transactions technology' (Barnett and Spindt, 1982, p. 4), could be accomplished if one knew the parameters of relevant utility or production functions (called the aggregator functions). But such functions are not known (see p. 71–4 above). Thus, aggregation is approached on the basis of index number theory, where there are no unknown parameters, but where prices of component quantities are required in addition to the quantities themselves.

Thus, the use of the quantity index dispenses with the use of an aggregator function, but cannot be compiled without both prices and quantities. To determine a change in aggregate service flows resulting from changes in component quantities, a quantity index must have prices as its weights. This reflects the fact that, in equilibrium, prices are proportional to marginal utilities.[21]

The price of the services of a durable is its user costs. Analogously, user costs of financial assets must be derived. As already mentioned (n. 18), such user costs have been computed and will simplify, when used in a quantity index, to $R_t - r_{it}$ (the expected maximum available yield R on any monetary asset during holding period, less own rate of return r on asset i during that period). Unless services accrued from a monetary asset i, the asset would not be held. The user costs are thus the equivalent of the price paid for the monetary services. They are not, as will be shown below, used as a weight in the Divisia money index, but are prices used with all of the quantities in computing weights.

The index selected is the Tornquist–Theil Divisia index, which defines the single-period growth rate of the aggregate as a weighted average of the growth rates of component quantities. The weights are value shares, representing the contributions of component monetary assets to expenditure on services of all components. User costs are used as prices in the evaluation of the value shares. The formula for the resulting aggregate, together with a simple example illustrating its application, are given in the appendix to this chapter. Working through the example should make the basic meaning of the monetary quantity index clear.

Simple sum aggregates would be the same as Divisia aggregates only if own rates of return on all component assets were identical, suggesting that the components would be perfect substitutes. This, however, is not likely to be the case, especially with 'broad' aggregates. If the rate of interest on a component changes, then, in the case of the Divisia index, all 'substitution effects' will be internalized (by definition) and the aggregate will not change; it will change only if the rate of interest has an 'income effect' (that is, when the level of utility, or monetary service, changes). A traditional aggregate cannot internalize the effects of substitution following a change in interest rates on a component (Barnett, 1982, pp. 690–1; Barnett and Spindt, 1982, p. 7).

The weights in the monetary-quantity index will change, as interest rates entering the calculation of the weights (and user costs) indicate. A rise in the general interest rates (indicated by R) will increase weights on liquid or transactions balances and will induce holders to reduce the proportion of such assets in their portfolio. However, if interest rates were to be paid on some hitherto non-interest-bearing assets, then this would lower their user costs and increase their holding and they would receive less weight (relatively to remaining non-interest-bearing assets, whose holding would decline). Substitution by wealth-holders would terminate only when the marginal return on each asset becomes equal. *The weights are likely to be most reliable in the absence of restrictions on interest rates, such as ceilings or cartel arrangements.*

The above properties of the index make it useful to study the effects of financial innovations on the 'transactions technology' (Mills, 1983, pp. 20–1). However, as will be seen from the next section, a difficulty with financial innovation is to identify whether, as well as to what extent, it has actually taken place: whether new financial instruments should be put in the domain of monetary assets, or whether financial institutions should be relabelled 'monetary' institutions, because of changes in their contribution to the flow of monetary and financial services. Thus, the index essentially offers a *method of aggregation*; it is, however, capable of showing us, over time, the changes in the contribution of identified assets to the 'moneyness' which it reflects.

We referred above to the ability of the monetary-quantity index to distinguish immediately between the 'moneyness' interest-earning demand deposits and interest-free deposits. It will be argued in the last part of the book that an important characteristic of financial innovation is the generation of differentiated, but sometimes *congeneric*, 'monetary' services or instruments, designed to overcome certain legislative technicalities, but serving otherwise as sources of an *identical transactions service*. Some new interest-bearing deposits have the transactions characteristics of traditional demand deposits; a statistical measure such as the Divisia 'money' would clearly distinguish between the transactions services of the two.

Comparisons of the simple sum aggregates with the corresponding Divisia aggregates show that the narrow aggregates (M1) do not differ a great deal, but that the differences between the aggregates increase as they are broadened by the inclusion of new components. Thus, as one would expect (see the appendix to this chapter), the simple sum totals are higher than the Divisia for the higher-level aggregates (M3 and L in the USA; £M3 and PSL2 in the UK), reflecting the fact that assets more distant from the transactions properties of the hard-core money (legal tender, demand deposits) yield more limited monetary services, but have relatively higher store-of-value characteristics.[22]

3.4.2 *The optimal monetary aggregate*

The preceding section was concerned essentially with the method of aggregation of financial assets. Barnett (1982) also outlined a procedure to identify the 'best' or the optimal level of monetary aggregation.

A three-stage selection process is proposed. The first is the selection of 'admissible component groupings' to classify assets in the monetary set into separable component subsets. A measure of substitutability between assets is sought through the properties of utility or production functions with monetary assets as arguments (see section 3.3.3). Stringent conditions of separability must be met in the selection of the admissible component groups (Barnett, 1982, pp. 695–6).

The components of each aggregate must include currency (legal tender), but must exclude non-monetary assets. A prior definition of monetary assets is assumed. 'In attaching a name to an aggregate, such as food or money, a prior definition of the components' domain must be selected' (Barnett, 1982,

p. 697). It is in the realm of the conditions for grouping the components that research programmes are incomplete (Barnett, 1982, p. 707; Goldfeld, 1982, p. 717). Problems are encountered most frequently in trying to isolate sets of assets in aggregates intermediate between the 'narrow' and very broad aggregates (such as L in the USA and PSL2 in the UK).

The second stage proceeds after the selection of admissible asset groupings, and refers to the selection of an aggregation formula. As mentioned, Barnett's choice is the Divisia index. When the aggregation is completed, the result is a hierarchy of aggregates nested about currency (legal tender).

Stage three is concerned with the choice of 'best' aggregate out of the available hierarchy. The theoretical choice falls on the highest-level aggregate, which internalizes substitution effects between assets. It is also preferred by virtue of the fact that, in choosing a lower-level aggregate, 'we are omitting factors of production from the economy's transactions technology'. Thus, the broadest aggregate does not leave out important information about the economy's flow of transactions services. Methodologically, the identification of the real-life counterpart of the 'money' of economic theory, by using the three-stage approach, is superior to the empirical approaches discussed earlier and to the approach which follows.

There is, however, an alternative third-stage procedure. This refers to the 'empirical' approach to the selection of the optimal 'money' using the criteria discussed earlier, namely, selecting the one that works 'best' in meeting macroeconomic policy objectives (see section 3.3). It is suggested that, provided that first two stages in the selection are completed, the choice 'by results' is acceptable, for it only completes the process of selection rather than constituting the sole criterion of the 'definition' of money. This, however, modifies the circularity objection, but does not eliminate it completely.

A. Spanos (1984), in an experimental study, attempted an eclectic approach reminiscent of the last-mentioned approach to optimal money identification. He called measuring 'moneyness' by using a weighted average (section 3.3) the 'multiple indicators' (MI) approach, and measuring money by relating money to macroeconomic results (section 3.2) the 'multiple-cause' (MC) approach, and he suggested a framework – 'multiple-indicator multiple-cause' (MIMIC) – which combined the two. 'Money' was measured by estimating the 'liquidity' content of components of PSL2 in the UK (for 1963–81) by considering 'liquidity' to be 'the latent variable'.[23]

The results resembled those obtained for broad aggregates by the Divisia index method, with 'money' components of PSL2 having the highest degree of liquidity, followed by savings deposits in non-bank institutions and time deposits in banks. The deployment of a simple sum aggregate as a monetary target was discouraged.

The empirical evidence presented by Barnett indicates that, by the criteria of macroeconomic performance, the broadest aggregate – Divisia L – is superior to the lower-level aggregates (Barnett, 1982, pp. 702–6). This was somewhat at odds with Cagan's (1982) study, which, using the criterion of minimizing the variability of the velocity of circulation about a time period, isolated the Divisia M1 aggregate as the 'best'. Existing evidence in the USA suggests that, on the whole, Divisia aggregates perform better (have better predictive capacity) than the simple-sum aggregates.[24]

The protagonists of the 'Divisia money' have little doubt that the Divisia money targets should replace the present targets. Barnett (1982, pp. 706–7) could not conceive of any further potential use for any simple-sum aggregates. The replacement of M1 by Divisia M1 could be useful, though he considered that the replacement of higher-level aggregates by the Divisia L would offer the best solution for targeting purposes. 'The components of Divisia L should permanently be defined to include all of the money market. Then new money market assets would be incorporated immediately by the definition of the aggregate.' This provision was made to account for financial innovations, although, as will be shown in Part III below, this may not be such a simple matter.

3.4.3 A critical evaluation

The advocates of the monetary-quantity index confidently pronounce the traditional aggregates as fit only for some accounting purposes to monitor the liability structure of banks (Barnett *et al.*, 1981, p. 504), but inappropriate for economic analysis. They can barely restrain themselves from sounding the funereal beat of what they think must be an inevitable march of the aggregates into eternal oblivion.

The index number approach to monetary aggregation, suggested by Barnett and his colleagues, is very appealing and is being experimented with in other countries including the UK (Mills, 1983). Its theoretical arguments are convincing, but practical issues remain. For instance, how does one take into account the fact that financial assets may yield different services to different holders, households and firms? Which assets should be included in the aggregates? (This issue is further discussed below.) How does one identify the user cost (or the rental price) when the benchmark interest rate (the maximum alternative rate) is not easily found and the own interest rate itself may have to be estimated?[25] However, issues such as these are common to most empirical problems in economics.

At this stage of the development of Divisia 'money', a general critical appraisal is difficult. Procedures surrounding the 'optimal monetary aggregates' are not yet widely understood and remain to be challenged by researchers (Berkman, 1980b, p. 151). There are, however, some difficulties with these aggregates which can be identified already. Some serious computational problems have been raised above. The study of the demand function for money has been fraught with problems of specification and data. Such problems would not be any less with Divisia L (or Divisia PSL2 in the UK).

But it is on the supply side that the difficulties might be considerably more forbidding (Goldfeld, 1982, pp. 719–20). What is the supply function of Divisia L? How does one approach the control of a monetary-quantity index which incorporates numerous assets of financial institutions which exhibit different behavioural and often statutory characteristics? In connection with this question, it should be noted that, so far, in the debate on monetary targeting, the 'causality' aspect has been highlighted in empirical studies, while the 'controllability' issue has been ignored (section 1.1.3).

Attempts to use the traditional control by interest rates, which would affect user costs, is likely to be more difficult than the current control. Moreover, as the Divisia 'money' is purely a statistical money, it cannot be traced out through the flow-of-funds interrelationships. It would be impossible to provide the asset counterpart, such as that for £M3 in the UK (see section 4.3), which forms the basis for controlling the aggregate. Barnett's answer to problems concerning the control of money follows the traditional monetarist prescription: use the monetary base control. This is substantiated by evidence that the long-run monetary base multiplier for Divisia L is stable (Barnett, 1982, pp. 692–3). However, abstracting from the not inconsiderable problems of controlling the monetary base itself, it is not clear what the relationship between the base and the chosen Divisia aggregate would be if the base were to serve as the instrument for policy (this aspect of monetary control will be elaborated in the next part of the text). This particular weakness, however, is not peculiar to the Divisia 'money'.

Economists have always been careful to present 'practical men' with clear and often simplified concepts or measures with which they could readily identify, and which they could proceed to execute. The proliferation of different measures of money already confuses not only the practical men, but also many practitioners of economics. Lombra (1982, p. 393) observed that considerations of definition, measurement, analysis and control of monetary aggregates, using a variety of paradigms, are viewed by both students and central bankers as 'akin to trying to solve the Rubik's cube blindfolded'. The adoption of statistical measures of money, as opposed to the more familiar measures, may add to these difficulties. However complex the M1, L and £M3 and PSL2 might be to comprehend, they can be explained easily in terms of adding the deposits of different institutions with which people are familiar (Berkman, 1980b, p. 152).

It might be more difficult to overcome the culture shock of the Divisia 'money' in terms of our perception of both its supply and its demand. In this respect, the reaction on the part of central banks, the financial community and politicians to the notion of a Divisia 'money' and its control would be of interest, for the introduction of such a variable into the policy process depends as much on this reaction as it does on the technical qualities of the new statistical money.

Thus, in the realm of measuring or identifying the money of macroeconomics, the monetary-quantity index research programme has probably been the most promising. Given the characteristics of 'monetary assets', the simple-sum aggregation is somewhat simplistic, and the Divisia index aggregation is intellectually more satisfactory. However, echoing Goldfeld (1982, p. 719), 'the Divisia indexes are promising but have perhaps been a bit oversold'.

Appendix

The mathematical formula given below can be found in most sources quoted in this section (e.g. Barnett, 1982, p. 690) and the simple example given below is similar to that in Barnett and Spindt (1982, pp. 6–7).

Q_t is the value of the aggregate during period t and $G(Q_t)$ is its growth rate between period $t-1$ and t. q_{it} $(i = 1 \ldots \text{n})$ is the quantity of asset i held during period t and $G(q_{it})$ is its growth rate between period $(t-1)$ and t. p_{it} is the user cost of asset i during period t.

$S_{it} = p_{it}q_{it}/\sum\limits_{j} p_{jt}q_{jt}$ is the expenditure share on the services of monetary asset i.

$\quad\quad S^{\star}_{it} = 0.5(S_{it} + S_{i,t-1})$ is the average share over two periods.

$\quad\quad S^{\star}_{it}$ $(i = 1 \ldots \text{n})$ act as weights.

Given the above, the growth rate of the Divisia quantity aggregate, $Q_{t'}$ is the weighted average of the growth rates of the component quantities:

$$G(Q_t) = \sum\limits_{i=1}^{n} S^{\star}_{it}G(q_{it}) \ .$$

Single period changes, beginning with a base period, can be cumulated to determine the level of the aggregate in each succeeding period.

Example

The derivation of a growth rate of an aggregate between two years may be illustrated with a hypothetical example. Let us consider two financial assets: currency (C) with zero own rate of return and a saving deposit (D) with 10 per cent own rate this year (t) and 8 per cent last year $(t-1)$. Let the maximum alternative interest rate available to the deposit holder be 25 per cent in t and 20 per cent in $t-1$. Let the holding of C be (in £million) 220 in t and 200 in $t-1$, and holding of D, 125 in t and 100 in $t-1$.

Thus the growth rate $[G(q_{it})]$ of C is 10 per cent or 0.1 and the growth rate of D is 25 per cent or 0.25. The growth rate of the Divisia aggregate is a weighted average of the two growth rates. This can be found in the steps shown below. On the left-hand-side, the development of the formula is provided with the corresponding applications of data given in the example above illustrated on the right-hand-side.

$$p_{it} = R_t - r_{it}$$

To find weights, we first need user costs p (viz. the difference between the maximum alternative rates and own rates). The user costs (see formula in note 18) of C in t is 0.25 (viz. $0.25 - 0$) and in $t-1$ is 0.2 (viz. $0.2 - 0$). The user cost of D is $0.25 - 0.1 = 0.15$ in t and $0.2 - 0.08 = 0.12$ in $t-1$.

$$p_{it}q_{it}$$

Expenditure on services of C is
in t $0.25 \times 220 = 55$ and
in $t-1$ $0.2 \times 200 = 40$
Expenditure on services of D is
in t $0.15 \times 125 = 18.75$
in $t-1$ $0.12 \times 100 = 12$

$$\sum_j p_{jt}q_{jt}$$

Total expenditure on services is
in t $55 + 18.75 = 73.75$
in $t-1$ $40 + 12 = 52$

$$S_{it} = (p_{it}q_{it})/\sum_j p_{jt}q_{jt}$$

Share of C in total expenditure
in t $55/73.75 = 0.75$
in $t-1$ $40/52 = 0.77$

$$S_{it}^\star = 0.5(S_{it} + S_{i,t-1})$$

Weight of C $0.5 (0.75 + 0.77) = 0.76$
By a similar procedure for D
Weight of D $0.5 (0.25 + 0.23) = 0.24$

$$G(Q_t) = \sum_{i=1}^{n} S_{it}^\star G(q_{it})$$

Growth rate of Divisia aggregate
$(0.76 \times 0.1) + (0.24 \times 0.25) = 0.136$ or 13.6 per cent

In contrast the growth rate of the simple sum aggregate is

$$(345 - 300) / 300 = 0.15 \text{ or } 15 \text{ per cent .}$$

The simple sum growth rate is higher because there is no recognition of the fact that a unit of currency provides more 'moneyness' than a unit of savings deposits.

Notes

1 For useful reading in this area see F–S (1970, part I); Brunner and Meltzer (1971); Goodhart (1975, ch. 1); Davidson (1978, ch. 6); Fisher (1978, ch. 2); Casson (1981, ch. 4).

2 In Laidler's (1969) article it has not been made clear how demand 'stability' can be measured by 'predictability' (p. 515), and how it can indicate 'substitutability' between assets (time and demand deposits) (pp. 515–19).

3 Comments on the interpretation of stability draw heavily on discussions and an article of my colleague, Guy Judge (1983).

4 Used, for instance by Laumas and Mehra (1976), who utilized the Cooley–Prescott (1973) technique of varying parameters' regression in estimating the demand for money function. See also Judge (1983, pp. 3–5).

5 For an extension of the formulation and its use with British data see Mills (1983, pp. 7–9).

6 See references in chapter 1, n. 15, and especially Feige and Pearce (1977, pp. 441–8) and Judd and Scadding (1982).

7 Some components of money aggregates are, and some are not, subject to explicit payments of interest. Often 'money' is assumed not to bear interest at all. Increasingly, 'own' rate of interest on money is estimated and utilized in empirical studies. One approach is to estimate 'own' rate by a weighted average of actual interest rates paid on various components of money aggregates (Artis and Lewis, 1976). More frequently, returns on 'money' are estimated from both explicit and implicit rates. There are differences of detail in approaching such calculations, especially where interest rates are imputed (see Klein, 1974; Startz, 1979). For a review of sources see Ewis and Fisher (1984, pp. 41–2).

8 Various methods of overcoming this difficulty have been attempted, including a derivation of a weighted average of various interest rates. See n. 7, and Chetty (1969, p. 272).

9 The regression equation used by Lieberman (1979, p. 241) was:

$$\ln M = \beta_0 + \beta_1 \ln T + \beta_2 \ln r + \beta_3 \text{ time}$$

where M was a money aggregate; T, volume of transactions measure; r, rate of interest and the time trend. It may be interesting to note that Lieberman (1977) estimated that demand for money, other things being equal, decreased owing to technological change at the rate of 1.5–2.5 per cent per year (p. 317).

10 Discussion of the methods of the identification of 'money' is not comprehensive; it leaves out some purely statistical approaches such as factor analysis (see Koot, 1975; 1977).

11 The utility function chosen was

$$U = (\beta_1 M^{-p} + \beta_2 T^{-p})^{-1/p}$$

where M represents money holding and T, money value of time deposits in the next period.

The budget constraint is derived by assuming that the utility maximizer has M_0 dollars and wishes to allocate them between M and T. If T is the cash value in the

next period and i is the rate of interest on T in the current period, then
$$M_0 = M + T/(1+i) .$$
As ordinal utility is used, β_1 is assumed to be one. Elasticity of substitution between M and T is $1/(1 + p)$. Using the indifference curves to aggregate money,

$$M_a = (M^{-p} + \beta_2 T^{-p})^{-1/p}$$

where M_a is adjusted money. If M and T were perfect substitutes then $\beta_2 = 1$ and $p = -1$ and $M_a = (M + T)$. Other parameter values would indicate less than perfect substitutability.

12 Chetty's generalized CES utility function is given as

$$U = (\beta M^{-p} + \beta_1 X_1^{-p_1} + \beta_2 X_2^{-p_2} + \ldots + \beta_n X_n^{-p_n})^{-1/p}$$

where X_s are various near-money assets. Budget constraint is given by

$$M_0 = f(Y, r_1 \ldots r_n) = M + X_1/(1+r_1) + \ldots + X_n/(1+r_n)$$

when $r_1 \ldots r_n$ represent respective yields on near-money assets, Y is income, and M_0 total cash holding allocated between M and X_s. (Chetty, 1969, p. 276–8). The function is maximized subject to the constraint and partial elasticities of substitution between M (money) and X_s (near-moneys) are then estimated (pp. 278–80).

13. A high degree of substitutability between financial assets supported earlier results by T. H. Lee (1966), who, using both time-series and cross-section data, rejected in turn the results of E. L. Feige (1964) (using cross-section data). Lee found that savings and loans deposits were even better substitutes for demand deposits than time deposits. He thus substantiated the G–S thesis and argued for a definition of money which was broader than the broad definition of F–S.

14. *American Economic Review*, vol. 62(1) (1972), contains comments on Chetty's study (Lee, pp. 217–20; Steinhauer and Chang, pp. 221–5; Chetty's reply, pp. 226–9). See also Feige and Pearce (1977, pp. 459–61), Donovan (1978, pp. 676–82); Boughton (1981b).

15. Theoretical specification starts with the postulate that the household sector wealth W_t issues from money M_t and assets $X_{i(t)}$ carrying effective interest rates $r_{i(t)}$:

$$W_{(t)} = M_{(t)} + \Sigma X_{i(t)} (1 + r_{i(t)}) .$$

Households maximize W_t subject to the monetary transaction constraint:

$$T_{(t)} = f(M_{(t)} X_{i(t)}) \qquad i = 1, \ldots, n .$$

The functional form for the 'transactions technology' is initially posited to be:

$$T_{(t)} = (\beta_{(t)} M_{(t)}^{-p} + \Sigma_i \beta_{i(t)} X_{i(t)}^{-p_i})^{-1/p} .$$

Thus, in M–W, money holdings appear in this transactions cost constraint rather than the utility function, as in Chetty.

16. Indeed, the utility function suggested by Boughton (1981b, pp. 376–81) is not a CES (which is strongly separable and homothetic) but a GES (generalized elasticity of substitution) function, which is homothetic but not strongly separable.

17. The filtering of data is a contentious issue. F–S (1970) suggested this method and used it in their 1982 work. Serious objections to this procedure have been raised essentially on the grounds of loss of information, which might distort conclusions (Hendry and Ericsson, 1983).

18. The general formula for the user cost (rental price) p of asset i in period t is

$$p_{it} = f(R_t, \tau_t, p_t^\star) (R_t - r_{it})$$

where

$$f(R_t, \tau_t, p_t^\star) = p_t^\star (1 - \tau_t)/[1 + R_t (1 - \tau_t)] \,,$$

R_t is the maximum available one period holding yield during period t; r_{it} is own rate of return on asset i during the same period; τ_t is the marginal rate of tax during t; and $p_t^\star$ is the true cost of living index during t (see Donovan, 1978, pp. 684–6; Barnett *et al.*, 1981, p. 498). In computing the monetary quantity index (to be discussed later), the formula reduces to $p_{it} = R_t - r_{it}$ as $f(R_t, \tau_t, p_t^\star)$, being independent of the selection of i, is cancelled out (see also Barnett and Spindt, 1982, pp. 3, 7).

19. This study also gives a good introduction to problems of separable functional structures on which further research is being urged (see e.g. Barnett, 1982, p. 707).

20. Three principal contributions, each well documented, are recommended to the reader: Barnett *et al.* (1981); Barnett and Spindt (1982); and Barnett (1982). The main British work on 'composite monetary indicators' is Mills (1983); also of interest is Bailey *et al.* (1982).

21. See Barnett and Spindt (1982, pp. 2–3). For a more systematic exposition see Barnett (1980a, pp. 28–41).

22. See Barnett and Spindt (1982, pp. 13–17); for the UK see Mills (1983, pp. 54–6). In the UK the two measures for M1 in 1963–81 period coincide until the mid-1970s and then gradually diverge.

23. A latent variable is defined as 'any theoretical variable which does not correspond one-to-one to a particular observed data series' (Spanos, 1984, p. 126). The estimated latent variable (liquidity) was (p. 137):

$$\zeta_t = 0.829y_{1t} + 0.248y_{2t} + 0.310y_{4t}$$

Where $y_1 = \Delta \ln$ (currency + sterling sight bank deposits), $y_2 = \Delta \ln$ (time deposits + certificates of deposit), and $y_3 = \Delta \ln$ (savings deposits in building societies, etc.).

24 So far the UK evidence is much less clear – see Bailey *et al.* (1982); Mills (1983, pp. 33–8).

25 See n. 7 above. See also a discussion between E. K. Offenbacher (p. 55–6) and W. A. Barnett (pp. 57–9) in *Journal of Econometrics*, vol. 14 (1980).

—4—

Monetary Aggregates in the UK

4.1 Evolution of money supply series

In 1980, referring to the simple-sum monetary totals in the USA, the advocates of the Divisia money measures hoped that 'they soon can be permitted to rest in peace on library shelves marked "the history of economic thought"' (Barnett, 1980b, p. 59). But in 1985, in both the USA and the UK, 'official' money measures were still simple sum aggregates. A brief account of the evolution of monetary aggregates in the UK is given below, highlighting the selection of financial assets for aggregation and the selection of aggregates for monetary targeting.

Official publications of money supply statistics emerged as a result of two main influences: (1) a plea of the Radcliffe Committee for better banking and monetary statistics, and (2) the rise of monetarism. The Radcliffe Report (1959) was responsible for a general improvement in financial statistics, whereas monetarism inspired the concentration of attention on the identification and measurement of the stock of money.

Until 1970, only one 'definition' of money was in official use. This was the 'broad definition' corresponding to M3, introduced in that year. It was based not so much on the *a priori* concept of money as a medium of exchange, which had often been emphasized in the theoretical literature, but on institutional characteristics, namely, on the fact that the institutions whose deposits were included in the stock of money belonged to what was considered to be 'the banking sector' (BE, 1970, p. 321)

Official statistics of the stock of money, in the now familiar form, were first introduced in 1970. Regular publications of money series began in *Economic Trends* (first in September 1970), *Financial Statistics* (first in September 1970) and *BEQB* (first in December 1970). Explanatory notes on the stock of money statistics invariably stress that there is no single, universally accepted, definition of money, and that any definition must, therefore, to some extent be arbitrary and subject to review from time to time in the light of institutional changes.

86

The 'definitions' introduced in the publications were M1, M2 and M3. M1 consisted of currency and sterling deposits on current accounts of private residents. It was the narrowest 'money', representing most closely the immediately transferable purchasing power of the private sector. M2 was the intermediate 'definition', which added to M1 sterling deposit accounts of private residents and private deposits with discount houses. The broadest 'definition', M3, embraced M2. It consisted, in addition to currency, of all UK bank and discount house deposits denominated in sterling or non-sterling currency held by UK residents in both the public and private sectors (but excluded sterling balances held by non-residents).

Competition and Credit Control of 1971 extended certain monetary controls to banks other than the traditional deposit banks and thus, for monetary control purposes, removed the rationale for distinguishing between deposit banks and other banks. For this reason, M2 was discontinued from 1972 and thus official publications of the money stock were, for a time, confined to M1 and M3. After 1971 there were some 'modifications' of official monetary aggregates, made necessary by changes in monetary theory and policy.

Improved statistical returns and some changes in the components or contributors to monetary aggregates frequently modified the aggregates between 1971 and 1984. Some changes were due to new contributors to the aggregates (in March 1972 and 1973 and September 1983). Redefinitions of contributors to the money stock also affected data in March and April 1973 and in December 1975.

Changes in statistical returns were another cause of small modifications in the aggregates. For instance, an improved system of banking statistics was devised in mid-1975. This resulted in the introduction of new information which changed the content of monetary aggregates, M1 in particular, from May 1975. Current accounts were replaced by 'sight deposits', to include money-at-call and money placed overnight. This was done to enable funds placed by the UK private sector with discount houses, and falling within the definition of sight deposits, to be included in M1. The new returns also reduced the extent of estimation previously needed to compile the aggregates.[1]

A significant modification in aggregates (including those discussed below) occurred in November 1981, when the 'banking sector' (essentially, UK offices of all banks observing a common reserve ratio and discount market institutions) was replaced by the 'monetary sector' (consisting of banks and licensed deposit-takers under the Banking Act (1979), together with the National Girobank and Trustee Savings Banks, the Banking Department of the Bank of England and other institutions observing monetary control arrangements of August 1981).[2] From the end of 1981, 'definitions' of money were based on the new monetary sector. One of the more frustrating aspects of researching with monetary aggregates is the absence of a long, consistent 'money' supply series.

4.2   New 'definitions' of money

Following the decision to base monetary policy on monetary targets, some
new aggregates appeared. A new 'definition' of the money supply was added
in 1977. It was connected with changes in the statistical presentation of
Domestic Credit Expansion (DCE), which was first introduced in 1969.
Changes in the money supply can be generated by both domestic transactions
and external payments emanating from balance of payments surpluses or
deficits. A general notion of DCE is that it measures a change in the money
supply adjusted for the balance of payments. DCE was intended to be an
indicator of domestically created credit which led directly to changes in the
money supply (M3).

The essence of the 1977 change in DCE lies in the exclusion of some
foreign currency lending by UK banks in the private sector which was, until
then, included. As a result, foreign currency lending to the private sector was
entirely eliminated from DCE. The basic rationale for such a readjustment
was a change in the government economic strategy announced in the so-called
'December measures' in 1976. Monetary policy was to play a more important
role in the overall economic strategy and aim at a restriction in monetary
expansion. Initially, the new DCE was considered to be a good indicator of
domestic monetary pressure, and a short-term target of its growth was fixed.
Soon afterwards this was translated into targets for the new aggregate –
sterling M3 (£M3).

The emphasis on the sterling component of DCE was reflected in the new
'definition' of the money stock. Thus, from 1977, three official 'definitions' of
the money stock were published: M1, consisting of currency in circulation
together with all sterling current account deposits held by the private sector;
£M3, comprising currency in circulation plus all sterling deposits held by UK
residents in both the private and public sectors; M3, consisting of £M3 and
all deposits of UK residents held in non-sterling currencies (see figure 4.1).
Targets for £M3 became the proximate objectives of government monetary
policy (see section 1.1.3). £M3 was used as *the monetary target* in the Medium
Term Financial Strategy introduced in 1979.

The rationale for the choice of £M3 as the target variable may be of some
interest. One of the prerequisites of using an aggregate for policy purposes is
the availability of adequate information about it. Prior to 1977, the Bank of
England carried out much research on M3 (from which £M3 developed) and
thus had substantial experience of its behaviour. It found it to be a
'particularly interesting quantity to study' because it contained 'so many
different strands' (BE, 1973, pp. 196–201).

We may recall (section 1.1.3) that, to serve as a monetary target, an
aggregate must be controllable and must exhibit a stable relationship with the
ultimate variables. With regard to the first condition, M3, and then £M3,
were linked with certain key credit counterparts (discussed below), such as

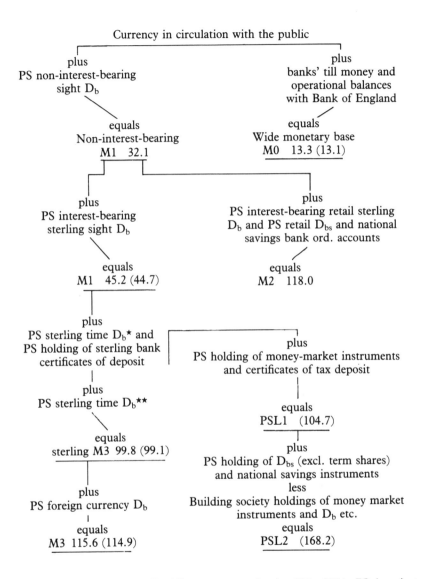

Currency in circulation with the public

plus
PS non-interest-bearing
sight D_b

plus
banks' till money and
operational balances
with Bank of England

equals
Non-interest-bearing
M1   32.1

equals
Wide monetary base
M0   13.3 (13.1)

plus
PS interest-bearing
sterling sight D_b

plus
PS interest-bearing retail sterling
D_b and PS retail D_{bs} and national
savings bank ord. accounts

equals
M1   45.2 (44.7)

equals
M2   118.0

plus
PS sterling time D_b* and
PS holding of sterling bank
certificates of deposit

plus
PS holding of money-market instruments
and certificates of tax deposit

plus
PS sterling time D_b**

equals
PSL1   (104.7)

equals
sterling M3 99.8 (99.1)

plus
PS holding of D_{bs} (excl. term shares)
and national savings instruments
less
Building society holdings of money market
instruments and D_b etc.

plus
PS foreign currency D_b

equals
M3 115.6 (114.9)

equals
PSL2   (168.2)

Figure 4.1 Monetary and liquidity aggregates in the UK, 1984. PS is private
sector, D_b, bank deposits and D_{bs}, building society deposits. Figures by the
aggregates refer to their totals as at the end of 1983. Figures in brackets are seasonally
adjusted; the others are unadjusted. One asterisk indicates an original maturity of up
to two years; two asterisks, an original maturity of over two years.
Source: BEQB, 24(1), March 1984, p. 79 and statistical tables.

the public sector borrowing requirement (PSBR) and bank lending, 'in a way that helps our understanding of the course of monetary developments' (BE, 1978, p. 36). These counterparts were also used as a basis for controlling the aggregate.[3] However, control of these has never been easy because of 'the sheer erratic variability of the counterparts of the money stock', which was well known to the central bank.

Before the 1970s, the relationship of M3 with income and interest rates (viz., the demand for M3) was stable, but this did not hold for the early 1970s following the credit reform of 1971 (BE, 1973, pp. 196–7). Thus, the ability of £M3 to explain or forecast developments in national income was suspect by the time it became the monetary target. 'On occasions the path of M3 can be significantly influenced by changing competitive conditions within the banking industry – conditions which can change for reasons quite separate from the course of nominal income in the economy, or the actions of the monetary authorities' (BE, 1978, p. 36). (This aspect will be emphasized in Part III.) Nevertheless, the Bank felt that, at the time, 'we have chosen best in selecting sterling M3' (p. 37). This statement can perhaps be better understood when noting that demand-for-money studies in the UK failed to indicate conclusively which aggregate is preferable on the basis of the second condition for targeting, namely a stable demand function (Allen, 1983, pp. 99–104).

The monetary targets in the first phase of the Medium Term Financial Strategy were overshot. An inquiry by a House of Commons committee (1981) revealed a considerable divergence of views of expert witnesses on almost every aspect of the targeting of £M3, ranging from the soundness of the underlying theoretical foundations of targeting to the techniques of control. However, the adequacy of £M3 as the target was questioned even by those who voiced an almost emotional attachment to it:

> As time goes on ... these aggregates all grow whiskers and begin to fray at the edges. I think there is a case for examining whether the thing [£M3] is correctly defined and whether one should not be looking at some other aggregates. On the other hand, there is, as with all other things, quite a lot to be said for continuity. Sterling M3 is an aggregate that everyone has grown to know and love, and there is something to be said for keeping on with it provided it is not providing a wildly wrong picture of monetary conditions in the medium-term.[4]

It seemed inevitable that a review of monetary aggregates for targeting purposes would take place. Two measures of private sector liquidity designated PSL1 and PSL2 were first introduced in July 1980, but they were preceded in 1979 by data on 'components of private sector liquidity', which were clearly their antecedents. The article introducing the new measures (BE, 1979) presented them without producing any coherent analytical justification for them. They appeared to have been introduced in order to bring together a variety of liquid assets in a similar manner as monetary assets had been aggregated; however, the aim was to stress *private* sector liquidity. The organizing principle governing the aggregation was to start at the 'monetary' spectrum and then to add to it in a manner which was theoretically not clear. 'Whereas the "money" block comes first, there is no natural order thereafter.' In effect, aggregates broader than £M3, but confined to the private sector sterling asset holding, came into being. PSL1 contained the M1 assets plus private sector holdings of sterling time bank deposits, certificates of deposit and money market instruments (such as Treasury bills) and certificates of tax deposit. PSL2 was PSL1 increased by private sector holdings of building society deposits less building society holdings of money market instruments and bank deposits (see figure 4.1). Thus, the new liquidity measures were more 'Radcliffian' in nature than £M3, but confined strictly to the private sector.

The emphasis on the private sector assets was pressed further in 1984, when £M3 (together with M3 and their component – PSBR) was redefined to exclude public sector bank deposits and certain other liquid assets. The analytical basis for this change is not clear. The redefinition, however, brought the totals into line with other monetary measures, none of which included public sector bank deposits. 'It removes from sterling M3 and M3 an element of no economic significance whose level is small but which can fluctuate by large amounts from month to month' (BE, 1984d, p. 78). An interesting corollary of this is that every act of privatization would raise monetary aggregates; thus the transfer, in 1984, of British Telecom to the private sector automatically turned some of BT's liquid assets into 'money' – raising £M3 and wider aggregates by about 0.5 per cent.

In 1981 the Chancellor announced that he wished to improve the information available about the narrower measures of money. To achieve this, a new aggregate, M2, was to be constructed to indicate more directly than £M3 the transactions balances in the economy (BE, 1982a). The new M2, which made its appearance in 1982, had no connection with the M2 deceased a decade earlier.

Essentially, the introduction of the new aggregate reflected the recognition that financial innovations, which will be elaborated later, made the other aggregates unreliable. For instance, some new transactions instruments, not included in M1, which was designed originally to measure the immediately transferable purchasing power, began to serve as transactions media or be related to money transmission services (discussed later). As interest rates rose, transfers tended to take place from M1 to new transactions media bearing interest rates. Thus, M1 movements tended 'to exaggerate the impact of such changes in interest rates on underlying monetary conditions' (BE, 1982a, p. 224). M1 was also said to include overnight balances held for investment rather than transactions purposes. £M3, on the other hand, included balances which were not stably related to movements in current expenditures and incomes in the UK. 'An intermediate aggregate was therefore sought which would identify those types of deposit that can most readily be used for transactions purposes.'

M2 is to be a measure of 'retail deposits', and thus includes currency and all deposits from which transactions settlements can be made by cheque or other methods such as standing orders. The institutional coverage of M2 was, at its inception, confined to the monetary sector, but it now includes retail accounts of building societies and ordinary accounts of national savings banks (see figure 4.1). The usefulness of M2 for purposes of economic analysis is not yet clear. Its usefulness for policy purposes would depend on the stability of its demand function and interest elasticity (Allen, 1983, p. 114).

Greater interest in narrower aggregates was also reflected in the attention given to the monetary base. This aggregate is often presented in textbooks as being the least controversial – consisting of the liabilities of the central bank and capable of being controlled with ease. In fact, there is no generally accepted definition of the monetary base, and it is possible to select different combinations of its components.[5] Its control also poses difficulties which are often overlooked in textbooks. As mentioned in section 2.3, attempts to influence its component parts involve a disturbance of the flow-of-funds, especially those related to the finance of the central government borrowing requirement.

In 1981 the Bank of England chose to define the monetary base, subsequently labelled M0, in terms of its 'wide' variant, consisting of currency held by the public, bankers' deposits in the Banking Department of the Bank of England and 'other liabilities' of the Bank. M0 was later added to the officially published monetary aggregates. At the same time, an increasing interest began to be paid to non-interest-bearing component of M1 (currency with the public plus sterling non-interest-bearing sight bank deposits), for reasons which will be explained in Part III. NIBM1 has now the status of a separate narrow aggregate (see figures 4.1 and 4.2). Figure 4.2 shows the values of narrow money aggregates since the birth of M2 in 1982.

In the 1982 Budget speech, after the target range for £M3 was announced, the Chancellor stated that other monetary indicators would be monitored, that the rate announced (8–12 per cent) would apply also to M1 and PSL2, and that attention would be given to the exchange rate, though it would not be targeted. During the subsequent year the Chancellor began to devote much interest to the newly mobilized M0, with the result that in 1984 it too entered the set of targeted M's.

The quick coming of age of 'little M0' as a monetary target caused some surprise, for it was generally thought that this aggregate, consisting predominantly of currency, was directly relevant neither to the control of the broader money supply nor to wider macroeconomic control. A Bank of England study in 1982 found that 'it has not been possible to find a stable econometric relationship between interest rates and cash balances in this country' (BE,

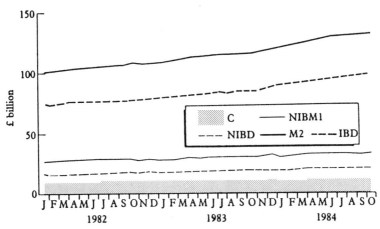

Figure 4.2 UK narrow money aggregates, 1982–4. C is currency in circulation with the public; NIBD, non-interest-bearing deposits; IBD, interest-bearing deposits; NIBM1, non-interest-bearing M1 = C + NIBD; M2 = NIBM1 + IBD.
Source: Bank of England Quarterly Bulletins, table 11.1.

1982b). Furthermore, the demand for cash was seriously overpredicted by the Bank in the early 1980s, possibly owing to the effect of financial innovations. One conclusion was that 'movements in cash are unlikely to be helpful as a guide to general economic or financial conditions'.[6] Thus, although it is difficult to identify a unifying theoretical framework in the recent target practice, it seems not unreasonable to suggest that it has proved singularly difficult to identify the money supply performing the macroeconomic control functions, and none too easy to control the identified aggregates.

Two target ranges for 1984/5 were announced early in 1984: for M0 (4–8 per cent) and the redefined £M3 (6–10 per cent), together with declining 'illustration ranges' for other components of Medium Term Financial Strategy until 1988/9. It was also stated that, in interpreting the behaviour of M0 and £M3, attention would also be paid to other indicators of narrow money, in particular M2, and the broad money, in particular PSL2, and to other available evidence such as the exchange rate. It is hard to say what particular economic theory is reflected in such a monetary strategy. It certainly has little in common with Friedmanite monetarist prescriptions or those of the new classical macroeconomics. In particular, it is not clear *what interrelationships are expected between the aggregates themselves and between each aggregate and ultimate macroeconomic objectives.* No coherent explanation of the strategy has been offered by monetary authorities.

We may conjecture, however, that the above approach to current monetary policy reflects the recognition that, in order to be able to judge 'monetary' conditions soundly, *it is necessary to analyse the whole of the financial sector*. In view of developments to be discussed in later sections of the book, such a position can be strongly commended. But in taking such a position, we do not need to construct monetary aggregates, or at least to attach unique macroeconomic characteristics to any selectively defined 'money'. Indeed, the Governor of the Bank of England admitted recently that, 'Because of the variability in the short-run monetary relationships, monetary targets have to be operated pragmatically. The course of the monetary target aggregates of itself thus provides only a first approximation to the overall assessment of monetary conditions, and to the appropriate policy reaction' (BE, 1984b, p. 476). Such a position would be consistent with financial theories outlined in section 1.2.2.

The full complement of money aggregates in the UK, showing interrelations between them, is summarized in figure 4.1. Figure 4.3 shows the levels of monetary aggregates in the UK (except M2, for which only a short series of data is available) between 1970(3) and 1983(2). Annual and quarterly growth rates (percentage changes) in the major aggregates for 1978–83 are depicted in figure 4.4(a) and (b), showing the differing growth patterns of the aggregates and revealing that, not infrequently, the growth rates moved in opposite directions. Certainly, since 1979 there does not appear to be any consistent relationship between the aggregates.

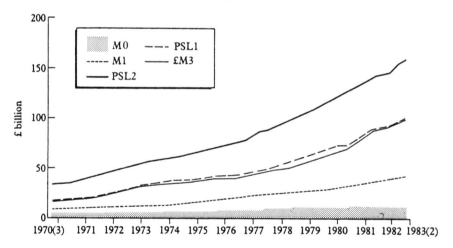

Figure 4.3   Monetary aggregates, 1970–83.
Source: Economic Trends, Annual Supplement, 1984.

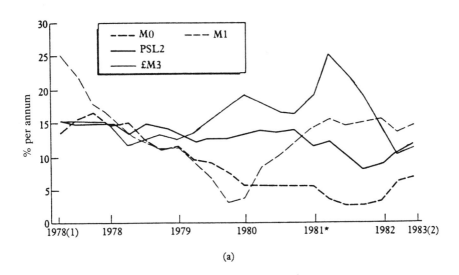

(a)

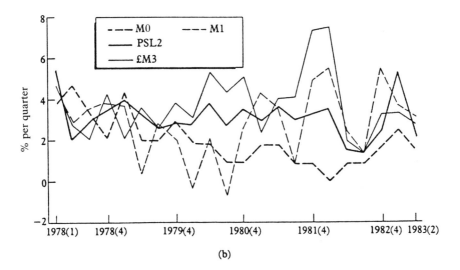

(b)

Figure 4.4(a) Annual growth rates of UK monetary aggregates, 1978–83. 1981 marks the redefinition of the monetary sector (see p. 87). (**b**) Quarterly growth rates of monetary aggregates, 1978–83.

Source: Based on quarterly data, seasonally adjusted. *Economic Trends*, Annual Supplement, 1984.

Figure 4.5 portrays annual growth rates of £M3, the principal targeted money supply in the UK, and nominal gross domestic product (GDP). £M3 lagged by two years is also presented (as £M3−8). Studies have shown that, in the 1970s, there was a statistical association between £M3, lagged by about eight quarters, and nominal national income. Clearly, this relationship appears to have broken down in the 1980s, with the tendency for the growth rate of the lagged £M3 to rise (until 1983) while the growth rate of GDP fell or remained stable. Close correspondence between this money aggregate (lagged or not) and GDP does not seem to exist any longer. However, heated debates continue on the interrelations between aggregates, on the association between them and nominal income or price level, and on the choice of the appropriate aggregate for targeting. These often yield perplexing results.[7]

To sum up, from 1976, when monetary targets were first introduced in the UK, the number of monetary aggregates rose from two to eight, and some modifications were made in the components of some of them. Different variants of the aggregates can be compiled by varying their component content. The experience of the USA with monetary aggregates was similar to that of the UK. Indeed, in 1979 in the USA there was a wholesale 'redefinition' of monetary totals (Simpson, 1980). (This will be discussed in Part III.)

The proliferation of different aggregates in the 1980s caused some bewilderment and cast doubts on the possibility of finding an indicative definition of the money of macroeconomics.

Figure 4.5 Sterling M3 and money income (GDP).
Source: Economic Trends, Annual Supplement, 1984.

Money is a theoretical construct devised by economists. It may not exist in the real world. Certainly it does not correspond to any particular statistical artefact, such as M1 or M2. It is a sobering thought that the New York Federal Reserve Bank has over 30 different definitions of 'the money supply'. [Gowland, 1982, p. 2]

S. Weintraub observed that:

Under the zeal for numerical magnitudes we have thus been bombarded with different aggregates, each containing a more inclusive assortment of liquid assets, such as M1, M2, M3, ..., Mn in bewildering profusion.... The numbering spiel can, under Socratic logic, ultimately prove that 'money' is something in the eye of the beholder as an economic version of beauty. [Weintraub, 1981, p. 469]

4.3 Counterparts of sterling M3

Monetary and liquidity aggregates are normally presented as simple sums of 'financial assets'. Strictly speaking, they are collections of liabilities of financial institutions (bank deposits, for instance, being a liability of commercial banks), and thus it is the liability side which is stressed. In any balance sheet, the liabilities – that is, the sources of funds – must be matched by assets reflecting the way funds are used to achieve the objectives of a business unit. In cases where an aggregate contains a significant portion of liabilities of financial institutions, it is possible to present that aggregate in terms of its corresponding asset structure. Focusing on the liability side may well be a useful way of measuring monetary changes and monetary pressure where financial institutions secure their liabilities and then essentially concentrate on the management of their asset structure. However, when institutions tend to adjust their liability side in response to lending commitments (asset formation) – that is, when 'liability management' (to be discussed in section 6.3) takes place – then it is more helpful to analyse the aggregates in terms of their asset structure.

In the UK, the 'money' for which the asset side has been developed is £M3. Using the asset counterparts, a change in £M3 can be simplified to the following identity:

$$\Delta \pounds M3 \equiv PSBR - PurPSD + L + EF - NDL$$

where PSBR is the public sector borrowing requirement; PurPSD is purchases of public sector debt by the UK non-bank private sector; L, sterling lending to the UK private sector; EF, external and foreign currency counterparts; and NDL, net non-deposit liabilities. Table 4.1 contains changes to the components of the identity between 1979 and 1984, which will be referred to in Chapter 6.

Table 4.1 Counterparts of changes in sterling M3, 1979/80–1983/4 (£ billion, unadjusted)

Financial year	Δ£M3	PSBR	PurPSD	L	EF	NDL
1979/80	6.5	+10.0	− 9.2	+ 9.3	−2.4	−1.2
1980/1	10.2	+12.7	−10.8	+ 9.2	+0.6	−1.5
1981/2	9.7	+ 8.6	−11.3	+14.9	−0.8	−1.7
1982/3	9.8	+ 8.9	− 8.3	+14.4	−2.8	−2.4
1983/4	7.6	+ 9.6	−12.5	+15.1	+0.1	−4.8

Sources: BEQB, 24(2), June 1984, table 11.3; *Financial Statistics*, June 1984, table 11.5.

Although the above expression is an identity and not a behavioural statement, it does reflect the notion that the formation of 'money' is an outcome of decisions taken by a variety of sectors and decision-making units (compare sections 2.3 and 2.4). It should be noted that, disregarding non-deposit liabilities, the counterparts may be grouped into the domestic component (DCE) (see p. 88) and the foreign counterpart (EF), measuring the net foreign payments outcomes. Thus,

$$DCE \equiv PSBR - PurPSD + L$$

and

$$\Delta£M3 \equiv DCE + EF .$$

The last expression is sometimes presented in a different approximation:

$$\Delta£M3 \equiv DCE + \text{reserve flows}$$

to indicate that the balance of payments and domestic monetary developments are linked through the reserve flows (Goodhart, 1979, pp. 144–6). However, the assets counterpart was first designed in conditions quite different from the present. The abolition of exchange restrictions in 1979 and the freely floating exchange rates brought about a situation where international capital transactions encounter few frictions, with the result that foreign and sterling currency balances, and foreign and sterling assets, have become much more substitutable in the portfolios of resident and non-resident economic agents. Thus, external demand for sterling is now more likely to affect £M3, especially through the finance of PSBR from sales of public sector debt to non-residents. Therefore an alternative presentation of the counterparts of changes in £M3 was introduced in 1983 and is published alongside the standard presentation (details in BE, 1983c). Basically, an attempt is now made to give greater recognition to the openness of the economy, to reverse the emphasis on DCE, and to identify the external finance of the public sector.[8]

As already stated, the ability to control the aggregate depends on the ability to influence the formation of its counterparts, and the existence of the asset structure of this monetary aggregate accounts, in good measure, for the faith shown in £M3 as a targeted total. It should, however, be stressed that the central bank does not directly control any of the counterparts and thus cannot, with any precision, influence the aggregate.[9]

4.4 Excluded liquid assets

In section 3.4.2 it was argued that, in order to construct monetary aggregates systematically, we need first to identify a domain of monetary assets, then, using some rigorous criterion, to select consistent and separable groupings, and finally, to aggregate these. As we have seen, the procedures used with the officially published aggregates are somewhat more arbitrary. The organizing principle seems to be to reflect, in the narrow aggregates, the monetary function of the means of transactions or payments (stressing the role of currency and banks as 'monetary institutions') with the higher-level aggregates progressively encompassing assets serving more as a store of value. The Bank of England has found it increasingly more difficult to define and interpret such monetary aggregates.

> While it is clear that there are special quanlities attaching to 'money' as a means of payment, it is much harder to define precisely what should actually count as money for purposes of analysis and policy. When one comes to the second attribute of money, store of readily accessible wealth, it is equally hard to draw clear distinctions. (BE, 1982c, p. 530]

There are liquid assets (defined as assets which can be quickly encashed without a serious risk of a capital loss) which are not included in any of the conventional aggregates, and indeed are even rarely considered as part of the domain of 'monetary' claims. For instance, assets denominated in currencies other than sterling are not considered as 'money' in most aggregates. It may be argued that, after the abolition of the exchange controls in 1979, and in the environment of convertible currencies in internationally integrated financial systems (to be discussed in section 5.2), public and private sector foreign currency deposits with banks abroad should qualify as monetary assets. They are not included in any aggregate, and private sector foreign currency deposits with UK banks are included only in M3, which does not play an important role in monetary management (compare section 4.2).

One of the most controversial assets not embodied in any aggregate is trade credit. Disputes concerning its 'monetary' characteristics and substitutability for bank credit continue intermittently and were particularly heated following the publication of the Radcliffe Report. Economists like Clower (1971, p. 18) maintain that '"money" should be considered to include trade credit as well as currency and bank deposits'. A recent contribution to the debate gave support to this view (Ferris, 1981).

Economists from Keynes onwards urged that unused credit lines (overdraft facilities and, more recently, credit cards) should, theoretically, be considered to be money. 'They represent sources that can be converted into liquidity, and in many cases they are more likely to be used to supplement cash than are certain short-term assets' (BE, 1982c, p. 534). Data on unused credit facilities are difficult to obtain, and data problems partly account for the exclusion of this asset from being considered in the 'money' domain.

As will be seen later (section 6.1.2c), one of the important instruments in the conduct of monetary control today is the bank bill, which is a commercial bill accepted (and thus guaranteed) by banks. Bill operations (purchases) by the Bank of England are increasingly used to smooth out cash shortages. Such bills are thus eligible for central bank discounting and are no less liquid or secure than, for instance, CDs (BE, 1982c, p. 535). Yet private sector holdings of such bills (£642 million at the end of 1983) are not included in 'monetary' aggregates, but only in the PSL aggregates.

There are other assets (like some building society shares) which are not part of any aggregate in spite of possessing characteristics associated with assets included in some monetary aggregates. These will be discussed in Part III, where it will be argued that, as a result of financial innovations and technological change, new liquid assets are created and previous demarcations between existing assets are becoming fuzzy.

Notes

1　For further information see additional notes to the tables in *BEQB* 12(4), December 1972, pp. 576–9; *BEQB* 13(2), June 1973, p. 261; *BEQB* 16(1), March 1976; *BEQB* 12(1), March 1972, pp. 77–8 and 153. For information on 1975 changes see 'New banking statistics', *BEQB* 15(2), June 1975, pp. 162–5.

2　For more details, see *BEQB* 23(4), December 1983; *Financial Statistics Explanatory Handbook*, 1984, p. 57. For brief details on the 1981 monetary arrangements see BE (1981, pp. 347–9) and *Treasury Economic Progress Report*, no. 137, September 1981.

3　'Any attempt to influence £M3 requires its counterparts to be influenced' (Goodhart, 1984, p. 132). See also Goodhart (1975, ch. 8); Artis and Lewis (1981, ch. 4); Allen (1983, pp. 104–8).

4　Comment made by Deputy Secretary of the Treasury, House of Commons (1981, vol. II, p. 327).

5　See 'The monetary base – a statistical note', *BEQB*, 21(1), March 1981, pp. 59–62; also useful is 'Measuring "narrow" money', *Treasury Economic Progress Report*, no. 163, December 1983, pp. 3–6.

6 On problems of monetary base control in the UK, see Foot *et al.* (1979), Coghlan and Sykes (1980); *Monetary Control*, Cmnd 7858, HMSO, 1980, Artis and Lewis, 1981, pp. 121–9. In the USA too there is considerable uncertainty about the efficacy of policy based on monetary base control (Bryant, 1983, ch. 5).

7 See, for instance, debates at a recent conference, in Griffiths and Wood (1984); especially the contributions by Budd *et al.*, pp. 75–119 with comment by Ormrod, pp. 120–8; and Bade and Parkin, pp. 241–86, with comments by Res, pp. 287–93, and Lomax, pp. 294–300.

8 The alternative identity, together with values (in £billion) for 1984(3) (*BEQB*, 24(4), December 1984, table 11.3) is:

$$\Delta \pounds M3 = PSBR - PurPSD - ExPSD + L + EF - NDL$$
$$2.4 = 2.6 \quad - 2.9 \quad - 0.5 \quad + 3.7 + 1.2 - 1.7$$

The symbols are as in the text except that ExPSD refers to external and foreign currency finance of public sector (increase −).

9 See references in n. 3; also Goodhart (1984, ch. 4).

— Part III —
Financial Innovations and Money

—5—

Financial Innovations and the Control of Money: US and UK Experiences I

5.1 Financial innovation process: a neglected subject

In the 1960s, money was said to have been 'rediscovered' in the process of the monetarist counter-revolution outlined in section 1.3. In the mid-1970s monetary policies in the West were redesigned: growth rates of money aggregates became intermediate targets for monetary authorities (see section 1.1). In the USA, the cradle of monetarism, financial innovations became a key reason for the redefinition of monetary aggregates late in 1979. M1, for many economists the closest to the macroeconomic 'money' variable, first became M1B then returned to its original designation of M1, only to be, in effect, suspended from use as a target, largely owing to the continuing process of financial change. It may well be redefined again.

The attitude of economists to financial innovation varies. For some, the instinctive reaction was to respecify the demand function for money, on the assumption that the function is inherently stable and it is only a question of an appropriate modification, which would take into account financial innovation, which is necessary (this is discussed in section 7.5). Some others became aware of our serious lack of understanding of financial innovations, of factors which induce them, processes which diffuse them and effects which follow them.

Technological innovation is concerned principally with the development of the real sector of the economy through increases in factor productivity. In chapter 2 we observed a long-run parallelism between real and financial development. We noticed that the performance of the main functions of the financial system, which include monetization and payments services, is closely linked with the real sectors. Indeed, financial innovation has been a concomitant of economic development from the inception of the modern financial system. It is not that economists were not aware of it; it is rather that, until financial innovation began to be blamed for causing parametric instability in the demand-for-money function, they failed to isolate it as a topic worthy of serious attention. The dominant paradigm of economic enquiry – that of neoclassical analysis, which is essentially timeless, emphasizing states of equilibrium rather than economic processes, as well as the artificial separation of the mainstream economics of money from the economics of the financial system – must bear some responsibility for this neglect.

Up to the mid-1970s, though the subject of financial innovation was neglected, it was not completely forgotten. As we shall see later, for a long time monetary economists had been well aware of the high degree of adaptability and elasticity of the financial system and its capacity to overcome obstacles and constraints which the economic environment imposed from time to time. Some of them were also well aware that such a characteristic of the financial system posed a potential threat to the efficacy of a monetary policy founded upon a statistically well behaved, but selected, relationship such as that between a monetary aggregate and nominal income. However, more concerted attention to this topic did not develop until after the mid-1970s.

The catalyst of the current interest in financial innovations is to be found predominantly in the difficulties experienced in the conducting of monetary policies. Financial innovations have become an accepted source of possible explanations of our empirical monetary puzzles. Only after they began to be suspected of seriously altering the commonly accepted relations between the money supply and interest rates and income did the attention given to financial innovations increase, revealing a serious need for research, a shortage of literature, and the absence of an analytical framework for investigation. 'The analysis of forces leading to financial market innovations is in its infancy' (Hester, 1982, p. 42).

The processes underlying macroeconomic change are essentially microeconomic. Yet the microeconomics of financial innovation remains in a state of almost complete neglect and is essentially confined to analyses of factors or conditions leading to innovations in financial instruments, markets and institutions. The process of innovation by financial institutions and the nature of diffusion of innovation are almost completely unresearched. The current literature on banking and finance affords evidence of only anecdotal and fragmentary nature. There is a need for systematic empirical studies on the subject. Questions which have been asked and investigated in the realm of technological innovation are still to be posed and seriously researched in the field of financial matters.

5.1.1 _Definitional complexities_

Schumpeter (1964, p. 62) defined technological innovation as 'the setting up of a new production function. This covers the case of a new commodity, as well as those of a new form of organization such as a merger, of the opening up of new markets and so on ... innovation combines factors in a new way ... it consists in carrying out New Combinations.' The new production functions incessantly shift existing cost curves. Product innovations, stressed by Schumpeter, are often distinguished from process innovations, which refer to technical advances and reducing the costs of production of existing goods and services, and involve an upward shift of production functions (Kamien and Schwartz, 1982, p. 2).

Similar distinctions are made in the realm of finance, where innovations can take the form of a widespread use of new financial instruments, or the emergence of new financial markets, institutions or practices. Just as the distinction with respect to technical innovation is not always clear-cut (e.g., computers may be classified with both product innovations and process innovations), one form of financial innovation is often associated with another. For instance, the emergence of the certificate of deposit (CD) in the USA was accompanied in 1961 by the creation of a new financial market which, by bringing buyers and sellers of CDs together and disseminating information, helped to evolve new financial practices in the money market (discussed in section 5.3.1a).

Schumpeter (1964, p. 59) distinguished between invention and innovation. 'It is entirely immaterial whether an innovation implies scientific novelty or not.' Invention does not necessarily induce innovation, and it is the latter that has importance in economic analysis. Freeman (1982) noted that 'An innovation in the economic sense is accomplished only with the first commercial transaction involving the new product, process, system or device although the word is used also to describe the whole process.' Both the stock of knowledge and the market potential are, therefore, considered to be necessary for innovation to occur. 'Innovation is a coupling process and the coupling first takes place in the minds of imaginative people. An idea "gets" or "clicks" somewhere at the ever changing interfaces between science, technology, and the market' (Freeman, 1982, p. 111).

In the sphere of financial innovation, it may sometimes be very difficult to isolate the process of accumulating knowledge and information and the first incorporation of these into commercial use. Invention and the generation of knowledge may not be well documented, as financial inventions are not subject to patent laws and protection.

Frequently, therefore, the emergence of a novel financial device or practice is obscure. New financial instruments or processes often remain unnoticed for some time, and information on them remains unrecorded or systematically gathered until wide diffusion has taken place (Hester, 1982, p. 43). This, as we shall see in section 5.3.1(b), was the case with repurchase agreements in the USA, which were used by security dealers in the 1950s but did not attract attention until they were adopted in large denominations by banks in the late 1960s.

Indeed, many financial innovations of recent years are not based on completely novel ideas or practices. Sometimes, at an appropriate moment, practices well known in one sector of the financial market spill over into another sector. This might indicate that market segmentation, often ascribed to financial markets, is not a chronic state, but is conditioned by the commercial environment. The recent use of variable interest loans as a device to cut risk associated with high and variable interest rates is often cited as a significant innovation; but variable interest mortgages have, for many years, been the common practice of UK building societies. Many economists regard the Eurocurrency system as a modern innovation dating from the late 1950s; however, the basic concept underlying the Eurocurrency system – that of transactions in currencies of third countries – was known in the City of London before the First World War. As we shall see below, it is often the *diffusion of innovation* that exerts significant economic effects rather than the innovation itself.

There is another problem in defining financial innovation, notably the distinction between innovative activity and an ordinary change such as a response to a price or interest rate variability. Schumpeter (1947, pp. 150–1) sought to differentiate between entrepreneurship and management. *Innovation* was seen as part of the entrepreneurial function and involved a *creative response*: whereas an 'adaptive response', or management response, referred to a reaction by industry to change within the range of existing practices, a creative response referred to *doing something outside the range of existing practice*. It is difficult to predict a creative response from existing facts by applying the ordinary rules of inference. Such a response shapes the course of subsequent events.

A precise definition of financial innovation which would result in a clear-cut distinction between the creative or entrepreneurial response and management reaction is likely to be elusive. Many financial developments are unmistakably 'creative' innovations, such as the appearance of new instruments (shares or CDs), new institutions (consortium banks), new markets (financial futures markets) and new processes (a switch from term lending to overdraft lending). Other cases, for example the shortening of maturity of lending in response to uncertainty brought about by inflation, may not be readily labelled as innovations.

5.1.2   *Inducement and diffusion*

There is some debate about the forces inducing technical innovation. Schumpeter stressed external events (such as wars) or intrusions from the supply side – autonomous inventions or innovations. The weight of evidence today, however, favours the demand-pull (rather than the supply-push) explanations associated with writers such as Schmookler (1966), though the concept of demand is rather general and imprecisely defined even in empirical studies (Rosenberg, 1982, esp. ch. 10).

Financial innovations too are likely, in general, to be explained as a form of adjustment to demand conditions and hence to conform to demand-induced innovation theories. However, more specific explanations are still in the stage of initial formulation. An attempt is made in chapter 7 to survey the existing state of knowledge on this issue.

An active role by the government in influencing the rate and direction of technological innovation is sometimes as strongly stressed as the demand-pull explanation. As will be seen later, the role of the government in financial innovations is quite different.

Little information has been published about the 'management' of innovation by financial institutions, the formulation of their innovation strategies, the extent to which such innovations are research-intensive, the organization of information and intelligence, the extent to which innovation is based on in-house research or consultancy arrangements, or about personnel and training policies and the scale of start-up costs. Though innovation has been recognized as a form of competition among, often oligopolistic, financial institutions, little is known about the relation between innovational effort and innovational output. The influence of market structure on innovative activity has been at the centre of empirical enquiries in the real sector, but in the realm of finance little systematic information is available. Equally scarce are investigations into the extent and nature of 'offensive innovation' (viz., innovation aimed at achieving or maintaining market advantage), and into the 'defensive innovation' strategies pursued by those who respond by imitating or improving innovations introduced by their rivals (terms used by Freeman, 1982, pp. 170 *et seq.*).

The diffusion of an innovation is often much more important than the occurrence of the innovation or the appearance of an invention. The literature on technical progress gives considerable attention to issues connected with the diffusion of innovations, the reasons for time lags (such as uncertainty, costs of adoption, lack of information), the process of learning and adopting original innovations by economic units, and the process whereby imitation is accompanied by further or secondary innovations and improvements, leading to 'swarms' or 'epidemics' of changes based on some basic innovation.

It is essentially this latter diffusion which has a significant industry-wide or macroeconomic impact. For a 'swarm' to occur, it hs been suggested that a combination of components is necessary (Kuznets, 1971, pp. 326–77): an invention or a new ingenious use of existing knowledge, which provides a framework for a succession of minor inventions and improvements; a supply of material capital, and in particular human capital, to ensure improvement and diffusion; and a large potential demand whose source is often a bottleneck in production process. Financial innovation may not exactly fit the pattern of its counterpart in the production sector, but as will be seen later, some financial developments do exhibit 'swarming' or surging characteristics.

Just as the mechanics of the diffusion of technical innovation is potentially relevant to the study of industrial policy (Davies, 1979), the mechanics of the diffusion of financial innovation may well be relevant to the study of financial and monetary policies. Yet few systematic enquiries into this aspect have been conducted. Only fragmentary illustrations can be offered.

There are factors which indicate that financial innovational diffusion has relatively short learning curves. Imitation seems to be easier in the financial world than in the real sector because there is less likelihood of the protracted learning processes which sometimes occur in the latter, and because the introduction of innovations may cost less.[1] Also, the absence of patent protection makes imitation easier and cheaper (compare Stoneman, 1983, pp. 16–17). Lower capital outlay and the availability of a mobile and intelligent labour force have been cited as reasons for a more rapid diffusion of financial change than technological change (B. Friedman, 1980, pp. 56–7). However, the existence of a multitude of regulations and conventions can act as an obstacle to innovation as well as a stimulus to innovative activity. The interaction between regulation and financial innovation and its diffusion will be elaborated in later stages of the text.

There are some fragmentary indications that, in relatively small-scale financial institutions, personal entrepreneurship and contact play an important part in the innovation and dissemination of innovative ideas. Redlich (1947) used US banking history to try to substantiate his thesis that economic development was largely the work of individuals. The role of personal contacts in diffusing banking ideas and practices in the USA was stressed.

Secondary banks in the UK, which developed rapidly in 1970s through their aggression and innovatory finance, were often masterminded by a single entrepreneurial personality, with able younger executives frequently being lured from more traditional banking establishments by generous financial incentives (Reid, 1982, p. 47). However, little seems to have been published on the generation of innovatory ideas, processes of imitation and diffusion of innovation in large banking houses in oligopolistic markets.

5.1.3   *Problems of classification*

Changes in the financial requirements of corporations, shifts in monetary policy and regulations, diffusion of technological innovations, competition and the breakdown of cartel agreements, exposure to the influence of international financial competition, changes in expectations, especially concerning the behaviour of inflation and interest rates – all are among the important factors which influence the occurrence of financial innovations or a change in their rate of diffusion throughout the financial system. Financial change has been so varied and widespread that it is impossible to give a comprehensive account of innovations which have occurred in the last few years.

Because of its varied nature, financial innovation presents considerable taxonomic problems. It also does not readily lend itself to a satisfactory treatment under any existing analytical framework. Our principal interest in financial innovations is in their impact on the measurement and controllability of 'money' and hence on policies based on monetary targets. The most sensible broad approach seems to be to separate those innovations which have a direct effect on the monetary aggregates from those whose effect might be indirect or even negligible.

Among innovations which have a direct influence on money aggregates and their control are those which generate new financial instruments serving as money substitutes, or, more specifically, as assets which are usable as means of making payments or settlements, but do not correspond to the theoretical construct of money conceived as a zero interest rate asset, or are not included in an official 'definition' of money. Their effect, in a given state of expectations, might be to change the parameters of a conventionally defined money demand. In terms of the analysis outlined in the appendix to chapter 1, such innovations might thus alter the size of the fiscal (a_1) and money (a_2) multipliers, with consequences for the relative efficacy of monetary control.

Some financial innovations are not directly connected with monetary aggregates, but are nevertheless relevant to the understanding of influences shaping the structure of the aggregates. In the USA these include one-bank holding company and credit programmes of agencies sponsored by the government (Hester, 1981, pp. 151–3, 162–5). In the UK they include the establishment of financial agencies such as Finance for Industry (in 1973) or Equity Capital for Industry (in 1976) or of public sector financial agencies such as the National Enterprise Board set up in 1975 (Wilson Committee, 1980, Appendices, pp. 475–85).

Another group of financial innovations belonging to the last mentioned category refers mainly to changes designed to give protection against risks principally associated with the uncertainty of the inflation rate or with high and volatile interest rates. They include switches from fixed to variable interest rate lending as well as the shortening of the maturity of debt. Such changes were quite widespread in the 1970s (BIS, 1983). It is problematical whether they constitute a 'creative response' or merely a sensible 'management response' (compare section 5.1.1). They have, however, brought a considerable change in the flow of funds and conditions attaching to intermediation.

Such practices were brought into more extensive use in economies other than the UK, where variable interest rate lending has been fairly commonly practised, especially by banks and building societies. But even in the UK the change was quite perceptible. It was closely related to the finance for industry. High nominal interest rates in the 1970s, together with the uncertainty of the future rates of inflation, made companies reluctant to borrow by the traditional methods of issuing debentures and other fixed interest bonds; most companies began to rely increasingly on medium-term and long-term bank borrowing at variable rates. Banks thus found themselves in a new role of supplying industrial finance less by the overdraft method and more by extending medium-term finance, either directly or indirectly through Finance for Industry or capital leasing. However, in spite of this, the average maturity of company debt between 1973 and 1981 decreased. The proportion of the debt repayable within one year rose from 30 to 37 per cent (BE, 1982g, p. 507). These aspects will be further developed in chapter 6.

Other financial practices in the above category are unmistakably innovatory. They include commodity or index-linked bonds and financial futures markets, which are briefly discussed below.

In the next two chapters, we concentrate on those financial innovations which are more directly linked with indicative *definitions of money*, or with the effect on the demand for such 'money'. However, it must be stressed that all innovations which affect the terms and conditions on which settlements, money transfers and financial intermediation take place must, in an interdependent financial system, have an effect on monetary aggregates, especially the high-level aggregates. Our aim is to examine a number of financial innovations relating to monetary policy mainly in the USA and UK. Our starting point, however, is the Eurocurrency market. A major innovation in itself, this has had an important influence on a number of important financial changes.

5.2   The international environment: Eurocurrency market

5.2.1   *The Eurocurrency market: a major innovation*

The development of the Eurocurrency system was perhaps the most important financial innovation of the post war period. It has had a profound effect on the world financial system as well as on the banking systems of major economies, especially in the USA and the UK. The practice of banks taking deposits and extending loans in currencies of other countries, which is the essence of the system, was known on a very modest scale before the war, but it blossomed only in the late 1950s to become a revolutionary financial innovation.

Basically, the Eurocurrency system refers to a market in 'wholesale' interest-bearing bank deposits denominated in currencies other than the domestic currency of the transacting banks. A systematic evaluation of the system is beyond the scope of this book.[2] The main aim here is to convey the general idea that the system is capable of being analysed in the framework of the theory of innovation. Its origin is to be found in the basic practice of lending in the currency of a third country, but historically is quite obscure. Such lending was brought into a more widespread commercial practice (viz. innovation proper) in the late 1950s, and then diffused, accompanied by 'swarms' of induced innovations (e.g. the Eurobond system), extensions (e.g. Asian-currency markets), improvements (e.g. use of information technology) and institutional innovations (e.g. consortium banking) to reach the complex and sophisticated state in which it is found today.

In the world of finance, the impact of the Eurocurrency system is comparable to that of coke smelting in the development of iron and steel, the steam engine in the development of railways, and the computer in information processing. This innovation has had a profound influence on novel financial developments in the domestic sphere, some of which will be discussed separately; it also has a bearing on the definition and control of the money supply, and indeed on the whole national financial management.

Explanations of the development of the Eurodollar system tend to highlight certain factors. Some propositions convey that it represented some natural extension of financial intermediation from the domestic to international sphere – a kind of international spill-over of the Gurley–Shaw hypothesis (McKenzie, 1976); others (mainly American) regard it as, in the main, an outcome of 'assymetrical monetary regulation' (Dale, 1984, pp. 12–13), a product of less stringent regulation imposed on the external currency portions of banks' balance sheets (Bryant, 1980, p. 101; Johnston, 1983, pp. 86–7), or even a deliberate development by banks to circumvent restrictive regulations at home (Wallich, 1982, p. viii). Certainly the fact that the market remained free from the regulations of any national or supranational central authority has made it a refuge for a number of 'oppressed' financial flows from regulated credit systems. 'If domestic banks are subject to policy regulations, financial intermediation will tend to emigrate' (Niehans, 1983, p. 547).

Though some factors were more important than others, it should perhaps be stressed that it was a *combination of circumstances* which induced the innovation. There was the underlying demand for capital generated by the successful recovery and expansion of European economies. This attracted international capital and was partly responsible for the expansion of all kinds of multinational business. Increases in output and international trade, in conditions of fixed exchange rates, resulted in shortages of liquidity, which the Eurocurrency system effectively supplemented. The growth of international banking and finance was thus a financial counterpart of the more general 'real' activity.

A major boost to international banking came in the shape of the dismantling of currency restrictions which had persisted after the war. The convertibility of international currencies in the late 1950s and the gradual abolition of other exchange restrictions removed a major barrier to the expansion of Eurocurrency transactions.

The largest component of the Eurocurrency system was the Eurodollar market, with its principal centre in London. As sterling, the foundation of London's supremacy as a world financial centre, began to shrink, particularly in relation to the dollar, financial markets in London began to operate increasingly in international currencies, especially US dollars (Robinson, 1972, pp. 196–7). By the mid-1960s, London had emerged as the world centre of the Eurodollar business.

The attraction of London was essentially related to its tradition and proven integrity as a financial centre, and above all to the relative freedom from regulations applying to foreign banks in London. Until the Banking Act of 1979, there was virtually no legal prohibition to setting up banking enterprises in Britain. Indeed, there seemed to have been a deliberate open-door policy towards foreign banking, including a policy to avoid imposing restrictive regulations on business carried out in non-sterling currencies, thus encouraging the inflow of overseas banks and Eurocurrency deposits (Grant, 1977, ch. 4).

The importance of the present position of the Eurocurrency transactions in the UK in relation to domestic financial flows is reflected in the flow-of-funds matrix in table 2.1 Row (16.3) indicates the 1983 change on the liability (deposit) side, and row (18.1) a corresponding change on the assets (lending) side. It should be borne in mind that most institutions operating in the Eurocurrency market are the same as those transacting domestic business. The degree of institutional integration in UK banking, and the extent to which sterling and foreign currency transactions are combined by individual institutions, may be gauged by examining the tables outlining the present anatomy of British banking in the appendix at the end of chapter 6, where the subject will be further elaborated.

Developments in the US economy undoubtedly contributed to the growth of the Eurodollar system, both in its early stages and, in an irregular fashion, subsequently through balance of payments outflows and Eurobranching connected with the circumvention of US capital and monetary restrictions imposed from time to time. The market remained highly integrated with the US markets, with movements in the US short-run interest rates (especially in relation to regulation Q) dominating the Eurocurrency rates (Johnston, 1983, ch. 5). However, the market was also influenced by conditions in Europe, and especially by speculative activity accompanying periods of changes in domestic monetary policies. Though there were occasions when national policies and institutional and statutory developments impinged on the workings of the market, in the longer run they predominantly enhanced its growth and the variety of financial practice.

The Eurocurrency market soon developed into a large, dynamic and highly flexible market. Not having a central bank, it was free from the usual interventions and market actions applicable to a national financial system. It became highly responsive to market stimuli such as differentials in interest rates and expectations of exchange rate changes, closely approximating the theoretical concept of a perfectly competitive market.

5.2.2 *Inter-bank operations: interdependence*

The market soon proved to be able to offer terms as good as, and often better than, domestic financial markets to both borrowers and lenders. It has developed an efficient organization dealing in large 'wholesale' amounts relatively cheaply. One of its chief characteristics is that it is predominantly an inter-bank market: of the total size of the Eurocurrency liabilities at the end of 1980, between two-thirds and three-quarters were inter-bank liabilities (for details see Ellis, 1981, pp. 354–6).

Banks are not always able to match quickly the inflow of deposits from savers with the available investment opportunities offered by customers and vice versa. This creates the basic precondition for the growth of inter-bank relations, particularly when communication is swift and transfer costs low. Such a development allows banks with surplus funds to deposit them with banks seeking funds for ultimate customers in the real sector. In a developed inter-bank system such as the Eurocurrency system, surpluses are usually onlent through a chain of banks until they reach a bank with a profitable outlet into the real sector.

The market offers a very efficient mechanism for transferring funds across national frontiers, including refugee funds escaping national regulations or seeking a more favourable regulatory environment. Two principal ways in which funds can migrate are by way of transfers between branches of the same multinational banking organization, and by way of inter-bank chains. The market thus adds to the efficiency of intermediation on an international scale by linking savers/depositors with investors/ borrowers in different parts of the world. Often, arrangements to transfer funds seeking profitable outlets can be electronically 'bleeped' over large distances and across national boundaries.

The Eurocurrency system is thus highly interdependent and responsive to market pressures. It is, furthermore, a parallel market, competing with domestic credit markets (Johnston, 1983, ch. 4). National economies, pursuing uncoordinated monetary policies for domestic motives, trigger off international financial reactions (this point is developed below). Equally, disturbances originating outside national frontiers do not leave domestic monetary policies immune from their effects (Frankel and Mussa, 1981). It is a market which illustrates an important characteristic of all financial or monetary systems in liberal capitalist economies, namely an extraordinary capacity to adapt to changing situations. This characteristic has been responsible for at least a partial circumvention of constraints imposed to manage internal financial flows. It has proved to be 'amazingly adept and innovative in developing monetary institutions and relations which not only permit but encourage evasion of government rules and controls' (Davidson,

1982, p. 228). Elsewhere, international banking in general was described as 'a complex scene in which corporations and banks seem able to exploit the regulations (or lack thereof) in one country to get around those of another' (Hester, 1981, p. 155).

The benefits of interdependence and flexibility on an international scale should, however, be related to a potential danger of interdependence: financial or liquidity difficulties of a participant in inter-bank operations are likely to have a quick chain reaction, leading to the risk of a serious banking crisis, particularly when confidence cannot be quickly rebuilt by a routine central bank intervention.

5.2.3   *The impact of Eurocurrency on national money management*

Economists were uncertain, and to a large extent still are, as to the theoretical framework which could be applied to explain the growth of the Eurocurrency system and its possible destabilizing influence. Some, regarding it as a self-contained banking system and applying the traditional single-coefficient multiplier analysis (section 2.3), stress the market's capacity for 'creating' Eurocurrency deposits and its potential for destabilization through excess liquidity. Most economists, however, tend to conceptualize the growth and effects of the market in terms of the portfolio adjustment approach, stressing its intermediating, rather than money-creating, potential. It is generally seen as an effective vehicle for mobilizing surplus funds in one part of the world and directing them to areas where funds are in demand.

Such an efficient market had a strong influence on the conduct of monetary policies in a world when these were largely uncoordinated. In conditions of fixed exchange rates, restrictive money policies by single economies, reflected in the rise of domestic interest rates relatively to interest rates elsewhere, often prompted an inflow of foreign currencies, causing monetary authorities to reverse the restrictive measures. The Eurocurrency system was the principal international vehicle which made the familiar Mundell mechanism (see e.g. Mundell, 1963) operate in reality. By 1971 its impact had contributed to the abandonment of the fixed exchange rate system (Bell, 1973, ch. 8). Floating exchange rates were in theory to offer independence to individual economies in the conduct of monetary policies, in the sense of enabling them to affect domestic nominal income by changes in monetary policy. This independence must, however, be qualified in conditions of 'dirty floats' (viz., where central banks influence exchange rate movement by deliberate actions on exchange markets), or where there is a high degree of substitution between domestic currencies and foreign currencies which is used to diversify portfolios of domestic wealth-holders (Miles, 1978).

The fact that the highest degree of financial innovation occurred in the USA and the UK is no accident. Both countries were closely linked with the development of Eurocurrency markets, and continue to be influenced by their operations. The Eurocurrency system has served as a channel of financial '*technology transfers*'. Bringing foreign banks with their different practices into contact with domestic banks enables the learning and imitation of such practices. This can apply to the use of technological devices, but more importantly to the use of different financial methods and instruments. For instance, the practice of term loans in the UK was largely copied by British banks from the US banks, which in turn learned from British banks the use of overdraft lending. Similarly, the issue in the UK of sterling certificates of deposits in the late 1960s, as will be seen later, constitutes an imitation of the US innovation of the early 1960s. From contacts with banking systems where there were fewer regulatory controls, US bankers gained the experience of more liberal banking (Robinson, 1972, pp. 289–90).

What has become known as 'liability management' (discussed below) in domestic banking was first practised by Eurobanks. Since the Eurocurrency market is a wholesale system, deriving much of its funds from the money market institutions and not from conventional deposits, it is no accident that liability management was developed primarily in those banking systems which had a considerable exposure to Eurocurrency business.

The extent to which Eurocurrency deposits, or other deposits denominated in foreign currencies, constitute substitutes to domestic monetary assets and should be included in money aggregates is a complex and disputed issue, touched upon in chapter 3. Empirical evidence is sparse and rather inconclusive (Boughton, 1979). Some economists stress the substantial impact of Eurocurrency markets on domestic liquidity, viewing their activity as a good substitute for domestic banking activity and hence regarding the markets as a supplier of near-monies alternative to domestic money (McKenzie and Thomas, 1983); they thus advocate an extension of monetary regulations to embrace the activities of Eurobanks (McKenzie, 1981). On the other hand, the inclusion of Eurodollar rates in the demand functions for money did not yield consistent results.

In studies carried out by M. J. Hamburger (1977), only in some cases, such as in the case of the UK's demand for M1, did the inclusion of Eurodollar rates (uncovered) improve the statistical properties of the function. The results were at least partly contradicted by J. M. Boughton (1981a, esp. p. 587). Ewis and Fisher (1984) found a high substitutability between foreign and domestic assets (see section 3.3.3). On the whole, however, there is little conclusive empirical evidence on the effect of international variables on the money demand functions or substitutability between assets denominated in foreign currencies and domestic financial assets.

What is clear, however, is that the Eurocurrency market is part of an efficient internationally integrated system which is likely to absorb pressures, at least in some degree, exerted by restrictive policies in individual countries. It also offers an alternative source of funds and liquidity for banks, large corporations and government agencies, as well as an additional set of opportunities alternative to domestic opportunities for surplus funds.[3] It is not likely to remain impervious to a change in conditions governing financial flows in domestic economies.

The treatment of foreign currency deposits in measuring monetary aggregates differs between economies, and the principles which govern the selection of such deposits are not clear. Narrow 'definitions' of the money supply as a rule exclude such deposits, but in some cases deposits held by non-bank residents in foreign currencies are included in the broader aggregates. Foreign-held deposits in foreign currencies are normally excluded (Johnston, 1983, pp. 66–71).

In the UK, overseas sector foreign currency deposits with the monetary sector (which are several times larger than the targeted aggregates) are not included in any aggregates[4] (see figure 4.1). They are almost completely matched by lending by banks in foreign currencies to the overseas sector (BE, 1982c, p. 534; compare also figure 2.1).

We may recall that private sector foreign currency deposits with the UK monetary sector are included only in M3, which has not been a targeted aggregate (see section 4.3). It is difficult to justify the non-inclusion of this asset in the aggregates, certainly £M3, after the abolition of the exchange controls in 1979 (BE, 1982c, p. 533). Indeed, UK residents' foreign currency deposits rose by a factor of 2.8 between 1979 and 1983 (to £14 billion in 1983, or about 14 per cent of sterling deposits with UK banks and cash). The 1979 deregulation also resulted in a parallel growth of overseas residents' holdings of sterling. As noted in section 4.3, together with more freely floating exchange rates, this brought about greater substitutability between currencies and between sterling and foreign currency assets in the portfolios of both residents and non-residents. This inspired the Bank of England to search for alternative 'definitions' of broad money. One of these included UK residents' holdings of both sterling and foreign currency deposits with UK banks; another encompassed overseas residents' sterling deposits with UK banks (approximately 21 per cent of £M3 in 1983) (BE, 1983c, pp. 526–8). However, in 1985 £M3 was retaining its vintage design.

In a highly integrated international financial system where currencies are fully convertible, all bank deposits, no matter in which currencies they are held, or whether they are held by residents or non-residents, should be considered as potential substitutes for sterling deposits (and hence regarded as part of the domain of monetary assets), and all are likely to be responsive to expectations of movements in exchange rates and to interest rate differentials between home and foreign deposits.

Thus, 'money' remains essentially 'defined' in terms of domestic financial claims. Given the extent of international integration, the interdependence in an open economy (Bryant, 1980) and the circumventive capacities of the Eurocurrency system, it is unlikely that the prerequisites of monetary targeting can be sustained.

5.3 Principal financial innovations in the USA

Financial innovation has been observed in all Western industrialized countries over the last two decades, although the extent and nature of its impact has varied (BIS, 1983). The highest degree of such innovation has occurred in the USA, essentially because all the factors that tend to induce innovations (mentioned earlier) were present. The particular exposure of the USA to financial change is often attributed to its historic attitude to banking. Though a bastion of free market enterprise, in the realm of banking the USA used regulation in profusion to alleviate the traditional American fear of 'money power', as well as to ensure that the financial system remained a public utility, immune from crises and panics. Unrelenting financial change rendered the newly defined M1 unreliable for US monetary policy purposes after 1982, and this has created pressure to 'redefine money' once again.

Recently, however, financial innovation has taken place in countries with much less pronounced reliance on regulation. In Canada, for instance, restrictions on competition by interest rates were removed by the 1967 Bank Act, and since then deregulation has not been a factor in financial innovation. Financial change there was a response to more intensive competition, high and variable interest rates, and the application of new technology. It centred around corporate cash management packages and new household deposit arrangements (BIS, 1983, p. 56; Freedman, 1983, pp. 101–3). These contributed to the effective withdrawal of M1 as a monetary target after 1982. Innovations in the UK can be ascribed partly to regulatory factors (though weaker than those in the USA) and partly to other forces which will be elaborated separately.

We shall begin with a brief discussion of some US financial innovations which have recently received considerable attention in economic literature, before moving, in chapter 6, to innovations in the UK, which have not been exposed to as widespread a debate. Issues common to both countries are discussed in both chapters.

5.3.1 *Money market instruments*

(*a*) *Certificates of deposit* A number of important innovations have occurred in the US money market. The term 'money market' is rather elusive, though in general it refers to large-scale, 'wholesale' borrowing and lending, usually involving financial institutions and large corporations. These transactions are normally carried out on the basis of certain financial arrangements or instruments. One such instrument is the certificate of deposit (CD), broadly described as a negotiable instrument certifying that a sum of money has been deposited with a bank issuing it and that, on the stated maturity date, the deposit will be repaid with interest by the issuing bank.

As with many innovations, a combination of factors accounted for the emergence of the negotiable CDs. During the 1950s, banks began to experience more intensive competition for deposits from savings institutions (such as savings and loans associations). Being at the time rather conservative, the banks were reluctant to accept large corporate time deposits, for fear of an abrupt withdrawal during periods of financial stringency. Large corporations began to raise funds by issuing commercial paper, which threatened direct intermediation through banks. Commercial paper began to displace government securities in the portfolios of large institutions. As the market for commercial paper improved and the general level of interest rates rose, the creation of large-denomination CDs was conceived as a way of protecting the market share of bank deposits.

The crucial boost to the development of CDs came in 1961 with the establishment of a secondary market for these instruments. From that time CDs became one of the main ways in which banks could mobilize temporarily free resources of large corporations on an unsecured basis. This way of borrowing protected banks from sudden withdrawals of funds during episodes of rising interest rates and stringent credit, and enabled them to meet the demand for advances from valued customers by operating the CD market.

To many investors, CDs represented a good substitute for government securities (e.g. Treasury bills), offering flexibility and often a higher yield. CDs thus became a valued addition to the menu of financial instruments which could be purchased by surplus units to diversify portfolios and utilize spare cash resources. Corporate treasuries in particular became more alert to the opportunities of earning income on their cash reserves as interest rates continued to rise. (This aspect will be discussed separately below.)

To banks, CDs represented a flexible way of raising resources from the money markets at a time when the competition for traditional deposits began to increase. The development of CDs was soon described as a 'revolution in banking' because it was associated with a move of banks towards greater independence from the influence of the monetary authorities and monetary policy (Gaines, 1967). Banks became more confident in soliciting the custom of large borrowers (financial institutions and corporations), knowing that they themselves could raise the necessary finance in money markets by bidding up interest rates. Large-scale borrowers increasingly looked for reliable credit lines undisturbed by credit shortages, however brought about. Banks therefore had to ensure that they had the capacity to lend, *even during central bank credit squeezes*.

CDs spearheaded the transformation in the traditional relations between the banks and the central bank. The ability of banks to raise wholesale funds by raising the interest rates on CDs made banks perceive the money market, rather than the discount window of the central bank, as the lender of last resort, thus removing the sharpness of the impact of Federal Reserve actions to influence aggregate spending. This was an important aspect of 'liability management', discussed in section 6.3 below.

For a time, the extent to which banks could operate CDs to neutralize monetary restriction was limited and they were judged to have only 'slightly weakened restrictive central bank operations' (Hester, 1981, p. 151). Their ability to meet the demand for loans by raising interest rates on CDs to accumulate the necessary funds was circumscribed by reserve requirements and a ceiling imposed by regulation Q, to which they could raise interest rates on CDs.

Regulation Q, which was generally applicable on deposits, was an impediment to interest rate competition and the ability to equate the demand for loanable funds with the supply. M. Friedman (1980b, p. 80) compared the regulation to a time bomb which had its greatest effect when inflation and interest rates were high. Normally, the monetary authorities raised the ceiling before it was about to become operational. However, to secure a reduction in credit, in 1966 the authorities resolved not to ease the restriction, and hence prevented the insulation of the market from the effects of the credit squeeze.

The shock of the decision to make regulation Q effective turned the attention of banks to an alternative source of supply of funds for onlending to credit-hungry customers. This came in the shape of the unregulated Eurocurrency market mentioned earlier. During this crisis, banks sampled the potential offered by the international market to mitigate the pressures of regulation Q.

There are two important consequences of the 1966 crisis which typify the behaviour of financial systems and stress the widespread interdependence discussed in chapter 2. First, regulation Q caused banks to seek refuge in the Eurocurrency system and at the same time vitally contributed to the growth of that system. The speed of adjustment was high and the learning period correspondingly short (Hewson and Sakakibara, 1975b). When regulation Q ceilings became binding again, banks knew how to overcome its effects by using the Eurodollar facilities. 'As far as the commercial banks were concerned, the Eurodollar borrowings, only an emergency resort in 1966, substituted admirably for CD market whenever it became immobilized by rate ceilings' (Wojnilower, 1980, p. 291). Indeed, in 1970 interest rate ceilings on CDs were liberalized, never to be used again as a tool of monetary control. They were later lifted completely for large-denomination CDs.

Second, the affliction of credit shortages in 1966 also produced a reaction from corporations, which began to seek assurances that in future the supply of funds would not be terminated abruptly. Overdraft facilities, rather than term loans, offered a way of safeguarding future supplies of credit regardless of short-term monetary conditions. Thus, corporate preference for overdraft lending increased; in 1980 unused credit facilities slightly exceeded demand deposits in banks (Wojnilower, 1980, p. 289), and in the subsequent year they exceeded M1 (Moore, 1983, p. 543). It was noted in section 4.4 that unused bank credit commitments – 'the invisible money supply', representing immediately spendable purchasing power – are not included in monetary aggregates.

Thus, the innovation of CDs and their diffusion and development was linked closely with other innovatory phenomena and management responses, all largely directed towards overcoming the sharpness of monetary restriction. CDs as a method of raising funds by banks continue to be developed. Issuers of CDs today seek to tailor them specifically to customers' requirements, for instance by allowing the investor to choose the date of maturity, or by mutually agreeing on intervals for computing interest rates (daily, quarterly, etc.).

(b) Repurchase agreements and the federal funds market   The federal funds market is one of the important money markets of the USA. It is a market which deals in reserves of the Federal Reserve banks. Immediately free federal funds (viz., funds not needed for purposes of a minimum reserve ratio) could be lent to institutions requiring liquid funds. The market grew rapidly at the end of the 1960s and especially after 1970 (Lombra and Kaufman, 1978, pp. 551–3). It became an important source of non-deposit funds to banks and other financial institutions and an important element in liability management by financial firms. It should be noted that the payment of interest on demand deposits was illegal in the USA. Rising interest rates thus increased the opportunity cost of holding idle funds by economic units and encouraged the growth of this type of market.

Sale and repurchase agreements (RPs, or repos for short) were arrangements which appeared on a small scale in the 1950s in the USA, whereby a security dealer sold US Treasury security or other federal funds instruments to a corporation, individual or government with a commitment to repurchase that security in a short period of time (often 'overnight') at an agreed rate of interest. They were not subject to interest rate ceilings under regulation Q or to minimum reserve requirements. The benefit to the lender was in the form of a yield on a balance which would otherwise be idle; to the borrower it gave the ability to meet pressing credit obligations. If the borrower was a bank, such a mode of borrowing could be used to remedy a reserve ratio deficiency without resorting to the help of the central bank.

The implications of such dealings in federal funds were noted in the 1950s (Minsky, 1957), but were not generally appreciated until large banks began to imitate these arrangements, thus substantially increasing the scale of RP operations. Periods of high short-term interest rates (1969, 1973–4) were particularly conducive to the growth of RPs as well as other forms of unsecured borrowing of federal funds from corporations, other financial institutions or government agencies. The net federal funds purchased by commercial banks rose from $0.3 billion at the end of the 1965 to $3.2 billion in 1970 and \$19.7 billion in 1975 (Hester, 1981, p. 157). At the end of 1979 the value of RPs was \$49 billion (approximately 12 per cent of M1), of which 41 per cent was overnight RPs (Federal Reserve Bulletins, table A13).

Transactions in RPs and unsecured funds had the following 'monetary' effects:

1 They permitted the lenders (e.g. corporate treasurers) in effect to receive interest on demand deposits.
2 They gave banks the means of competing by price for bank deposits.
3 They enabled overall expansion of bank deposits on the basis of a given supply of reserve funds simply by bidding up interest rates during periods of restrictive monetary policy.
4 Activity in such instruments, as in other instruments with which financial institutions manage their liabilities, contributed to the variability of interest rates.
5 They also contributed to the abandonment by the Federal Reserve in 1979 of interest rates as an instrument of monetary control in favour of a monetary base type of control.

It was widely recongized that dealings in RPs and similar instruments caused a slippage in monetary policy. Preventative measures considered included the imposition of a minimum reserve ratio on RPs or the abandonment of the prohibition on paying interest on bank current accounts (Lombra and Kaufman, 1978). The latter proposal was, indeed, advocated much earlier as a way of inhibiting financial innovations which economized on cash holdings (Marty, 1961, pp. 61–2). However, while agreeing that reserve restrictions might help, J. L. Pierce (1982, p. 781) commented that 'there is no protection against future innovations in money management that would develop to avoid reserve requirements'.

Some economists had little doubt that RPs represented a 'money' substitute (Hester, 1981, pp. 161, 171–5), but the Federal Reserve has been rather indecisive in its treatment of RPs as monetary assets. In 1979 it imposed reserve requirements on net federal reserves purchased, but relinquished them a year later. It did not include them in the 'redefined' narrow measures of money (M1A and M1B).[5] Overnight RPs were included in M2 and term RPs in M3 (see notes d and e to table 5.1 below).

(c) Money market mutual funds   The money market instruments discussed above represent 'wholesale' loans of large denomination which precluded the participation of households and small firms in their transactions. *Money market mutual funds* (MMMFs) overcame this gap in intermediation. These funds collect household deposits in small amounts (\$1000-plus) and invest them in short-term money market instruments, thus giving small investors some benefits from high market interest rates. They also provide a means of

avoiding interest rate ceilings when they become binding on deposits (Lawrence and Elliehausen, 1981). The customers of MMMFs can make withdrawals on demand, so that such funds provide services similar to those associated with demand accounts, but with a bonus of interest earnings.

Having started in 1972, their early diffusion was slow until 1978 when they began to grow rapidly. This rapid growth was linked with relative interest rates. Account holders in banks and savings institutions became unduly penalized by the interest rate ceilings binding on those institutions in relation to interest rates governing in the money market. The funds were also facilitated by technological improvements in money transfers, which will be discussed later.

The total of MMMFs at the end of 1977 was nearly $4 billion, which had nearly trebled by the end of 1978. Between 1978 and 1982 their balance increased by 23 times to stand at approximately 48 per cent of M1B (see table 5.1). However, in 1983 they showed a decline as a result of competition from new types of retail accounts discussed below. Like RPs, MMMFs were incorporated not in the 'transactions' aggregates, but in M2.

5.3.2 New deposit accounts

Banks and thrift institutions in the USA reacted to competition from the very successful MMMFs by innovating a variety of instruments designed to attract or retain their retail custom (BIS, 1983, p. 54). These included the new types of retail accounts, bearing the characteristics of demand deposit accounts but earning a money-market-related interest. We shall confine ourselves to only a brief discussion of these accounts.

In 1978 all US banks were authorized to offer *automatic transfer service* (ATS) accounts. The ATS provided an automatic transfer of funds from interest-bearing savings accounts into demand deposit accounts whenever this was necessary for making transactions from the latter. Low transfer costs, arising from the application of technological devices, made this possible. The accounts permitted holders to reduce transactions balances to the minimum; in effect, interest was now paid on balances previously held in demand deposits. The overall effect of such arrangements was to reduce the demand for non-interest-bearing money (such as M1A after the 'redefinition' in 1979).

ATS were classified as 'transactions' money and incorporated in M1B (part of 'other checkable deposits' in table 5.1) in the money 'redefinition' of 1979. They also had an effect on the minimum reserve requirement by member banks of the Federal Reserve system. Deposits held at ATS were subjected to the (lower) reserve ratio required on savings deposits rather than the (higher) ratio applicable to demand deposits, and hence had an expansionary effect on money aggregates such as M1B and M2 (Tatom, 1982, p. 24).

The *negotiable order of withdrawal* (NOW) is yet another monetary asset that has come into prominence in the early 1980s. NOW accounts refer to interest-bearing savings accounts in depository institutions (banks and savings establishments) from which withdrawals can be made by negotiable drafts rather than demand over the counter. They began on a small scale in the 1970s, and until 1976 their use was confined to New Hampshire and Massachusetts. In 1976 a wider use was authorized, but it was limited to North-eastern states. The 1980 Monetary Control Act permitted their spread nationwide, and it is from that year that their diffusion accelerated markedly. Only from 1980 were they included in M1B (later M1).

These accounts initiated a move towards interest-bearing accounts with chequing facilities, blurring the distinction between 'demand' and 'time' or 'savings' deposits. From 1981 banks and savings institutions nationwide began to offer interest-bearing accounts with limited chequing facilities, and from January 1983 Super-NOW accounts were authorized. These offer relatively high interest rates and full chequing facilities, but require a minimum balance.

In December 1982, permission was given to issue yet another monetary instrument, namely the *money market deposit account* (MMDA); like Super-NOW, it is not subject to interest rate restriction, can be opened by all depository institutions, and offers transactions services. However, the transactions facilities are more limited than those on Super-NOWs, and for that reason, while Super-NOWs have been included in M1, the MMDAs are part of M2.

It has been suggested that both MMDAs and Super-NOWs have been 'rushed through' Congress in order to enable banks and depository institutions to compete with MMMFs (Tobin, 1983a, p. 162). Whatever the reason, it appears that the US banking system is now moving towards transactions accounts yielding interest income.

Two economic effects of the above-mentioned innovations should be noted at this stage. The new facilities lower transactions costs to the holders of money balances. They also contribute to the increase in interest-bearing balances in money aggregates. In terms of the conventional demand-for-money analysis, they might thus be expected to decrease the demand for narrowly defined money as well as to alter interest rate sensitivity. We shall return to these issues later.

There is a considerable state of flux in the American classification of 'monies'; new financial instruments are being added to the newly 'redefined' aggregates in an arbitrary way. Distinctions continue to be made between 'transactions' (hence narrowly defined 'money') and 'savings' (hence higher-level aggregates) instruments without a convincing rationale. Indeed, the Monetary Policy Report to Congress (1983, p. 134) readily admitted that 'These distinctions are not clear-cut, and they illustrate the increasing

fuzziness of the dividing line between M1 and non-M1-type balances.' The
new accounts are offered not only by banks, but also by other depository
institutions, which thus play an increasingly important role in money
transmission services as well as in financial intermediation. The Chairman of
the Federal Reserve System, P. A. Volker (1984, p. 316) recently asserted
that it is indisputable that 'thrift institutions have essentially become
bank-like institutions'.

Financial innovations in wholesale and retail deposits have produced
considerable shifts of funds between aggregates and rather erratic growth
patterns (see tables 5.1 and 5.2 in the appendix to this chapter). Between
1980 and 1983, 'other checkable deposits', reflecting the growth in ATS and
NOW accounts, rose by a factor of five to nearly a quarter of M1. Between
November 1981 and November 1982 the average balance per account rose by
8.7 per cent (to $5500) and the number of accounts rose by 22.4 per cent (to
18 million) (Radecki and Wenninger, 1983, p. 8). In 1983, M2 swelled with
funds attracted by the new MMDAs. The structure of the aggregates is
changing in a rather unpredictable way in response to competitive and
deregulatory impulses. From table 5.2 we can see a very erratic pattern of
growth rates of monetary assets, particularly demand deposits and M1A.

The decline in non-interest-bearing assets in monetary aggregates is quite
noticeable. The decrease in demand deposits has been particularly striking.
Their ratio to both M1A and M1B (later M1) has fallen (see figure 5.1): in
1977 M1B was composed almost totally of non-interest-bearing assets; in
1983, only three-quarters of its components bore no interest (see M1A/M1B).
The ratio of non-interest-bearing M1A to higher-level aggregates is shown in
figure 5.2; 82 per cent of M2 now bears interest. It should also be

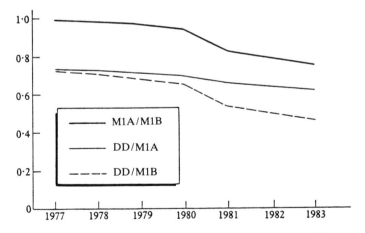

Figure 5.1 Declining ratios of non-interest-bearing 'money', USA, 1977–83.
Source: Table 5.1.

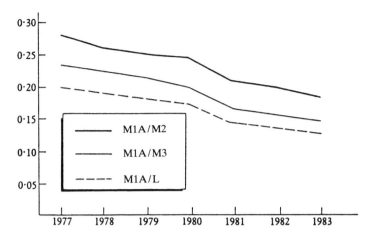

Figure 5.2 Ratios of M1A to higher-level aggregates, USA, 1977–83.
Source: Table 5.1.

remembered that the rate of interest on the components of the aggregates is mostly related to money market rates; thus, 'own' interest rate of aggregates varies because of the changing proportion of interest-bearing assets and under the influence of market rates.

The above-mentioned innovations caused the behaviour of M1 in relation to economic activity to diverge sharply from its historical trends, particularly after 1981 (Monetary Policy Report to Congress, 1984, p. 79). Uncertainties concerning M1 motivated the Federal Open Market Committee at the end of 1982 effectively to put M1 in abeyance as a targeted aggregate; in official terms, less weight is being given to M1, but more to M2 and M3, as indicators of monetary policy. On theoretical and empirical grounds, however, the use of middle-of-the-range simple-sum aggregates for policy purposes has been discouraged (compare section 3.4).

5.3.3 *Financial futures*

We now come to an innovation which has only an indirect effect on 'money', namely, financial futures (FF) trading. Futures markets in commodities or currencies have, for a long time now, been an established part of commercial life. FF markets are an analogous development, but relatively new.

Financial futures refer to agreements for deliveries of financial instruments at a specified date and at a price agreed at the time of contracting. Thus, a buyer contracts to purchase a security at a future date and a seller to deliver that security at a prearranged price. FF markets are arrangements whereby buyers and sellers of financial futures are brought together for the purpose of contracting in FFs.

The first FF market was set up in Chicago in 1975 at the initiative of the local Board of Trade to transact, in the first instance, securities of the Government National Mortgage Association. The immediate reason for this development was the high volatility of interest rates experienced in the 1973–4 period in the USA. It was at that point that the imitation of commodity and currency arrangements took place in the sphere of financial instruments to allow a hedge against losses caused by erratically fluctuating security prices. The diffusion which occurred subsequently testifies to the success of the innovation (Wojnilower, 1980, pp. 308–11). The Chicago market was extended to embrace other government securities (such as Treasury bills), CDs and other commercial paper. It is now increasingly becoming a market in international FFs, with Eurodollar banks from the USA and Europe participating in its dealings.

In 1982 the London International Financial Futures Exchange (LIFFE) was opened to enable financial institutions to trade in international FFs. The basic idea of the market is the same as that of its Chicago trailblazer, though its operations are organized on somewhat different principles (Blanden, 1983; Fitzgerald, 1983).

As already noted, the key reason for the successful development of FF markets was the risk faced by financial institutions because of fluctuating interest rates. A contributory factor was the growing habit of variable interest lending mentioned earlier. This inevitably shifted some of the risk on to the borrowers, who thus sought protection. The gradual deregulation, and the expected removal of all interest rate regulations, has also created uncertainty concerning future interest rate changes. Thus, by offering an opportunity to hedge against risk, the FF markets fulfil a basic role of a financial institution in reducing uncertainty at an acceptable cost. However, it should be stressed that such markets also attract speculators, and may contribute to instability in some parts of the financial sector.

An assessment of the economic impact of FF markets cannot be made with confidence. They are a new phenomenon in a generally changing situation. Their impact on money aggregates is not likely to be direct, but they alter the terms and conditions in an interrelated financial sector and are thus relevant to monetary management. At the microeconomic level, risk-averse financial institutions welcome the opportunity to insure against losses caused by interest rate shifts. Many institutions in the USA believe that FF markets will help them to improve the management of interest rate spreads in the new deregulated environment of the 1980s (Hale, 1983, p. 33). Indeed, dealing in FFs has for many banks become part of the balance sheet management to be discussed under 'liability management'.

It is in this protection against the effects of interest rate variations that we should seek the macroeconomic impact of the FF markets. 'The siren song of the financial futures markets is that they offer banks, builders, and all business the immunity to macroeconomic policies of restraint' (Wojnilower, 1980, p. 309). This may have an element of persuasive advertising, though early assessments of the macroeconomic impact do stress the danger of a *growing insensitivity of financial institutions to interest rate changes* (Hester, 1981, p. 167). Thus, FF markets, particularly in conjunction with the increasing floating rate lending, might make monetary control less effective by insulating the economy from the effect of official interest rates increases (BE, 1983a, p. 362).

5.3.4 *Corporate cash management*

Corporate cash management refers to a deliberate deployment of liquid assets in companies in order to maximize the return on the financial portfolio. Recent literature on financial innovation might give the impression that cash management is a relatively new phenomenon of the early 1970s, coinciding with high levels of interest rates. However, though its macroeconomic impact in recent years might have been greater than before, the basic idea of cash management is not new.

US corporations showed considerable interest in managing their financial surpluses and cash balances in the 1950s, especially at the time of rising interest rates. Indeed, high nominal interest rates often appear as a prime explanatory factor of innovations in cash management. Though this constitutes a plausible hypothesis, the relationship between interest rates and novel ways of using cash resources needs to be investigated further. The hypothesis has received some support in the USA, but there is apparently no evidence for it in the UK (BE, 1982b, p. 520). Improvements in cash management appear to be a process continuing even after interest rates start to decline (Gaines, 1967, pp. 99–101), and there is no indication to suggest that episodes of falling rates have discouraged innovations in cash management in more recent years. Thus, cash management is likely to be a more complex phenomenon than a simple reaction to high interest rates. As with other innovations, reliable evidence on inducement is lacking. While interest rates may be important, cash management innovations are also related to other factors, such as transactions costs, profitability and other innovations in the financial system.

Regular monitoring of changes in cash balances, accurate cash flow forecasts and the availability of means of quick and reliable funds transfers (all related to transactions costs) are among the essential requirements of effective cash management. All are sensitive to improvements in communications technology.

It was the search for profitable outlets for liquid funds by corporate treasurers which was partly responsible for the original development of RPs (Minsky, 1957, pp. 176–81) and also contributed to the creation of CDs. In the 1970s, it was the more intensive use of such instruments, of other financial innovations and, in particular, of the vastly improved communications and electronic funds transfers that resulted in more effective cash management, in innovations in cash management techniques, and in the provision of novel cash management services for corporate treasurers (Porter *et al.*, 1979, pp. 217–19).

It should thus be emphasized that the development of corporate cash management was an integral part of complex and interrelated innovatory processes involving the development of money markets, new financial instruments (CDs, RPs, MMMFs), new accounts (ATS) and new technology. It thus resembles more a *'cluster' of innovations* deployed by novel arrangements which permit corporate treasuries to develop new management methods.

Cash management in large corporations has encouraged banks and other agencies to supply cash management systems, which essentially provide electronic links between banks and their customers, giving corporate treasurers the facility to monitor accounts worldwide and transmit funds quickly.[6] These are now becoming very sophisticated, supplying a continuous flow of information and packages containing treasury management devices such as forecasting systems and automatic foreign exchange conversions. Such facilities make corporations even more alert to the financial environment and enhance their sensitivity to profit opportunities. They also enable corporate treasuries to conduct a sort of do-it-yourself banking from their own terminals. Paradoxically, banks have thus been helping companies to exercise banking functions. An important aspect of this development is the rising capability of companies to develop inter-company lending, thus bypassing the financial media reflected in monetary aggregates. Clearly, the traditional bank–company relationships have been changing, and the implications of such changes have hardly been investigated.

It is not clear what the future holds in the realm of cash management for large corporations. At the end of 1984 BP decided to organize its cash management in the foreign exchange department by setting up a non-deposit banking unit, BP Financial International, to offer specialized banking services to its branches and associated companies. There may well be other companies seeking profit opportunities in an in-house banking organization, replacing the financial services previously carried out by banks. Financial intermediation in the 1980s is likely to continue to evolve without leaving any part of the sector immune from change.

In spite of the threat to banks in this do-it-yourself banking by corporations, there is rivalry between banks offering companies appropriate cash management packages. The UK banks lag behind their US counterparts in the development of this service, although since 1982 some clearing banks have started to offer them.[7] However, cash management systems are available to UK corporations from US banks well represented in the UK.

Cash management is thus best looked at as a complex eclectic phenomenon permitting economies in money holdings. Improved information flows and forecasting procedures reduce uncertainty about cash flows and lower 'precautionary balances'; new financial instruments provide new profit opportunities; electronic devices enable switches of funds into higher interest rate media to be made quickly at low transfer costs. Viewed in the framework of the familiar transactions demand for money based on the inventory-theoretic approach, which essentially predicts the demand for money as an increasing function of transfer costs and a decreasing function of interest rate (opportunity cost of funds held in money),[8] improved cash management has been held responsible for the overprediction of the demand for M1 in the USA in the 1970s (Porter *et al.*, 1979).

A downward shift in the aggregate demand for a narrowly defined money is a plausible prediction resulting from cash management innovations in the company sector. However, in the sense that cash management innovations also shape the attitude of corporations to profit opportunities in the field of liquid asset management, and enhance their sensitivity to interest movements, they may also have an impact on the interest elasticity of the demand for money. Corporations have increasingly become sensitive to interest rate differentials, or 'spreads' – that is, the difference between their borrowing rates and the general rates in wholesale markets (viz. deposit rates). Corporate borrowing is said to be positively related to the decrease in spreads (indicating falling costs of intermediation). Indeed, in the UK the phenomenon of 'round-tripping' has been observed when the spread becomes temporarily negative, leading to an expansion of borrowing and redepositing, which is in turn reflected in the growth of £M3 (this aspect will be developed in chapter 6).

The extent to which corporate behaviour affects the macroeconomic interest elasticity of money demand depends on the ability of the authorities to influence interest rate differentials and the speed of response by the corporate sector. The ability of the authorities (as will be seen later) to influence *relative interest rates* is considered to be impaired. There is, however, little firm evidence on the effect on macroeconomic interest sensitivity, and more research is required to assess more accurately the relation of the management of financial portfolios by corporations and national monetary management. What is clear is that companies now have an effective capacity to seek relief from restrictive monetary conditions, not only in the domestic economy, but also abroad.

5.3.5 *A challenge to monetary orthodoxy*

Before leaving the examples of US financial innovations two points may be observed. First, in a situation of financial change, it is difficult to provide an indicative definition of money except perhaps in terms of the legal tender. If money needs to be defined, for instance for purposes of targeting, it does matter crucially *which measure of money is chosen*. Financial innovations are likely to result in different shifts of demand functions for different aggregates. Interest sensitivities of the functions also need a complete reinterpretation. The demand for individual financial assets is likely to be more sensitive to interest rate differentials. The interest sensitivity of aggregates too would depend on differentials between 'own' rates and the general level of money market rates manipulated by the authorities.

Broad aggregates are more likely to internalize the effects of interest rate changes, but the extent to which they represent 'money' is questionable. In this realm the Divisia money-quantity index would distinguish between changes in 'moneyness' (income effect) and would neutralize all 'substitution' effects (see section 3.4.1). In general, it is thought that, because of the rising content in all aggregates of assets whose interest rates are flexible and related to money market rates, the ability of the authorities to effect credit demand responses to a change in general interest rates has become more limited. Thus, in terms of the traditional demand function for 'narrow' money (such as M1A or M1B), financial innovations reduce interest rate sensitivity (steeper slope) and decrease the demand at each level of interest rates (as funds are attracted to interest-bearing instruments in high-level aggregates).

It is doubtful whether such changes to the demand are occurring in a regular or predictable way. Indeed, it is the sheer uncertainty and unpredictability of shift and slope changes which pose the main problem of monetary control (Pierce, 1984, pp. 392–4). In such a situation, the conduct of monetary policy based on using the growth of the quantity of money as an intermediate target must be viewed with serious scepticism.[9] These points will be further developed later.

Second, the innovations described here are only a selection of more widespread financial changes which are altering the structure and operations of the financial sector as a whole. For reasons which will be developed later, non-bank financial institutions (insurance companies, securities firms) are increasingly diversifying to deposit-taking and payments and funds transmission services. Less frequently, but noticeably, non-financial enterprises are also venturing into banking business. Thus, the phenomenon of 'non-bank banks' is challenging the traditional concept of 'banks'.[10] Volker (1984, p. 313), the Chairman of the Federal Reserve System, with some consternation summed up this situation: 'Deposit-like instruments and payments services are springing up in significant volume partially or wholly outside the framework of governmentally protected and supervised depository institutions.'

In this environment of financial flux, monetary authorities are increasingly sceptical about the reliability of customary monetary management and the textbook version of the two-stage process of monetary targeting (see section 1.1.3). There is no assurance that the transmission mechanism of orthodox monetary action designed to influence money and credit in the public interest is functioning, or whether financial innovations which impair its operations are consistent with the public interest. Expressing such doubts, Volker (1984, p. 312) observed that 'we have a system that is changing, helter-skelter, in response to a variety of economic and other forces, but with little sense of public policy issue at stake'.

Appendix

Table 5.1 US money stock measures and some components, 1977–83 ($ billion; averages of daily figures; not seasonally adjusted; end of December)

	1977	1978	1979	1980	1981	1982	1983
Demand deposits	247.0	261.5	270.8	274.7	243.6	247.3	251.6
M1A[a]	340.1	364.2	382.5	397.4	373.8	387.8	406.6
Other checkable deposits	5.0	9.4	18.2	27.4	78.5	104.1	131.2
M1B (M1 after 1981)[b]	345.1	373.6	400.6	424.8	452.3	491.9	537.8
Money market mutual funds[c]	3.8	10.3	43.6	76.6	186.8	233.6	178.5
M2[d]	1229.0	1409.0	1531.3	1635.4	1798.7	1967.4	2197.9
M3[e]	1464.7	1634.8	1786.0	1996.1	2242.7	2466.6	2712.8
L[f]	1726.7	1943.9	2159.4	2332.8	2605.6	2876.5	3184.7
Debt[g]				3946.9	4323.8	4710.1	5244.8
M1A/M1B	0.99	0.97	0.95	0.94	0.83	0.79	0.76
M1A/M2	0.28	0.26	0.25	0.24	0.21	0.20	0.18
M1A/M3	0.23	0.22	0.21	0.20	0.17	0.16	0.15
M1A/L	0.20	0.19	0.18	0.17	0.14	0.13	0.13
M1A/debt				0.10	0.09	0.08	0.08
Demand deposits/ M1A	0.73	0.72	0.71	0.69	0.65	0.64	0.62
Demand deposits/ M1	0.72	0.70	0.68	0.65	0.54	0.50	0.47

[a] M1A: demand deposits at all commercial banks other than those due to domestic banks, the US government, and foreign banks and official institutions, less cash items in the process of collection and Federal Reserve float, plus currency outside the Treasury, Federal Reserve banks, and the vaults of commercial banks, plus travellers' checks of non-bank issuers.

cont.

Table 5.1 *cont.*

[b] M1B: M1A plus negotiable order of withdrawal (NOW) and automatic transfer service (ATS) accounts at banks and thrift institutions, credit union share draft accounts, and demand deposits at mutual savings banks. M1A and M1B ceased to be published separately after 1981; M1B became simply M1. They came into being in 1979 as a result of the 'redefinitions' of money from 1980 onwards. Years 1977–79 are given for purposes of comparison.
[c] Included in M2.
[d] M2: M1B plus savings and small-denomination time deposits at all depository institutions, overnight repurchase agreements at commercial banks, overnight Eurodollars held by US residents other than banks at Caribbean branches of member banks, MMMFs and MMDAs.
[e] M3: M2 plus large-denominated time deposits at all depository institutions and term RPs at commercial banks and savings and loan associations.
[f] L: M3 plus other liquid assets such as term Eurodollars held by US residents other than banks, banker's acceptances, commercial paper, Treasury bills and other liquid Treasury securities, and US savings bonds.
[g] Debt: debt of non-financial public and private sectors.
Source: *Federal Reserve Bulletins*, tables A13.

Table 5.2 Growth rates of monetary assets and totals (percentage growth from 4th quarter to 4th quarter)

	DD^a	$M1A^b$	M1	M2	M3	Debt
1978	5.9	7.1	8.2	8.0	11.8	13.0
1979	3.6	5.0	7.5	8.1	10.3	12.0
1980	1.4	3.9	7.4	9.0	9.6	9.5
1981	−11.3	5.9	5.1 $(2.5)^c$	9.3	12.3	9.6
1982	1.5	3.6	8.7	9.5	10.5	9.2
1983	1.7	4.8	10.0	12.1	9.7	10.5

[a] Demand deposits.
[b] As in table 5.1; discontinued from 1981 onwards, but offered here for illustrative purposes.
[c] 2.5 per cent is the 'shift-adjusted' growth rate of M1; that is, 'old' M1B (born 1979, dead 1981, but living as M1), less an estimate of 'other checkable deposits' (e.g. NOW) which originate from non-demand deposit funds. The shift-adjusted M1 is supposed to be a purer 'transactions' money (see Tatom, 1982, pp. 25–6).
Source: *Federal Reserve Bulletin*, 70, February 1984, p.81; table 5.1 above.

Notes

1 A hint that financial innovations may have high set-up costs, and thus can be expected to occur in the portfolios of large institutions, has been given in Hester (1982, p. 43). Low capital intensity of financial innovations is mentioned without elaboration (e.g. B. Friedman, 1980, p. 57).
2 More information may be found in Hewson and Sakakibara (1975a); McKenzie (1976); Dufey and Giddy (1978); Llewellyn (1980); and Johnston (1983).

3 An examination of tables in the appendix to chapter 6 does bring home the fact that the UK and overseas banks carry out, albeit in different proportions, essentially the same business in sterling and in foreign currencies.

4 In 1984, overseas sector deposits in the UK in foreign currencies were over six times as large as M1 and nearly three times as large as £M3 (see tables 6.7 and 6.9 below).

5 The inclusion of RPs into M1B would have stabilized M1B's velocity of circulation (Cagan, 1982, pp. 664–7).

6 Some systems (e.g. Citicash Manager of Citibank, MARS of Morgan Guaranty) are available to the UK companies.

7 Midland Bank was the first of the clearers to offer an electronic cash management service based on a US computer network and systems, and a year later Nat West began to supply a similar service through its Nat West Network.

8 Using Miller and Orr's (1966, p. 425) formula for the inventory theoretic model, the long-run average demand for money $M_d = 4/3(3t\sigma^2/4i)^{1/3}$ where t are transfer costs, σ^2 variance of daily cash flows, i interest rate (as explained in the text). It is postulated that the 'swarm' of financial innovations relevant to cash management would reduce t and σ. The sensitivity to i is a problematical issue (Porter *et al.*, 1979, p. 217; Judd and Scadding, 1982, pp. 999–1000).

9 Few American economists doubt that financial innovations have been mainly responsible for the uncertain or confusing situation in US monetary policy. Some, however, attach substantial contributory blame to erroneous control procedures by Federal Reserve authorities (e.g. Friedman, 1982). J. L. Pierce (1984) argued that financial innovations were the main factor in the mid-1970s, but that between 1979 and 1982 the procedures of the authorities were more destabilizing than the innovations which could have been predicted.

10 For instance, Sears, Roebuck and Co., a large retail chain, has been developing financial services. In 1978 it earned almost as much from offering such services as did the Bank of America Corporation (Clausen, 1980, p. 93).

—6—

Financial Innovations and the Control of Money: US and UK Experiences II

6.1 Innovation-inducing developments in the UK

6.1.1 *Regulatory changes*

In both the USA and the UK, there has been a strong tendency to free the financial sector from restrictive regulations. Circumventory activity, increasing competition (including competition from overseas banks), and the electoral preference for parties espousing the *laissez-faire* spirit have all contributed to this tendency.

In the USA the deregulatory processes resulted in the 1980 Depository Institution and Monetary Control Act. New proposals for deregulation have been announced and are widely expected to be implemented. These would remove further barriers which demarcate the activities of financial institutions. They are expected to permit banks, in effect, to extend their activities into non-banking business such as insurance, dealing in some types of securities, and managing mutual funds. On the other hand, they are also expected to allow other financial institutions to diversify into traditional banking operations. The possible consequences of deregulation are now widely debated.

In the UK, too, it is anticipated that the deregulation which has already taken place will soon be followed by further moves to free financial institutions, and in particular building societies, from the constraints of some rather old rules. Deregulation normally generates, at least in the short and medium term, greater competition and further innovation as a form of competitive action.

In the UK, public pressure for more competition in the financial sector, designed to achieve a system more responsive to the needs of a changing economy and to improve allocative efficiency, has manifested itself strongly ever since the publication of the Radcliffe Report (1959). The recommendations of that report have been reinforced by various other inquiries into the financial system, increasingly advocating liberalizing reforms. Only a very general account of regulatory changes is given below to serve as a background to innovatory changes discussed later.

The National Prices and Incomes Board (1967) advocated a more competitive banking system which would regain a leading role in capital markets, mainly on equity grounds; it also urged the extension of monetary regulations to non-bank institutions. The Monopolies Commission Report (1968), which pronounced against a proposed duopoly in commercial banking, drew attention to the absence of price competition in banking and criticized the wastefulness of some methods of oligopolistic competition such as branching (more specifically, 'over-branching'). The Select Committee on Nationalized Industries (1969) pressed the Bank of England to foster competition in the financial sector so as to improve the overall allocative efficiency of the economy. The Crowther Committee (1971) recommended the withdrawal of direct controls on consumer credit and pronounced against fragmentation in the credit market: consumer credit was to be granted by all financial institutions. In these reports, competition was directly linked with increased efficiency.

The reports were supported by academic studies, some of which attempted to measure the loss of resources caused by the operation of the price cartel by banks, and urged the abolition of all traditional central banking controls on banks, such as the minimum reserve requirements (Griffiths, 1970, 1972). Thus, deregulation, or more precisely decontrol, was seen as a way of enhancing the efficiency of banks. At the same time, the acceptance of the conventional wisdom that the demand-for-money function was essentially stable helped to alleviate fears of a possible loss of control over monetary growth and of the dangers of instability.

Competition and Credit Control (CCC) of 1971 was a major UK financial reform;[1] it abolished the main impediments to competition in the monetary sector by withdrawing the use of direct monetary controls (such as ceilings on deposits) and dissolving the cartel arrangements which prevented rivalry by price among banks. The newly created 'eligible reserve assets' ratio was to apply to all banks and not just the clearing banks. The move towards a freer, if not free, market was further emphasized by the announcement that, henceforward, credit allocation was to be 'primarily determined by its cost'.

The 1971 measure was an expression of faith in the free market philosophy and an exhortation to greater enterprise in financial markets. It encouraged banks to be more innovative in the management of both their assets and their liabilities. In particular, it increased their appetite for meeting competition for deposits by mobilizing funds by means of money market instruments and interest-bearing deposits. (These aspects are analysed separately below.)

Only the principal effects of CCC are briefly sketched here. The credit reform coincided with an expansionary economic policy. The initial implementation of the allocation of credit 'by cost' was to make the minimum lending rate (MLR), a successor to the Bank rate, behave rather passively, until 1978, by following rather than leading the money market. This contributed to a situation where the interest rate structure favoured expansion. Changes in MLR involved a 'bias towards delay', in the sense that the rate readily came down, but its rise was frequently delayed owing to its unpopular political repercussions (such as its effect on house mortgages and business confidence). Bank lending rates (e.g. overdraft rates) to prime customers tended to lag behind money market rates (e.g. rates on CDs), encouraging borrowing from banks in order to redeposit ('round-tripping') or buy money market instruments, thereby boosting high-level money aggregates (Gowland, 1978, pp. 56–9; Goodhart, 1984, p. 103).

CCC was followed by dynamic rises in bank deposits, the money supply, interest rates and inflation. Between 1971 and 1973 the M3 measure rose by 61.5 per cent and the £M3 equivalent (£M3 was not used until 1976) by 58.5 per cent. Undoubtedly, the expansionist policy contributed to these results. However, much blame was laid on the 'permissive regulatory environment' in which clearing banks set out vigorously to 're-intermediate', that is, to recapture the business they had lost during the years when monetary restriction was directed primarily at them. 'Their record of intermediation and innovation over this period [1971–3] has no parallels in British banking history' (Chesher *et al.*, 1975, p. 37).

The newly liberated market forces and entrepreneurial zeal contributed to the famous 'secondary banks crisis' (Reid, 1982). The secondary banks, perhaps the most innovative of the institutions at the time, relied for their lending, much of it for commercial property development, on funds raised in the money market. They were also perhaps the first manifestation of the dangers involved in 'liability management', which will be examined later. They developed outside the reach of the supervisory and prudential standards applicable to the established banks, and, in their rapid expansion in the early 1970s, often transgressed these standards. The 1973–4 crisis of the secondary banks was prevented from spreading to the remainder of the banking system by a rescue action – the 'lifeboat' – by the other banks, guided with strong determination by the Bank of England. 'A principal lesson of these years has been that any system of control sets a premium on avoidance and circumvention; and that prudential regulation is not immune from it' (BE, 1983b, p. 368).

The immediate policy reaction to the financial expansion of the early 1970s was a retreat, in December 1973, from the CCC principles in the shape of the establishment of a supplementary special deposits scheme (known as the 'Corset'), which imposed ceilings on the 'interest-bearing eligible liabilities' (IBELs) of banks and a resolve on the part of the monetary authorities to review the prudential arrangements applicable to financial institutions. The former measure involved banks and finance houses placing non-interest-bearing supplementary deposits with the Bank of England if their IBELs rose faster than a rate specified by the Bank. The Corset was designed essentially to discourage the raising of 'money' in wholesale markets (viz., to counteract 'liability management') in order to finance more profitable lending, thus preventing interest rates from rising and getting completely out of control.

The effect of the Corset on interest rates and on the expansion of £M3 is not easy to assess because of the simultaneous operations of other monetary actions (open market operations and MLR). It was, however, quite soon avoided and circumvented by financial institutions: by resorting to such measures as the increased use of the commercial bill market (the 'bill leak'), where depositors were, in effect, assisted by banks to supply their surpluses to borrowers outside the banking system (hence 'disintermediation'), whereby credit rose at a given level of £M3; by building up an appropriate asset structure in anticipation of the imposition of the Corset; or by the switching of sterling business from the UK to overseas financial centres (Hall, 1983, pp. 30–43; Coakley and Harris, 1983, pp. 200–1). The application of the Corset thus distorted financial flows (and hence monetary aggregates), and by the time it was first relaxed and eventually abolished in 1980 its effectiveness was severely eroded by avoidance.

The new minimum 'eligible reserve assets ratio' too was proving to have little or no restrictive force upon which the authorities could rely in trying to implement a more stringent monetary policy. Like its predecessor, the 'liquidity ratio', it consisted of a bundle of assets, the acquisition of some of which could easily be arranged by banks which were becoming increasingly skilled at the management of their assets and liabilities. As eligible reserve assets included money at call, Treasury bills, local authority bills and commercial bills, securing a desired level of such assets was not difficult, with the result that the Bank of England did not have an effective liquidity leverage to implement a restrictive policy (Morgan and Harrington, 1973).[2]

The abolition of the Corset was part of the second wave of liberalizing reforms which came shortly after the election of the Conservative administration, whose broad economic strategy was based on monetarist principles. In October 1979 exchange controls, that is, restrictions on transactions relating to investments in foreign currencies, were removed after 40 years in operation. This opened the economy even further to international influence and strengthened its integration with world financial markets (compare section 5.2.3).[3]

A Green Paper on Monetary Control proposed new monetary arrangements which were implemented in August 1981.[4] In effect, they swept away the remaining continuous monetary controls and changed the operation of the MLR. The requirement that banks maintain a minimum reserve assets ratio was abolished. The only remaining requirement of this sort was left for technical reasons: banks and licensed deposit-takers (created by the 1979 Bank Act) were asked to hold 0.5 per cent of their eligible liabilities with the Bank of England, and, in addition, the London clearing banks were to keep at the Bank whatever operational balances they thought necessary.

The practice of announcing MLR was discontinued to remove the 'bias towards delay' in operating the discount rate. The Bank would respond to bids and offers from the market, making public the rate at which it had done business. In its interest rate operations, the Bank would aim to keep short-term interest rates within an undisclosed band which would be moved from time to time. Those arrangements were to give the market greater flexibility in interest rate operations and thus greater influence on the structure of interest rates. They were also to remove interest rate stickiness which encouraged 'round-tripping'.

Thus, the effects of the reforms between 1971 and 1981 were to free banks, and some other institutions, from the impediments to competition and innovation, to which they had been previously subjected, mainly in the name of monetary control. The Bank of England was left essentially with interest rates as a weapon of control, but without any traditional continuously binding restrictions such as the reserve ratio. This was deemed sufficient to influence the money stock.

It should be reiterated that, from 1971 onwards, the underlying intellectual or theoretical basis for the liberalizing reforms was the acceptance of the thesis, consistent with monetarist teaching, that the freeing of financial institutions from regulatory constraints would improve the allocative efficiency of the financial system, and that the demand-for-money function was inherently stable. Thus, the removal of monetary controls, including the Corset, was not associated with a loss of overall monetary control: with a stable demand for money, changes in the money supply were expected to yield predictable results.

6.1.2 *Competition*

(*a*) *The impact of the Eurocurrency market* In some countries, Eurobranches of foreign banks provided a significant element of competition to indigenous banks, not only for international, but also for domestic business, thereby encouraging innovation. This was of particular importance in the UK, the principal centre of the Eurodollar market (see section 5.2.1).

By the end of the nineteenth century, the British banking system dominated the financial system of the country. It should, however, be remembered that at that time commercial banks financed mainly the working capital of the economy; external long-term capital requirements of industry were supplied mainly through the stock exchange. The banking system, which had emerged through a lengthy process of amalgamations, had an oligopolistic structure. The units were relatively large and stable, but were not fully alert to intermediation opportunities in the economy. In particular, they seemed not to be aware of the potential offered by the mobilization of savings from relatively low-income households. Government initiative and encouragement was largely responsible for filling the gaps in intermediation by shaping the non-bank sector of financial institutions under various enactments such as Trustee Savings Bank acts, Building Societies acts and Friendly Societies acts. Thus, the financial system which emerged in the postwar period was highly segmented. Financial institutions belonged to associations (such as the Committee of London Clearing Banks, Building Societies' Association) which regulated the behaviour of their members.

Different sets of financial institutions operated under different laws, regulations or customs which reflected the origins of the institutions and often the role of government initiative in bridging various gaps in the provision of financial services (Sheppard, 1971, ch. 1). The segmentation of the financial system was also encouraged by different fiscal advantages enjoyed by various holders of securities or deposits. Interest rates were set by agreement between members of associations or institutions or in accordance with some predetermined formula. Thus, there was little or no price competition between various groups of financial institutions, and considerable barriers to entry into cartelized associations existed.

Lending and borrowing was largely demarcated between various institutions. The government seemed to be content with the system, as it facilitated both monetary control and control over the flow of finance in general. But such a system did not readily respond to new challenges. Indeed, new intermediation (such as Industrial and Commercial Finance Corporation) was again created with the strong support of the Bank of England (nationalized in 1946) or else came from new hire purchase companies. In such a segmented market, liability management was largely irrelevant – indeed, the term was virtually unknown. Financial institutions received their deposits and managed their asset portfolios so as to reconcile profitability and risk, taking into account the constraints imposed (often by 'moral suasion') by the authorities. Asset management was the essence of banking. (These terms are explained in section 6.3.)

The catalyst of competition between institutions was the increasing penetration of the financial sector by overseas banks and the development of the Eurodollar market, with its centre in London. Previously, inconvertible currencies and exchange restrictions had kept out competition from overseas banks. However, the convertibility of currencies and the lifting of major exchange restrictions in the late 1950s, together with the rapid rise of Eurodollar transactions, marked the beginning of a growing rivalry from overseas banks. Deposits of these banks remained fairly stable up to 1957 at £0.7 billion. They rose in the next five years by more than a factor of three to £2.4 billion (Sheppard, 1971, p. 15). At the beginning of the period deposits in foreign currencies were a very small proportion of total deposit liabilities, but by 1962 they constituted 12 per cent of the total and by 1967 30 per cent; by 1972 they surpassed sterling deposits, constituting 53 per cent of total deposits, and in 1979 they rose to 69 per cent (Wilson Committee, 1980, appendices, table 3.11).

The activities of foreign banks began an erosion in demarcation boundaries, encouraged innovation and generated pressure for regulatory change (discussed earlier). The banks began to challenge indigenous institutions for domestic business, making them more sensitive to price competition and financial opportunities. 'The dominant domestic institutions, the banks, the insurance companies, the building societies, and savings banks, were forced to compete more aggressively to retain their market shares' (Sheppard, 1971, p. 16). Clearing banks, the largest and possibly the most conservative of the lot, did not escape the pressure of general competition from foreign banks and from the much smaller, but infinitely more aggressive and enterprising, indigenous merchant banks. Novel developments in the wholesale markets followed, stimulating innovative methods of managing liabilities and assets, which will be discussed later. Indeed, the 1960s were an important decade of innovation and growth, but this was not seriously perceived generally until the early 1970s, and then only in specialist literature (Einzig, 1971; Revell, 1973; Grant, 1977) rather than in mainstream economics.

In a relatively short space of time, British clearing banks were transformed from essentially domestic intermediaries into international banks. Competition with overseas banks, most of them large multinational banks, began to force them to diversify into activities previously alien to them. Some of the activities in which they began to take part, directly or through subsidiaries or affiliates, were quite removed from traditional banking (leasing of equipment, factoring). Others encroached on the preserves of other institutions (merchant banking, insurance broking).

In the more traditional banking activities, the competition from foreign banks was formidable. In the early 1970s foreign, and in particular American, banks began to increase their penetration of corporate finance by medium-term lending, and even began to bid for retail deposits. Citibank became practically indistinguishable from typical clearing banks.

The British banking system has been exposed to competition from foreign banks more than any other banking system. Foreign banks now heavily outnumber indigenous banks (Revell, 1983b, p. 153). As may be seen from tables 6.6–6.15 in the appendix to this chapter, Britain now has, in effect, an international banking system, in which monetary control, *designed essentially to control sterling liabilities of the private monetary sector only*, looks increasingly fragile, considering that traditional bank and foreign exchange regulations have been removed.

The general anatomy of the contemporary banking system is reflected in tables given in the appendix. Of the liabilities of the banking system, over 70 per cent are in currencies other than sterling (table 6.6). Nearly 74 per cent of deposits and CDs are in such currencies (table 6.7). Overseas banks supply 15 per cent of sterling deposits and over 61 per cent of other currency deposits in the UK (tables 6.8 and 6.9). On the lending side, overseas banks are responsible for 23 per cent of lending in sterling and for 15 per cent of sterling advances of the UK private sector. They also lend 71 per cent of advances in currencies other than sterling to the UK private sector (tables 6.14 and 6.15). Though the overseas banks are characterized by a different structure of their liabilities and lending, there appears to be no difference, in principle, in their activities in the UK, and they remain rivals to the indigenous banks in both the domestic and overseas fields of activity.

(*b*) *Competition between indigenous institutions* Banks also faced increasing competition from other financial institutions which challenged their near monopoly in traditional banking services. In the realm of administration of payments and money transmission, they faced competition from the National Giro, Trustee Savings Banks and, more recently, building societies. The same institutions, together with national savings facilities and overseas banks, provide a strong challenge for retail demand and savings deposits.

The competition between banks and building societies deserves a special mention. Building societies expanded steadily and quickly after 1970 (see table 6.1) to become key financial intermediaries for the personal sector. Between 1970 and 1982, the number of current accounts in banks rose by a factor of 1.8 (to 31 million); the number of share accounts in building societies rose by a factor of 3.5 (to 37 million) (Johnston, 1984, table 2). In the mid-1970s, the near-monopoly position of building societies in the supply of housing finance was challenged only by the public sector, and by the late 1970s and in 1980 they accounted for over 80 per cent of housing debt outstanding. Banks and insurance companies played a relatively small part in this market. Building society interest rates were 'recommended' by the

Table 6.1 Growth of building societies, 1970–83

Year	No. of branches	Staff (thousand)	Shareholders (million)	Borrowers (million)	Assets Current prices (£ billion)	1983 prices (£ billion)
1970	2016	25.2	10.3	3.7	10.8	49.0
1980	5684	52.7	30.6	5.4	53.8	67.0
1983	6672	61.2	37.7	5.9	85.9	85.9

Source: HM Treasury, *Building Societies: A New Framework*, July 1984, Cmnd 9316, HMSO, table 1.

Association of Building Societies (ABS) and observed by its members. They were kept reasonably low, with mortgage rationing being the normal behaviour. Rivalry between societies manifested itself essentially by competitive branching and, increasingly, through advertising and innovative high-interest or premium accounts.

The abolition of the Corset and the second wave of deregulation of banks, mentioned earlier, fundamentally changed both the competition between banks and building societies and the competition between building societies themselves. Banks, finding it progressively more difficult to compete for corporate finance, and being goaded by deregulation into becoming more aggressive, entered the housing mortgage market with remarkable and quick success. By the end of 1983, they accounted for over 15 per cent of the housing debt outstanding, while the share of building societies had dropped to 75 per cent from 82 per cent in the years 1978–80 (table 6.2). Indeed, in 1982 banks captured 36 per cent of net mortgage advances, though the proportion fell during the next year to about 25 per cent (table 6.3).

Reaction from the building societies was swift and resolute. A diversification of activities, which they had been considering with increasing interest during the 1970s, now became their key target. 'Senior management of some of the larger societies had become affected by the more aggressive, competitive and innovatory spirit prevailing elsewhere in the financial system. . . .' (BE, 1983b, p. 371). Their new-found aggression became especially evident in the area of price competition. ABS began only to 'advise' interest rates, but the members no longer adhere to uniform rates. Political pressure has mounted to release the societies from antiquated legal restrictions which hamper their competition with banks. In January 1983, ABS published a document relating to this issue. The 1984 Green Paper (H. M. Treasury, 1984) was the government response to it. Briefly, the government proposed to grant the societies limited powers of entry into the traditional activity of banks. On the liabilities side, it proposed that 80 per cent of funds should be raised from the societies' members and only 20 per cent from the money market and other sources. On the assets side, 90 per cent of total assets, other than liquid and fixed assets, should represent advances to members, secured by the first mortgage on borrower-occupied property. These propositions would go some way towards satisfying the aspirations of the societies. Some innovative responses by the societies to competition will be discussed below.

The intrusion of banks into the housing market had an important 'monetary' effect at the time when £M3 was to be constrained as part of the Medium Term Financial Strategy. Together with other factors (e.g. abolition of the Corset) (Hall, 1983, ch. 8), it contributed to £M3 overshooting its target range. Between February 1980 and April 1981, £M3 expanded by 18.5 per cent exceeding the top limit of the target range by 68 per cent and its mid-point by 106 per cent. In the equivalent period of the subsequent year, £M3 rose by 13 per cent, the respective overshooting being 30 and 63 per cent.

Table 6.2 Loans for house purchase of the personal sector (amounts outstanding at the end of the year)

Loans from:	1975 £ bil.	%	1978 £ bil.	%	1979 £ bil.	%	1980 £ bil.	%	1981 £ bil.	%	1982 £ bil.	%	1983 £ bil.	%
Building societies	18.9	75.6	31.7	82.3	37.0	82.2	42.7	81.6	49.0	79.4	57.1	75.2	68.2	75.2
Public sector	3.3	13.2	3.4	8.8	3.8	8.4	4.5	8.6	5.1	8.3	5.9	7.8	5.8	6.4
Banks[a]	1.3	5.2	1.8	4.7	2.4	5.3	3.0	5.7	5.4	8.7	10.7	14.1	14.4	15.8
Insurance companies	1.5	6.0	1.6	4.2	1.8	4.0	2.1	4.0	2.2	3.6	2.2	2.9	2.4	2.6
Total (A)	25.0	100.0	38.5	100.0	45.0	100.0	52.3	100.0	61.7	100.0	75.9	100.0	90.7	100.0
Total financial liabilities of personal sector (B)	40.3		62.7		75.4		86.2		102.1		123.1		144.7	
(A)/(B)	62.0		61.4		59.7		60.7		60.4		61.7		62.7	

[a] Includes Trustee Savings Banks, which in 1982 were transferred to the new 'monetary sector'. Their loans were negligible in 1975, £15 million in 1978, £23 million in 1979, £116 million in 1980, £298 million in 1981.

N.B. Figures do not always add up exactly due to rounding off.

Source: Financial Statistics, June 1984, July 1984, tables S5, S15.

Table 6.3　Loans for house purchase: net advances

	Total (£ bil.)	Building societies (% of total)	Public sector (% of total)	Banks[a] (% of total)	Insurance companies (% of total)
1979	6.5	81.6	5.7	9.2	3.5
1980	7.3	78.5	9.8	8.1	3.6
1981	9.5	66.8	6.5	25.8	0.9
1982	14.1	57.7	6.3	36.0	0.0
1983	14.6	75.7	−1.4	24.7	1.0

[a] Including Trustee Savings Banks, which in 1982 became incorporated in the monetary sector. Their advances were £7 million in 1979, £93 million in 1980 and £182 million in 1981.
Source: *Financial Statistics*, July 1984, table S5.

Thus, banking (and hence 'money'), during a period of stringent policy, was able to expand into a new asset market without much difficulty. The resulting distortion of £M3 (see Figure 4.4(a) and (b)) made the monetary authorities place greater emphasis on PSL2, which includes the greater part of building society liabilities (BE, 1984b, p. 476). This episode raises the question of the 'monetary' nature of both bank and building society deposits (Goodhart, 1984, p. 157). Anticipating a further impetus to competition between banks and building societies, the Governor of the Bank stated that: 'In these circumstances all the aggregates, not only the various definitions of narrow and broad money, but also the wider liquidity measures, are liable to be subject to unforeseen distortions' (BE, 1984b, p. 476). The intrusion resulted in an important change in the 'asset content' of the 'money supply'. A further change in this field followed a reorientation of the banks' lending which resulted from a combination of a change in corporate finance and the authorities' tactics in trying to hit monetary targets.

Since the 1950s British companies have experienced a decline in retained profits, which had been a major source of their investment finance. Thus, they have had to rely increasingly on external sources of funds for investment. Traditional external sources had been issues of shares or debentures on the capital market. However, inflation and falling profits often made it both expensive and risky to resort to new issues. Furthermore, the preference of the personal sector has shifted decidedly away from holding direct investments such as shares and debentures. These had to be absorbed by institutional investors (such as pension funds, insurance companies, investment and unit trusts), whose liabilities were increasingly held by the personal sector. Industry in turn began to rely more on the supply of bank loans.

The customary short-term lending by banks for working capital changed. Increasingly banks began to orientate themselves towards the supply of industrial finance, mainly medium-term. Contractual term-lending at the expense of overdraft lending was a concomitant of this trend. In the late 1970s, 40 per cent of all non-personal lending was term-lending (Wilson Committee, 1979, vol. 3, pp. 75–7). The division of function, accepted as 'normal' in the past, between the capital market supplying long-term funds and banks supplying short-term credit, ceased to be clear-cut (Revell, 1983b, pp. 143–8). Competition to provide industrial finance was related to the need for banks to resort to wholesale borrowing on the money market. This important aspect will be developed further below.

(*c*) *The impact of monetary policy*   Monetary policy, designed to confine monetary growth within a targeted range, also altered the pattern and nature of intermediation. If we confine our attention to £M3, for which asset counterparts are available (see section 4.3), we can follow more clearly the effects of the strategy of the money supply control. One objective of the monetary authorities was to exercise a fiscal restraint designed to lower PSBR as a proportion of GDP. However, PSBR is very unpredictable and not easy to control. To curb the expansion of £M3 *at a given PSBR*, monetary authorities endeavoured to prevent the finance of PSBR from being reflected in the measure of the money supply. This was done by funding the borrowing requirement through sales of marketable (mainly stocks) and non-marketable (national savings) debt. Till 1976, much of PSBR remained unfunded, but since then the funding of the debt has been much more substantial.[5] Indeed, in the financial years 1977/8, 1981/2 and 1983/4, there has been a substantial overfunding of the debt (negative values in table 6.4).

Table 6.4   Unfunded PSBR and Bank of England commercial bill purchases
(£ billion)

| | | | *Sterling lending to private sector* | | |
Financial years	*PSBR*	*Unfunded PSBR[a]*	*Total[b]*	*BE bill purchases[c]*	*Other monetary sector*
1979/80	10.0	0.8	9.3	0.8	8.6
1980/81	12.7	1.9	9.2	2.0	7.2
1981/82	8.6	−2.7	14.9	4.2	10.7
1982/83	8.9	0.6	14.4	−0.8	15.2
1983/84	9.6	−2.9	15.1	3.6	11.5

[a] PSBR − PurPSD in table 4.1 above.
[b] L in table 4.1.
[c] Purchases of commercial bills by the Bank of England Issue Department.
Sources: *BEQB*, 24(2), June 1984, table 11.3; *Financial Statistics*, June 1984, table 11.5.

Table 6.5   Central government borrowing requirement (CGBR) and its finance
(£ billion)

		Principal ways of financing[a]				
		Sterling borrowing from non-bank private sector				
Financial Years	*CGBR*	*Total*	*Stocks*	*Non-marketable*	*Sterling borrowing from monetary sector*	*External and foreign currency finance*
1979/80	8.3	8.8	8.3	−0.1	−0.2	0.2
1980/1	12.7	11.9	8.9	2.5	2.2	0.3
1981/2	7.6	12.2	7.1	4.4	−1.8	1.5
1982/3	12.7	10.0	4.5	3.9	−0.8	2.7
1983/4	12.2	13.1	9.9	2.9	0.6	1.0

[a] Only the main ways of financing are listed; for further details see the source.
Source: *BEQB*, June 1984, table 7.

The main element in PSBR is the central government borrowing requirement (CGBR). Table 6.5 shows the main ways of financing CGBR. The key role of borrowing from the non-bank private sector in financing CGBR is strongly evident. Much of the debt is financed by selling government stocks. To attract investors, the government adopted new marketing methods and innovative stock design, including indexing and floating rate stock issues (Dennis, 1982, pp. 281–90; BE, 1983d, pp. 182–3). The investors are principally the non-bank private sector, consisting essentially of financial institutions, mainly insurance companies, pension funds and building societies. (The three absorbed 72.6, 74.8 and 88.3 per cent of stocks shown in table 6.5 in the years 1980/1, 1981/2, 1982/3, respectively.) The stocks purchased by the non-bank sector shown in table 6.5 represent the bulk of the net official sales of stock.[6] On average, the term to maturity of stocks has been falling, with the sales of stocks maturing within five years rising and the sales of long-term stocks falling.[7] This form of financing government debt directly competes with the medium-term finance which banks have been extending to industry.

The non-marketable borrowing, shown in table 6.5, refers mainly to National Savings, where the issues of national savings certificates on which the government chooses the rate of interest, redemption conditions and tax conditions is an important medium of attracting funds. National Savings are directly in competition with building society deposits and the savings accounts of banks. Again, *the mode of government borrowing increases competitive pressure in certain parts of the financial sector.* Thus, to avoid the 'monetary' consequences of the financing of government deficits, increased competition developed for medium- and long-term finance in personal and industrial sectors.

The policy of funding, and in particular of overfunding of government borrowing requirements, has had an important impact on financial flows and an overall effect on the liquidity of the economy. The financing of government debt by issues of longer-term claims has contributed to the relative decline of Treasury bills, the traditional instrument in smoothing operations by the central bank to relieve liquidity shortages at desired interest rates in the money market. As a result, the proportion of Treasury bills in bank portfolios has declined. Bank deregulation at first lowered and eventually swept away the usual liquidity requirements (see section 6.1.1), making banks decrease their cash and liquid assets cushion to become more sensitive to liquidity changes in the financial system and more reliant on short-term market borrowing ('liability management'). At the same time, as industrial and personal customers, in spite of the recession, increasingly turned to banks for finance (some of it 'distress' finance), shortages of liquidity became persistent.

To alleviate this situation, there has been a revival of classical commercial bill finance with interesting 'monetary' consequences. The issue of a bill of exchange is, in the first instance, a way of supplying short-term funds to industry and commerce. A bill accepted by a reputable financial institution becomes a liquid security eligible for discounting (see 'bank bill' in section 4.4). In 1981 the list of banks eligible for discounting at the Bank was extended, thus widening the scope of the Bank's operations in bills (BE, 1982d; 1982f). The Issue Department of the Bank of England increased its holdings of UK commercial bills from a low level in 1979 to £0.4 billion in 1980, £2.9 billion in 1981 and £7.6 billion in 1982 (*Financial Statistics*, June 1984, table 527D).

The Bank developed two distinct operations in commercial bills, one through the Issue Department (which is part of Public Sector – see table 2.1, row (11)) and the other through the Banking Department (which is part of the 'monetary' sector – see section 4.1). The operations (e.g., purchases of bills from the money market) of the latter produce a shift within the holdings of the monetary sector, that is, *within* a counterpart of 'money', without adding to the deposit liabilities of the monetary sector. However, purchases of bills by the Issue Department have in recent years played an important part in relieving the financial and liquidity pressures imposed on the private sector by the funding policy. Column 5 in table 6.4 shows substantial increases in the purchases of commercial bills by the department, particularly during periods of large overfunding. The acquisition of such bills implies, in effect, central bank lending to the private sector, which would otherwise have to be provided by banks – the Bank refinances industrial and commercial lending. Such operations affect the size of 'sterling lending to UK private sector', which is a 'money' counterpart (see section 4.3), and its impact is shown in table 6.4.

Two important points should be mentioned in this context. First, operations in commercial bills have been used as a way of relieving both financial and cash shortages in the private sector. Operations through the Banking Department are a way of relieving cash shortages without a direct effect on the quantity of money (though possibly with some indirect effect through influencing interest rates). In the early 1980s the turnover of bank bills increased substantially; by a factor of over 4 in 1980, and in 1981 by a factor of 2.5 (BE, 1982f, p. 88), to become one of the principal instruments of market control.

Second, operations in bank bills allow the authorities a measure of control over short-term interest rates. Indeed, both funding and bill transactions afford a means of influencing both long- and short-term rates. Bill purchases, together with operations in other money market instruments, also provide a framework for controlling the monetary base which consists mainly of cash (BE, 1982f, p. 94; 1984c, pp. 488–9). It should, however, be remembered (see section 2.3) that a deliberate intervention to achieve a desired quantity of 'base money' would imply a ripple effect on financial flows mainly through effects on interest rates; as the authorities cannot achieve both a desired quantity and a price effect, the result might well be a loss of control over interest rates and an uncertain effect on the domain of 'monetary' assets.

Thus, the monetary strategy recently adopted has resulted in a *redirection of financial flows*, creating competitive pressures, and hence encouraging innovation in some parts of the financial sector. The authorities had to offset some of the effects of some of their operations designed to have restrictive monetary effects and to adopt *not altogether planned* adjustments in their activities. The decline of a market in one instrument (Treasury bills) has been replaced by a surge in another (bank bills). Overfunding in the interest of meeting monetary targets has made intermediation more complex and has contributed to private borrowers relying more on bank finance. Now the Bank is looking for ways of encouraging the private sector to meet more of its external financial requirements from long-term financial markets, possibly by twisting the structure of interest rates to raise short-term and lower long-term rates. Discussing such issues of monetary policy, the Governor of the Bank stressed the constraints imposed upon the authorities by the *changeable nature of the financial system* and by the *limitations of our knowledge and understanding of it* (BE, 1984b, pp. 480–1).

The general conclusion in this section is that, in the 1980s, a virtually completely open and internationally integrated financial economy has emerged in the UK, influenced increasingly by deregulation brought about by an ingenious evasion of old constraints and a political preference for free market economics. It is highly competitive, with government operations, designed to finance fiscal deficits and control money aggregates, adding to the competition in some parts of the market. The interdependence between the financial and monetary sectors should be stressed. Various chain reactions can be identified: the challenge of overseas banks affected indigenous institutions and, in particular, banks; the banks reacted by moving to meet the needs of industrial finance and by developing non-traditional areas of finance including lending to the housing market; the response to competition by the building societies in terms of innovative services (to be discussed) has been accompanied by strong pressure for the abolition of regulations restricting their activity.

Our attention has dwelled on banks, the traditional suppliers of 'money'. *Financial* change, however, now affects *all sections of the financial system*. In 1984 the Governor of the Bank of England spoke of the tide of innovation and competition sweeping through the system, leaving no institution, including insurance companies and the Stock Exchange, immune to it (BE, 1984a, p. 198). 'Overlapping activities' of financial firms are becoming more common, and the trend towards mergers between different varieties of financial intermediaries setting up department-store-type entities raises serious issues concerning both 'monetary' control and the nature of future regulation.

6.2 Main UK innovations

6.2.1 *Parallel markets: inter-bank business*

The 'money market', as noted in the previous chapter, is a term, often loosely used, referring to arrangements whereby 'wholesale' funds are lent and borrowed. The UK's traditional money market embraced markets in such instruments as money-at-call, Treasury bills and commercial bills. In the 1960s, alongside these established arrangements new markets began to develop. These 'parallel markets' embody the Eurocurrency transactions and transactions in sterling instruments. As the Eurocurrency market has been mentioned earlier, we shall concentrate here on developments in the sterling parallel markets, consisting of transactions in such instruments as the local authority temporary debt, deposits of finance houses, sterling CDs and inter-bank deposits.

In the late 1950s the sterling parallel markets hardly existed; of the total value of instruments in the London money markets outstanding at the end of 1957 (£5.1 billion), over 89 per cent were traditional instruments and the remainder consisted of mainly the local authority temporary debt. In 1962, of the total of £6.5 billion, the traditional market absorbed 70.7 per cent with inter-bank deposits having a small share (7.8 per cent) of the total. Five years later the respective figures were £9.2 billion, 60.3 per cent and 14.2 per cent.

The UK clearing banks were at first reluctant to participate in the inter-bank market. 'It is an unbreakable convention of English deposit banking that no bank may be seen to borrow from another, whether it is the Bank of England or another bank' (Revell, 1972, p. 429). In fact, inter-bank relations were developing, indirectly, through brokers. Competition and Credit Control of 1971, however, gave an important boost to the market by allowing inter-bank balances and holdings of CDs to be used as offsets in the calculation of eligible liabilities serving as a basis for monetary controls. From that time, parallel money markets became fully used by all banks, including the more conservative clearers.

By 1972 parallel markets dominated the sterling money markets; of the £18.3 billion of balances outstanding, the traditional markets absorbed only 30 per cent; the inter-bank market absorbed 27.7 per cent and the newly developed sterling CDs, 27.0 per cent. In 1979 the corresponding figures were: total, £44.7 billion; traditional markets, 27.9 per cent; inter-bank deposits, 36.7 per cent; sterling CDs, 8.2 per cent; local authority debt, 12.7 per cent (Wilson Committee, 1980, appendices, table 3.70).

An interesting inter-company parallel market emerged in the late 1960s as a direct consequence of credit squeezes on banks and in particular, ceilings imposed on bank lending. In essence, large corporations with temporary surpluses lent directly to credit-seeking corporations. Banks, not able to lend themselves, often acted as agents, bringing the lender and borrower together in a financial activity which, by dis–intermediation, bypassed central bank credit restrictions. No data were available on the size of the market, but it was not considered to have been large (Einzig, 1971, pp. 76–8; Wilson Committee, 1980, appendices, p. 507). As noted in section 5.3.4, modern cash management methods enhance the capacity of large corporations to borrow from and lend to each other.

Parallel money markets have increased flexibility within the monetary sector by allowing banks to utilize quickly, albeit at a price, new sources of funds. The Bank of England's view was that 'The market adds to the efficiency of the banking system; and well developed markets in inter-bank funds and certificates of deposit must strengthen the system as a whole by improving its ability to mobilize funds quickly in response to unforeseen calls' (BE, 1972, p. 495).

However, like their counterparts in the USA, the *UK parallel markets have also increased the circumventive powers of banks*. During the periods when restrictions on lending applied, they provided a means for transferring resources from banks with surplus resources, which had reached their credit ceilings, to others which still had scope for lending. Even when no direct restrictions applied, the markets offered a way of bidding up resources to meet profitable lending opportunities. This aspect will be discussed further in connection with 'liability management' by banks.

In the UK, the inter-bank market is the largest of the sterling parallel markets. It refers to dealings between banks in 'wholesale' amounts (usually

£250,000 and over) on an unsecured basis for an agreed period (usually between 'overnight' and three months). It provides an additional cushion between the traditional discount market and the banks, and offers scope to participants to utilize their reserve assets and to manage their liabilities more effectively. Its ultimate source of liquidity is the discount market, for which the Bank of England acts as the lender of last resort.

The current interrelationships of banks with the UK monetary sector are reflected in the tables in the appendix to this chapter. For example, 24 per cent of sterling deposits in banks are by UK monetary sector; 5 per cent are sight deposits (table 6.8). Of deposits in foreign currencies, 19 per cent are by UK monetary sector (and 16 per cent are CDs) (table 6.9). The proportion of UK monetary sector deposits in the total sterling deposits of different banks varies (tables 6.12 and 6.13). For instance, in UK retail banks only 11 per cent of sterling deposits are by the UK monetary sector; but the respective figure for other British banks is 49 per cent. A large proportion of sterling deposits of foreign banks, particularly Japanese banks, is derived in this way.

The introduction in the UK of CDs represented, as mentioned in section 5.2.3, a financial 'technology transfer', arising from close international banking contacts. Dollar CDs (more specifically, 'London dollar negotiable CDs') were first issued in 1966 by London-based US banks, and later by indigenous banks, to become the most important negotiable instrument traded in the foreign currency market (for evolution see Robinson, 1972, pp. 219–22).

In 1968, following an amendment of the Exchange Control Act, the first sterling CDs appeared to extend the inter-bank market in unsecured sterling funds and add to its flexibility (BE, 1972). They could be issued by a UK office of a British or foreign bank. London discount houses formed the main market for them. The ultimate holders of CDs were mainly other UK banks, other financial institutions and large non-financial companies. In 1972 banks held about 60 per cent of the total holding.

Before 1971, interest rate cartel arrangements inhibited British clearing banks from participating in the sterling CD market. The removal of this restriction in the 1971 credit reform, together with an arrangement whereby CDs and other inter-bank balances could be used as offsets in the calculation of eligible liabilities, gave a strong incentive to the banks to start issuing CDs. Liability management was considerably facilitated, if not encouraged, by this measure. Thus, the 1971 reform boosted the market in sterling CDs (and M3, of which it was a component); but, above all, it enabled the banks to operate and compete much more freely in wholesale markets.[8]

The functions of this innovation *vis-à-vis* the central bank influence on the banking sector are analogous to those discussed earlier in relation to CDs in the USA (see section 5.3.1(a)). They added to the traditional liquidity buffer, that is the discount market, a secondary liquidity buffer within parallel markets (Wilson Committee, 1979, p. 97). Sterling CDs are included in all broader aggregates (see figure 4.1).

6.2.2 *New deposits and financial 'packages'*

In the UK, the development of novel interest-bearing substitutes for traditional current accounts, and thus of interest-earning 'transactions' money balances, has lagged behind that in the USA. However, it is now in full swing, resulting in many innovative accounts which combine the characteristics of the American ATS, MMMF and MMDA accounts, together with other novel features. Unlike their US counterparts, UK financial institutions are not inhibited by regulations from offering interest on demand deposits.

There is very little reliable information on the quantitative impact of these new accounts. It might, at this stage, be modest, but the pace with which new techniques of mobilizing finance are developing is increasing, as is the ingenuity of their design. The information below has been gathered essentially from the financial press. Many new financial schemes are now in the process of being 'remodelled' to keep up with competition. The main innovators are building societies, licensed deposit-takers (LDTs), unit trusts and smaller banks.[9]

New high-interest cheque accounts combine the features of a savings account and a variable interest rate (often related to money market rates) with a chequing account sometimes free from bank charges. Among the more interesting innovations in the UK are the money funds, also known as 'high-interest cheque accounts' or 'money market bank accounts'. A selection of such accounts is listed in n.9.

Most institutions offering such accounts require a minimum investment, which normally varies from £100 (Citibank Savings) to £2500. Chequing facilities are available, though there are sometimes restrictions on withdrawals and the use of cheques. For many depositors such accounts are hybrids, representing reasonable substitutes for both current and savings accounts. The traditional distinction between accounts is becoming blurred.

The payment of interest on current accounts is not a novelty in British banking; the Co-operative Bank, for instance, pioneered such a facility. Smaller banks appear to be more enterprising in this field. Not all clearing banks have responded to the challenge of these accounts (see n. 9). Midland Bank, in 1982, was the first to do so. However, it is a matter of time before the remainder of the High Street banks produce similar arrangements. In 1984, both the Midland and Barclays announced 'free banking' for customers whose current account remains in credit.[10]

In 1971 more than two-thirds of M1 consisted of non-interest-bearing accounts, the remainder being mainly currency. In 1975 private sector sterling sight non-interest-bearing deposits accounted for 55.6 per cent and interest-bearing deposits for 10.6 per cent; in 1985 (first quarter) the respective proportions were: 42.6 per cent and 33.9 per cent.[11] Values for

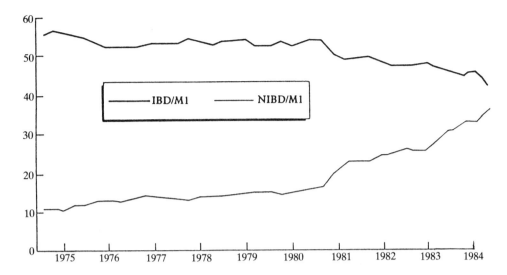

Figure 6.1 Interest-bearing (IBD) and non-interest-bearing deposits (NIBD) in the UK, as a percentage of M1, 1975(2)–1985(1).

Sources: Bank of England Quarterly Bulletins, tables 11.1; *Financial Statistics*, tables 7.1. (see Note 11)

quarters between those dates are shown in figure 6.1. These do not take into account increases in 'free banking' facilities on current account, or new 'transactions' accounts, on which interest is payable. The higher content of interest-bearing deposits in M1 increases its 'own' rate of interest. This makes M1 less responsive to general interest rate changes influenced by the authorities as part of monetary control. In terms of the money demand analysis, holdings of M1 (as indeed of other aggregates) become less interest-rate-sensitive. This is analogous to the situation already discussed in connection with cash management (section 5.3.4) and will be further developed under liability management in section 6.3.

Building societies have been particularly active in developing new services for investors. They are now enhancing their role as savings institutions and increasingly extending their facilities into banking services. Their inroads into banking activities are likely to be further encouraged by recommendations contained in a recent Green Paper, mentioned in section 6.1.2, which envisages the removal of old legal constraints on such activities.

The plan to reform the organization of the Bankers' Clearing House, announced at the end of 1984, is expected to offer the societies, as well as other banks whose services are not very different from those of clearing banks (e.g. Citibank, Standard Chartered), the benefit of direct cheque-clearing. At the moment, although the House is undoubtedly a public utility, it is owned by the Committee of London Clearing Banks, and the restricted membership acts as a barrier to entry. The proposed reform is likely to relax, if not remove, this barrier.

As early as 1973, the Governor of the Bank of England observed that 'Share and deposit accounts with building societies are used by many people in much the same way as they might use a deposit account with a bank' (BE, 1973, p. 194). Indeed, many people have used them to perform some of the basic functions of bank current accounts. And yet such accounts have never been incorporated in any monetary aggregates narrower than PSL2, which emerged in 1979 (see section 4.2). But since that time, building societies have been the most innovative institutions attracting non-marketable funds. Liquidity characteristics of ordinary shares and deposits have increased; but their share of building society deposits has gone down in favour of high-interest accounts and term shares with early withdrawal facilities (BE, 1983b, p. 371). 'In practice, for some purposes ordinary accounts are like sight deposits with banks, and high-interest accounts – which have developed since 1979 – are similar to seven-day deposit accounts....' (BE, 1982c, p. 535). Yet neither is included in £M3; their combined total in 1982 was approximately half of £M3.

Furthermore, there has been a rapid development of term shares with early withdrawal facilities.[12] These shares, whose characteristics resemble high-interest deposit accounts, were made available in 1981 and became very popular with investors, who increased their holding of such shares from £3.7 billion at the end of 1981 to £12.9 billion at the end of 1983. The latter sum was equivalent to the 13 per cent of £M3. Yet such shares have not so far been included in any aggregate, *not even in PSL2*. It seems that the monetary aggregates have never quite caught up with innovations and the consequent changes in the liquidity characteristics of new building society deposits.

There is a theory of bank behaviour which claims that banks do not operate like the textbook profit-maximizing firms. Instead, they seek to develop 'customer relationships' which ensure that they maximize profits, over a medium-term, from all the services offered. The 'customer relationship' depends upon the 'bundling' of services (including 'free banking') without attaching specific charges to individual facilities (Revell, 1983b, pp. 154–6).

More recent innovations by financial institutions seem to emphasize this point. Building societies increasingly have been offering services which encroach on the traditional domain of banks – easy cash withdrawal, credit, bill settlement, standing orders and the means of money transmission. In theory, they are not permitted to develop banking services, although, as already stated, legislation is expected to enable them to do so. But even without such legislation, they have made some inroads into traditional banking or have overcome such restrictions, often by co-operating with other financial institutions.

Some societies, including the Halifax (650 branches) and Leicester (244 branches), offer cash dispensers; more societies plan to do so. Many of them also supply credit cards such as Visa or Access with any of their accounts. Some provide chequing accounts, but without cheque guarantee cards: Abbey National, with 677 branches, has a Cheque–Save account; Halifax has a Deposit–Cheque account; Town and Country, with 70 branches, has a Moneywise account.

Perhaps the most interesting innovations are those where building societies enter into arrangements with banks, LDTs or Giro to offer a variety of combinations of traditional building society facilities with different degrees of banking services including full current account and personal loans or overdrafts. Some of these arrangements involve a complex package of financial services yielding the combined advantages of both a bank current account and building society interest-bearing account. These include the Alliance's Bank–Save account and Nottingham's Homelink.[13]

Each of these packages incorporates a different mixture of services and a design of arrangements to suit its depositors. Bank–Save, for example, caters for customers able to deposit at least £500. It supplies them with chequing and savings accounts each offering associated facilities. A part of the initial deposit is transferred from the savings account to a current account, which is automatically (as in ATS accounts in the USA) topped up when it falls to £100 (the amount required to avoid bank charges). The services also include a Visa credit card and overdraft limits. Essentially, the arrangement enables depositors to earn interest on balances which would otherwise remain 'idle', at negligible transfer cost.

Homelink is an innovative scheme which utilizes Prestel to link the building society and the Bank of Scotland with the customers and their shopping, travel and holiday outlets. It gives access to Barclays Bank ATMs (see section 6.4) and cheque cashing in some other banks. It thus 'bundles' both society and banking services with 'home shopping'. It also enables the society to expand without having to open new branches.

The 'bundling' of financial services is not confined to banks or building societies. Some high-interest chequing accounts mentioned earlier also constitute packages. Save and Prosper's Premier account, for instance, offers money market rates of interest on sums equal or in excess of £1000, together with a current account with unrestricted use of cheques and standing order and direct debit facilities. There is also an automatic and unsecured overdraft provision. With the Visa Premier Card, which is also supplied, cash can be drawn out at any Visa bank branch. Such withdrawals are not subject to the usual charges, but go through special Save and Prosper accounts. The full Visa balance is automatically settled from the Premier account once a month.

Some accounts offer facilities akin to corporate cash management schemes discussed earlier, but on a smaller scale and with extended facilities appealing to smaller investors. In 1983 Hambro Life devised a much more comprehensive Financial Management Programme for investors with £25,000 or more. This combines banking, credit and insurance facilities and financial management.[14] Packages even wider than this, adding, for instance, full house-purchase facilities, do not seem to be far off.

The packaging of financial services, together with arrangements for joint venture or co-operation between some financial institutions, may well be a precursor of a more fundamental organizational and structural integration in the financial industry of the future. For our purposes here, it must suffice to conclude that the conventional current account, or a non-interest-bearing sight deposit, which has been the foundation of traditional commercial banking and a key component of the narrow or transactions 'definition' of the money supply, is being submerged by interest-bearing equivalents from a variety of sources other than banks. In retail finance it is increasingly being offered as an element in a package deal which further obscures the orthodox distinctions between monetary and financial services. Financial institutions in general are increasingly attempting to meet customers' preferences by tailoring financial services to fit them. This involves intense competition by price (by size and mode of payment of interest rates), by withdrawal facilities, by the size of the initial deposit required, by arrangements for bank charges, by chequing and cash dispensing modes, by loan and overdraft arrangements, by automatic management of transactions balances, by additional services – financial or non-financial – and, indeed, by the ability to design packages of the above services. *The technology of payments and settlements is in a state of flux and is increasingly interlinked with other services.*

6.3   Liability management

6.3.1   *Microeconomic impact*

In a general sense, the activity of any business enterprise can be analysed in terms of asset and liability management designed to achieve the objectives of the enterprise. Thus, it may be perfectly understandable that, in the banking firm, the traditional conflict involved in the reconciliation of motives of profitability on the one hand and risk avoidance and liquidity on the other must be resolved by asset and liability management.

However, in recent years the term 'liability management' has crept into popular use to signify an important shift in the nature of the traditional management of a financial firm. It is thus an important innovation, or, more precisely, a 'swarm' of innovations, in a sense similar to Eurocurrency markets or corporate cash management, which have developed since the late 1950s. This has its microeconomic as well as macroeconomic implications.

Increased competition has forced financial institutions, and in particular banks, to diversify their activities and change their business strategies (section

6.1.2). This refers both to the assets as well as the liabilities side of intermediation, but it is on the liabilities side, or, more specifically, the deposits side, that the change has been particularly acute.

Traditionally, banks tended to adjust the level of their lending (assets) to the funds (deposit liabilities) at their disposal. Particularly in the case of the UK clearing banks, when price competition was restricted, balance sheet management was rather passive on the deposits side; banks had a steady supply of customary deposits derived basically from their superior position in the payments system of the economy. This steady *pool of deposits* for each bank represented a limit to which assets could expand. The funds were then allocated on the assets side between various activities to ensure appropriate levels of primary and secondary reserves and of earning assets. Such an approach to banking is sometimes called 'asset management' in juxtaposition with 'liability management'.

Basic changes on the lending side of banking have already been discussed. With reference to table 6.10 in the appendix to this chapter, we can summarize the essentials of the sterling asset structure before concentrating on liability management. Currency holdings, bills and lending to the London discount market account for less than 6 per cent of sterling assets; the secondary liquidity buffer consists essentially of lending to the UK monetary sector (21 per cent in 1983); advances to the public sector and investments account for only 8 per cent of assets; and the most important earning assets are advances to the UK private sector (47 per cent), some financing medium- and long-term loans to industry (see section 6.1.2). Though innovative lending methods were developed (leasing, flexible rate advances), it is on the liability side that change was most pronounced.

The competition for deposits described earlier forced banks to reorientate their management and to search for sources of funds other than primary deposits. They thus had to pay more attention, simultaneously, to the state of *both* sides of the balance sheet. It should be stressed that this reorientation in bank behaviour developed along with other changes already discussed. New instruments and practices, together with new markets, appeared, largely bypassing the traditional regulatory framework or forcing deregulation. In the USA, RPs, federal funds, CDs and other arrangements in wholesale and retail markets facilitated a more active attitude to 'buying deposits' at market-related rates. The influence of exposure to practices in the Eurocurrency market, where inter-bank activity is widespread, should not be overlooked.

In the UK, banks received a significant encouragement to compete more aggressively for deposits from the 1971 reform. The authorities, alarmed at the subsequent expansion of bank deposits, retreated from the position of 1971 in the shape of the Corset, whose basic purpose was to confine the scope of liability management and gain greater control over the market (section 6.1.1). However, evasion and other pressures accounted for the abolition of the Corset in the 1980s, and banks regained the freedom to 'buy money' on wholesale markets; approximately 30 per cent of total sterling deposits came from the UK monetary sector and CDs. Banks had to adapt to the new markets and competition by price to promote their market shares. The 'pool of funds' method of operations gave way to liability management, which in a *narrow* sense refers to meeting the demand for loans even when the traditional deposits are insufficient, by raising the necessary finance in wholesale markets.

Thus, instead of simply adjusting assets to the available funds, banks seek custom and then adjust liabilities to meet the demand. In short, *the supply of funds adjusts to the demand for them.* In this connection, it is believed that the difference between the rates charged on prime loans and the short-term rate paid for deposits reflects the cost of intermediation. The lower the spread between the rates, the lower the cost of intermediation, and the larger is likely to be the volume of funds attracted (Goodhart, 1984, p. 165; Tobin, 1983a, p. 164).[15]

In a *broad* sense liability management signifies a changed attitude to banking. From rather passive mobilizers of traditional deposits, banks, particularly in the USA, have turned into aggressive operators in the money markets. The basic purpose of this strategy is to endeavour to expand permanently investible funds available to banks and to improve market shares.

The 'pool of funds' method of operations has been superseded by a 'forecasting method of management' (Rohlwink, 1984). This involves, basically, estimating the future values on both sides of the balance sheet as well as the future movements in these values. On the asset side this includes liquidity management, and on the liability side the ability to raise funds to meet the commitment of the customers and take advantage of new profit opportunities.

In this connection, distinction has been made between short-term liability management, designed to strengthen reserve positions, that is the ability to purchase liquidity to supplement liquidity stored in cash and liquid assets, and generalized liquidity management, referring to sustained initiatives to enhance the inflow of investible funds (Kane, 1979). The latter was interpreted as a series of regulation-induced innovations comprising the specific innovations referred to earlier. Such an interpretation of liability management might be somewhat too broad. It does, however, bring home the idea that, like corporate cash management, liability management consists of a 'swarm' of innovations, alive and striving, and closely interrelated with financial developments elsewhere.

Indeed, the two swarms of innovations are related and can interact to frustrate the operations of monetary authorities and produce an unexpected and possibly perverse impact on monetary aggregates. A good exmple of this is the phenomenon of 'round-tripping' (noted first in section 6.1.1), which was observed particularly vividly in the UK in the early 1970s, but still continues to occur from time to time. Essentially, 'round-tripping' refers to corporate treasuries borrowing at a lower rate from banks and lending the proceeds back to the banks at a higher rate via the wholesale markets. This curious situation can occur when the authorities, in attempting to restrict monetary expansion, operate in the open market to reduce reserves. Companies taking advantage of the 'fixed' interest on overdrafts (these may be 'fixed' in relation to bank base rates, whose adjustment in turn may be related to MLR, which lags behind the movement in wholesale market rates) borrow funds from their banks and redeposit them in the money market, where interest rates rise owing to official operations. Banks react to reserve shortages not by reducing lending but by 'liability management', that is, by bidding funds from the market to accommodate borrowing by their clients (Allen, 1983, pp. 98–9).

In this connection, three points should be emphasized. First, once again, the wide interdependence and alertness of economic agents in today's financial markets emerges clearly. No one financial innovation can be analysed adequately in isolation from others and from the underlying market situation. Second, corporate treasurers have an important role to play in interest rate arbitrage and have the capacity to react to exploit market rigidities and frictions. Third, phenomena such as 'round-tripping' are likely to occur only where, given the underlying flexibility and contestability of the markets, some, possibly custom- or regulation-induced, rigidities remain. The realization of this point formed part of the rationale for liberalizing reforms in the UK after 1979, in particular those referring to the operation of MLR (see section 6.1.1).

It should be stressed, again, that liability management also involves ensuring that funds are available *even during periods of credit stringency*. Financial institutions try to ensure that funds are to be found in the wholesale market whenever the need arises. This can be done by building up a reputation in the market through lending funds whenever possible so as to be able to borrow funds more easily when the need arises; by developing credit lines with other banks; by diversifying the sources of credit so as not to rely excessively on one credit supplier; and by seeking new sources of funds of appropriate maturities. The use of financial futures markets (section 5.3.3) increasingly gives financial institutions a measure of protection against unpredictable movements in interest rates in wholesale markets.

Modern methods of balance sheet management rely increasingly on the efficient supply of information and good forecasting facilities. These are provided with growing efficiency by new methods in information technology (to be discussed in section 6.4). Thus, banks today have developed management systems which make them increasingly immune from direct or even proximate effects of traditional central bank action, and *corporate bank customers expect a steady supply of funds even during periods of restrictive monetary policy*.

So far, the term 'liability management' has been explained mainly in relation to banks. With the growth of competition and deregulation in general, however, all financial institutions have become more active in trying to accommodate their customers or grasp investment opportunities by ensuring more reliable or more controlled access to sources of finance. This is true in particular of building societies, which up to 1980 were often content to ration mortgage finance whenever their 'pool' of lending funds was insufficient, and when their competition by price was inhibited both by the ABS cartel and by 'moral dissuasion' by the government, anxious to avoid increases in mortgage rates. The intrusion of banks into the mortgage markets and the funding efforts of National Savings (section 6.1.2b) fundamentally changed the attitude of the societies to competition.

Liability management of a new style has already emerged and is likely to develop in the next few years. Clearly, the more aggressive building societies are no longer prepared to tolerate a loss of potential custom to a rival because of externally or internally imposed restrictions on their ability to balance supply with demand. The cartel arrangement has by now effectively disintegrated. After 1979, building societies began to borrow in the wholesale markets by issues of negotiable bonds, sterling CDs (first in 1983) and marketable term shares. Raising funds in the Eurocurrency system is also contemplated (Phillips, 1983, pp. 12–16). The innovative response of building societies to competition in general is not expected to make the task of controlling monetary targets any easier.

6.3.2. *Macroeconomic impact*

We do not yet have a complete understanding of the macroeconomic implications of liability management together with other financial innovations closely related to it. Some implications, however, are emerging.

The financial system has become less dependent on the central bank as the lender of last resort, in the sense that it is now easier for financial institutions to equate the demand for funds with the supply by operating in the wholesale money markets. By the same token, the capacity of financial institutions to circumvent central bank operations or regulations has increased. The significant degree of interdependence in the financial sector may indeed hinder or inhibit the authorities in undertaking restrictive or remedial action in parts of the financial sector for fear of wider repercussions. Thus, the supervisory role of the central bank has become more difficult.

However, it is the implications which have already been touched upon in connection with company cash management (see section 5.3.4) which present the main concern for the future efficacy of monetary policy. First, we need to remind ourselves of the standard theory of money supply and demand discussed in earlier chapters. Money is presented as a 'bank' asset, usually bearing zero interest rate; less restrictively, it bears a fixed nominal interest rate. The demand for money incorporates an endogenously determined interest rate on money alternatives. The authorities, in attempting to alter the money supply, relied on deposit rates being stable and on their ability to influence market rates, inducing changes in credit. Thus, it was the *ability to influence relative interest rates* which mattered.

However, before liability management, it was sufficient for the authorities simply to concentrate on manipulating the level of general market rates, as this would, in effect, involve changes in relative rates. Liability management implies that money's 'own' rate can vary with the general market rates. Thus, the authorities' ability to affect relative interest rates has been impaired, particularly with higher-level aggregates containing a significant proportion of instruments whose rates are related to market rates or can be altered as part of offensive increases in rates by institutions attempting to attract funds to cover loan commitments (Goodhart, 1984, ch. 5). The demand for funds by the private sector is a key determinant of the response to a general interest rate movement of the whole financial sector, and with liability management this response is increasingly sluggish.

The main effect of this, in terms of the traditional analysis, is to make the demand for money less sensitive to interest rates, that is to make the *LM* function more perpendicular, implying less influence of variables entering the *IS* function on income but greater interest rate variability following changes in these variables. In terms of the expenditure and monetary multipliers in the *IS–LM* framework, such a change would decrease q, making the expenditure multiplier a_1 fall and the money multiplier a_2 rise (see appendix to chapter 1, especially the discussion of equation (A1.18)).

Some critics of current developments in money markets, and of the deregulation permitting such a situation, see them in terms of a move towards a perfectly interest-inelastic *LM* – for some time held as a natural or desired phenomenon of quantity theorists and monetarists. 'If nature does not provide one, then super-monetarist policy would be in order' (Tobin, 1983a, p. 157).[16] Further macroeconomic implications (within the *IS–LM* model) will be outlined below, but first we shall concentrate mainly on the implications for the definition of money and its control.

The tendency towards a less interest-elastic demand-for-money function has already been noted in connection with the impaired ability of the monetary authorities to affect relative interest rates. Attempts to pursue monetary control in such a situation may lead to considerable interest rate volatility. The nominal level of interest rates can no longer serve as a reliable instrument of monetary control. What should also be stressed is that the sensitivity of the demand for various individual 'monetary' assets to interest differentials, that is, the sensitivity of banks or customers to interest rate spreads, has not declined. On the contrary, it has increased with financial innovations improving the awareness of profit opportunities and with the lowering of transactions costs arising from technological change (to be discussed later).

Thus, together with a decline of the interest sensitivity of the demand for money (however defined) caused by liability management, cash management, and a higher content of interest-earning assets in money aggregates, we also have a shift of funds between different aggregates at a particular level of general interest rates. This may be brought about by changes in interest differentials, 'redefinitions' of money components, or regulation and deregulation. In section 5.3.5 we posited a downward shift (decline) in the US M1, on the assumption that funds escaped from M1 into instruments included in higher-level aggregates. With changing financial circumstances (competition, financial innovation, deregulation, technological change), different shifts between aggregates are likely.

With regard to the UK, M1 was expected to fall in conditions of liability management in response to a general rise in interest rates which affect the 'wholesale' deposit rates included in broader aggregates (Goodhart, 1984, p. 155). Elsewhere, higher interest rates on sight deposits within M1 (hence higher 'own' rate) were said to have attracted new funds into M1 (Johnston, 1984, p. 7). In an attempt to implement a restrictive monetary policy using £M3 as the target in 1979, the authorities attempted to raise interest rates, with the effect that interest-bearing liquid assets embodied in the aggregate attracted funds from elsewhere. The aggregate thus showed an 'untargeted' rise. 'The harder the brakes were applied, the faster the car seemed to run' (Niehans, 1982, p. 11) (compare section 6.1.2b).

Theoretically, the demand for an aggregate is likely to shift depending on whether new funds are likely to be attracted to it or whether there would be a net escape of funds in a given set of circumstances. Thus, the impact of liability management and associated innovations is likely to be uncertain and unpredictable. The fall in interest sensitivity may be accompanied by an upward or a downward shift (as shown in figure 6.2) in the demand schedule of an aggregate. Given a menu of aggregates, there are likely to be relative shifts in the aggregates, making the relationship between them difficult to predict and interpret.

Thus, liability management and other innovations change the slope of the demand function – a tilt from M_{d0} to M_{d1}. They may also cause either a fall (M_{d2}) or a rise (M_{d3}) in the demand at every given level of interest rates. The final position of M_d would be difficult to forecast. In terms of the *IS–LM* analysis (see the appendix to chapter 1), both expenditure and money multipliers (a_1 and a_2) are likely to be changeable, with the general tendency towards a relative rise in a_2 and a further effect on national income resulting from uncertain shifts in the demand for 'money' (caused by a change in M_0 in equation (A1.15) in that appendix). These effects on the demand for money help us to understand some of the results of the empirical work discussed in chapter 3, and in particular the observation of an increasing interest

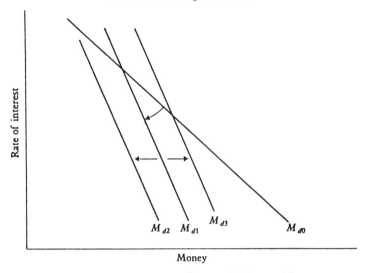

Figure 6.2 Liability management: effect on the demand for an aggregate.

inelasticity of the demand-for-money function and an instability of the function observed in the 1970s.

As noted above, the wider macroeconomic implications of innovations are frequently analysed in the *IS–LM* framework, where the *LM* incorporates the traditional money supply and demand schedules. 'As deposits come to bear competitive interest rates, monetary theory – models of money supply and demand and of the transmission of control measures and shocks through financial markets to the real economy – will have to be rewritten' (Tobin, 1983a, p. 162). Without disagreeing with this, one does wonder whether it would be desirable, or indeed possible, to rewrite monetary theory while retaining the paradigm of money supply and demand which poses no less perplexing questions. It would be most difficult to find an aggregate whose information content would be meaningful without possessing a good knowledge of developments in an interdependent financial system as a whole, and it is rather unlikely that a stable relationship of such an aggregate, or any other 'money' aggregate, with macroeconomic variables would endure under pressure from policy measures. This theme is developed in chapter 7.

6.3.3 *Potential instability*

Before leaving liability management and financial innovation in general, we should observe that there are other issues, with which we cannot deal fully and which arise from the changing characteristics of financial structure. One of them is the problem of general financial stability, which has in recent years received attention particularly in the light of some large bank failures.

The growing interdependence of banks and financial institutions through inter-bank connections in Eurocurrency and domestic wholesale markets implies greater reliance on a more speculative deposit base than the retail deposit base of traditional banking, and this is causing some anxiety. Bank failures have taken place in both the UK and the USA; in the latter, although the *average* number of bank failures has not risen, the size of insolvent banks has risen appreciably (Maisel, 1981, pp. 3–9, 140).

Financial institutions are quick to run for cover when faced with financial shocks or uncertainty. This has been observed in the case of the UK secondary bank crisis, the first manifestation in Britain of the dangers of liability management (see section 6.1.1). A similar run for cover has been noted in connection with bank failures in the USA, the latest (1984) being that of Continental Illinois (primarily a wholesale bank). Clearly, the potential for financial crises exists, though the subject is hardly ever mentioned in mainstream macroeconomics. This is perhaps because modern financial crises have been less frequent and acute than the crises preceding the Second World War and so far have been dealt with rather effectively by central bank initiatives or interventions. Economists generally accept that 'Financial crises are a childhood disease of capitalism, not an affliction of old age' (Goldsmith, 1982, p. 42).

Conventional modes of thought have, however, been challenged in this field by economists such as Kindleberger (1978) and Minsky (1977, 1978, 1982). 'The monetarist–Keynesian debate leaves little, if any, room for instability of credit and fragility of the banking system, or impacts on production and prices when the credit system becomes paralysed through loans rendered bad by falling prices. . . .' (Kindleberger, 1978, p. 72). Minsky is even more critical of current economics preoccupied with modelling 'village-fair' economies rather than economies 'with a Wall Street' (1982, p. 16).

Kindleberger's financial fragility thesis rests essentially on an extreme version of the 'financial theory' of money discussed in chapter 1: control of the money supply, however defined, is futile, as there is an infinite possibility of credit expansion given a fixed monetary base. Minsky's financial instability hypothesis regards finance as essentially speculative in character, with cash-flow relations shaped in periods of stability, which over time encourages risky practices ('stability is destabilizing'). Liability and corporate cash management, for instance, can be taken to a limit, at which point an otherwise robust financial system becomes fragile. Minsky thus advocates not policies of money control but policies 'to diminish the weight of speculative finance in the economy' (1977, p. 152).

The above propositions have not been integrated into a unified macroeconomic theory. They do, however, remind us of some of the important issues arising from sophisticated financial systems increasingly removed from the effectiveness of the traditional function of the lender of last resort. It also reflects a wider anxiety that, as the financial system acquires an enhanced capacity to create new liabilities or manage liabilities more effectively, it becomes harder to define money and hence to control it satisfactorily. There is also a fear that current methods of portfolio management by financial institutions, by increasing their exposure to liquidity crises, make them much more dependent upon prompt action by monetary authorities designed to 'bail them out' and prevent a bank panic (Kane, 1979, pp. 165–72). On the other hand, in the knowledge that the authorities would be wary of permitting the unfortunate externalities of a bank failure to develop into a panic, banks or other financial institutions might unduly rely on being 'bailed out' and become less prudent (the so-called 'moral hazard thesis').

Indeed, the study of the nature of stabilizing factors such as the role of the government sector and the lender of last resort in a financially fluid and resilient economy deserves more attention than is afforded by the standard framework of discretion *v.* rules-of-behaviour debate. Certainly the relative risks of insolvency and illiquidity in the new competitive, innovative and deregulated environment need to be reassessed (Maisel, 1981).

Almost unnoticed, the role of the central bank has been shifting from orthodox monetary management towards control of a microeconomic nature in the financial system. The function of the lender of last resort is fulfilled less in terms of maintaining the general liquidity of the financial system and more as a form of 'parental responsibility' and prudential supervision (McClam, 1982). In the UK, the traditional approach to bank supervision was to evolve more formal arrangements from voluntary and informal arrangements. The aim in the 1980s has been to interfere as little as possible with 'soundly managed companies' and to supervise more actively companies 'which need it'. The approach has been described as 'sailing with a fairly light rudder', but being 'mindful of the Charybdis of prudential laxity' and of the 'Scylla of overbearing regulation'. However, it seems that the Bank is now moving towards less flexibility and more firmness in supervision (BE, 1982e). Clearly, in the present competitive and innovative financial environment, the task of the supervisor is at once more vital and harder than in conditions of market segmentation.

6.4 Technological innovations

6.4.1 *Pervasive influence of modern technology*

Discussing a commodity money economy at the end of the last century, Wicksell (1936) observed that:

> It is at once clear that the purely physical conditions under which money can be paid and transported set a definite limit to the magnitude of the velocity of

circulation. Money cannot circulate faster – at any rate in a pure cash economy – than a messenger boy can run; its speed cannot exceed that of a mail van, train, or steamer to which is consigned the cash used for making a payment. [Wicksell, 1936, pp. 54–5]

In contrast, today large values of debt can be settled over vast distances in minutes. Technological change in the financial industry has been much quicker than our perception of its economic implication. It has been a major factor in bringing about the international financial integration discussed in section 5.2, and has been a common factor in financial innovations embraced by corporate cash and liability management.

Current technological change is all-pervasive. The purpose of this section is to outline the impact of computer and information technology on the financial innovative process and to point out its main economic implications. Economists have, in general, neglected the technological aspect of monetary economics, particularly in studies of the demand for money. Though it is clear that changes in financial technology have had a profound effect on the operations and structure of the financial system, there have been few investigations into its impact, and mainstream macro- and monetary economics continue to portray macroeconomic relationships on the assumption of static technology. Consequently, accounts of the diffusion of modern technology in the financial industry, of its determinants, processes and influence on financial innovations, tend to be impressionistic rather than systematic.

Increased competition and the adverse effect of inflation on the costs of financial services, which have been among the most labour-intensive of service industries, have undoubtedly prompted the move by financial institutions towards the widespread use of computers and telecommunications. The introduction of new technology has not been just a means of lowering the operational costs of banks and other financial institutions, but also has played a crucial role in all major financial innovations, although the precise processes by which the adoption of modern technology was linked with financial innovations are not well documented. High technology is also likely to play a part in financial developments in the foreseeable future.

In our discussions on individual financial innovations, references were made to the enabling role of new technology. Indeed, computer and information technology, often embraced within the acronyms EFT or EFTS (electronic funds transfer systems), have had a substantial impact on financial 'products' (instruments), processes, markets and institutional change. Uncertainty and the ability to grasp new profit opportunities are of key importance in financial behaviour. Today, information can be bleeped electronically to financial institutions over vast distances; communication networks also enable economic agents to react to messages quickly by pushbuttoning funds inside or outside national boundaries without recourse to written orders or traditional financial documents. Access to information networks and other computerized financial gadgetry is making it easier for financial and non-financial units to diversify their financial products or services. New technology is expensive, but it gives scope for economies of scale inviting co-operation, mergers or wider participation in order to spread the cost of investment in new systems over a wider range of users and/or services.

6.4.2 Payments system

The financial industry, and in particular retail banking, is relatively labour-intensive (Revell, 1983a, p. 57). Payments are among the financial services which engage a considerable proportion of bank staff; according to the evidence presented to the Wilson Committee, in the late 1970s 60 per cent of the staff employed in banks were engaged in money transmission work. Technological innovations have been responsible for changing both the nature and the cost of payments services. It should be remembered that such services are often closely linked with the availability, storage, retrieval and transmission of information.

In retail banking, the use of cash dispensers and the more modern automated teller machines (ATMs), introduced in the early 1980s, is now quite widespread.[17] Such systems are developing into large networks, and new networks (both national and international) are planned for the future (for instance, by a link consortium of building societies, unit trusts and LDTs). This is one example of modern technology where sharing is economical, has taken place, and is planned to expand. Participation in ATM networks enables small financial intermediaries to gain access to customers without having to open new branches (compare section 6.2.2). Transactions using ATMs have lower unit costs to suppliers than conventional services over the counter, and enable banks on average to lower bank charges (Marti and Zeilinger, 1982, pp. 11–13).

Many ATMs now offer the basic facilities of cash dispensing and balance reading, but new systems are developing which supply additional services, such as transfers between accounts, ordering of cheques, and loan applications. In the future they are likely to provide a kind of do-it-yourself, push-button, electronic, basic retail banking service, more flexible in terms of access than the existing service. No longer confined to the 'through-the-wall' arrangement in banks, they can be located on remote sites and in establishments not related to financial institutions and not constrained by normal opening hours.

The use of the credit card facility is another development made possible by modern technology. In the UK the number of such cards issued rose by a factor of 8 between 1970 and 1980 and by 22 per cent in the first two years of the 1980s.[18] The credit card represents an example of modern retail intermediation *par excellence*. It is an innovation which combines the services of traditional settlements (cash, cheque) with loan facilities in a simple, convenient and relatively safe way. It is thus a cheque and loan substitute for transactions purposes. It is, of course, only an intermediate arrangement, as the debt must be settled periodically with the credit card company. But, in the process of settlement, the user has the option of choosing an interest-free loan for a short period or an interest-bearing loan for longer periods. The provision of credit cards is not confined to financial institutions; retail outlets offer their own cards, predominantly, but not exclusively, for in-store settlements.

An extension of 'plastic card banking' in the shape of EFTPOS (Electronic Fund Transfer at Point of Sale) is planned to provide the automatic settlement of bills incurred in trade outlets through a system of EFT based on the use of a plastic card (Nicholas, 1982, pp. 26–30; Marti and Zeilinger, 1982, pp. 13–23). The scale of this development is difficult to predict at this stage.

The above innovations reduce costs of settlements by displacing paper and people from processing settlements. They also reduce the costs of setting up or participating in the provision of payments and settlement services by new entrants.[19] They thus enable a variety of agents, not necessarily financial, to develop innovative retail financial services, thus making financial markets more contestable, by facilitating entry and exit. The term 'contestable' markets is used in the sense in which Baumol (1982) proposed it. The theory of contestable markets is increasingly employed to explain behaviour in financial markets, and in particular the existence of large oligopolistic units, seemingly unable to exploit their market power and exhibiting competitive pricing behaviour (Davies and Davies, 1984). *Technological advance in general makes financial markets more contestable and susceptible to easy entry and exit and 'hit-and-run' entrants.*

The introgression of building societies in the UK into 'banking' services, described in section 6.1.2, is due largely to technological innovations in retail settlements. As already noted, Sears Roebuck, the largest retail chain in the USA, is also forcing its way increasingly into the provision of financial services, and in 1985 a similar intention was announced by Marks and Spencer in the UK. Such financial innovations might also enable households to manage their cash balances more effectively, contributing to a slowing down in the growth rate of the public's cash holdings relatively to that of consumer expenditure and personal disposable income, and to overpredictions of the demand for currency in circulation with the public (approximately 90 per cent of M0) by the forecasting equations of the Bank of England (BE, 1982b; Johnston, 1984, pp. 6–11).

In the realm of wholesale payment and transfers between financial institutions, EFTS, involving automated inter-bank settlement and electronic fund transfers, increase the speed of settlements and reduce their cost. Wholesale settlements are carried out largely by automated systems, such as

New York's CHIPS (Clearing House Interbank Payments System). Much international inter-bank dollar transfer is carried out through this system. The dominant fund transfer system in the USA – the FedWire (Federal Reserve Wire System) – has rapidly increased the value of its transactions, by a factor of 5 between 1950 and 1960 and again between 1960 and 1970, and by a factor of 6.4 between 1970 and 1980 (Frost, 1982, p. 48).

In the UK, BACS (Bankers' Automated Clearing Services), the EFTS set up by the clearing banks, became operational in 1969 to deal with company settlements and transfers such as payroll payments and standing orders, and currently processes over 12 million money transfers per week. CHAPS (Clearing House Automated Payments System), first used in 1984 to make electronic transfers for banks in the City, will in the future be extended to wholesale transfers (over £10,000) throughout the country. Settlements are carried out in a day.

EFTS, enabling payments to be made between two parties or to a third party in response to an electronic rather than a paper instruction, have been an essential feature of financial innovations, particularly in the realm of inter-bank activity, displacing the more time-consuming cheque and other manual forms of payments. The development of the new financial instruments such as RPs, MMMFs or NOW, and of the high-interest chequing accounts and 'packaged' services mentioned earlier, would not have been possible without electronic or wire transfers and modern information technology. These enable financial institutions to take advantage of investment opportunities quickly and to lower transactions costs, thus contributing to a reduction in the demand for non-interest-bearing 'money'. BACS transactions, for instance, cost about one-third of the equivalent paper transactions (Marti and Zeilinger, 1982, p. 44). Automatic transfers, from interest-bearing into customers' current accounts, and 'sweep' accounts, from which excess transactions balances are swept into interest-bearing accounts, further accentuated this trend. The marginal transfer costs of such arrangements must be very close to zero. We shall return to the question of declining transactions costs in chapter 7.

A concomitant of the revolution in money transfers has been the revolution in information technology. This has made possible better access to information and more cost-effective storage, processing and retrieval of data, as well as better cash-flow forecasting for purposes of liability and cash management, discussed earlier. Manual handling and accounting of transactions has been replaced by automated accounting and data processing. Such systems have also enabled financial institutions to cope at a relatively low cost with frequent alterations in the financial environment, for instance with numerous changes in interest rates, taxes and exchange rates. This has yielded benefits to managements in the form of management information and to customers, both personal and corporate, in terms of up-to-date knowledge of cash balances and investment opportunities, contributing to a reduction in uncertainty and the ability to maintain lower transactions and precautionary balances.

6.4.3   *Common factors in financial innovations*

The drive to decrease transactions costs in order to develop financial activity previously restricted by reserve requirements and interest rate ceilings is sometimes seen as a key reason for the development of international markets (Niehans, 1982, pp. 19–20). Indeed, EFTS have played a crucial role in international transactions by providing a high level of information and the capacity to move funds quickly without the impediment of geographical or national boundaries (compare section 5.2). Such transfers often help to bypass regional or national monetary restrictions. The Eurocurrency market could not have developed to its present level without such facilities. Improvements in such facilities are continuously taking place.

In 1977, SWIFT (Society for Worldwide Interbank Financial Telecommunications) became operational. Principally a network for sending information and inter-bank instructions rather than a fund transfer or settlement facility, by 1981 it linked to over 900 banks in 39 countries and, by 1983, to more than 1000 banks in 42 countries. The network processes over a quarter of a million transactions per day. With its increased use, the cost of entry into the network and costs per transaction were significantly reduced (Frost, 1982, pp. 49–51).

New technology has contributed greatly to international financial integration. Wojnilower (1980) gives a graphic description:

> Thanks to improvements in electronic communications, the financial community has been molded into much more of a 'crowd'. Trading floors have always consisted of crowds in the literal sense. Now, however, the crowd has been extended to embrace all market participants who want to join. The video screens that transmit instantaneous news and price information are standard equipment everywhere. [Wojnilower, 1980, p. 313]

The potential for circumvention of national regulations or restrictions has thereby become that much greater. Resorting to international or offshore markets now constitutes a standard method of relieving domestic financial pressures.

We should also recall that developments in new technology have played a vital part in corporate cash management. Indeed, they have led to a new form of intermediation. Banks supply corporate treasurers with information and settlement systems and means of EFTS, which enable them to manage liquid assets and arrange transfers of funds directly within and across national boundaries.

It has already been mentioned that modern technology has made financial markets more contestable by reducing the costs of entry and exit. It has also opened, to personal and corporate customers, less costly access to different forms of financial intermediation. Customer loyalty has played an important part in the stability of financial institutions, especially to commercial banks offering traditional payments services. With increasing outlets for intermediation, better awareness of the availability of alternative systems and an increasing isolation of customers from their bankers caused by more widespread and more remote pushbutton or plastic card payments operations, customer loyalty is being tested. More footloose customers might seek financial services which would satisfy their particular preferences, thus increasing further competitive pressure on financial institutions.

Modern technology, furthermore, has enabled financial institutions to diversify into activities not traditionally associated with them. This has been particularly visible in the realm of payments and fund transfers, where the monopoly of banks has been significantly eroded by the intrusion of building societies, LDTs and even retailers. This has provided financial institutions with new means of competitive aggression.

It was noted that one important characteristic of the new technological innovations in finance is the potential for economies of scale. These have been largely responsible for an increasing degree of co-operation, or 'marriages of convenience', between financial institutions and for a tendency towards a greater diversification of services. The sharing of various financial networks and packaging of financial services, discussed earlier, are an important illustration of this. Such activities, together with receding regulatory restrictions, help to reduce the traditional demarcations between institutions.

Both competition and experience of localized co-operation are likely to lead to further, more far-reaching, structural changes, giving greater scope for financial innovation. Various forms of association and mergers are already developing between financial institutions which might lead to universal banking or financial supermarkets. Banks have shown considerable interest in linking up with jobbing firms, insurance companies and even estate agencies. It seems that successful future intermediaries will be those which adapt their organizational structures in a way which would enable them to make the best use of technological potential. It is most likely that, in a future institutional set-up, the distinction between the 'creators of money' and the intermediaries or 'banks' and other financial institutions would become even more meaningless than it is now.

To conclude, the technological advances deployed in modern finance have been a common denominator of all major financial innovations. They have had a strong impact on the macroeconomic demand for narrowly defined 'money', largely by reducing transactions costs. Indeed, a view has been expressed that the only fundamental change in financial industry is 'technological innovation', which reduces transactions costs (of storage, retrieval and transmission of information); all other changes are merely 'adaptive innovations', consisting of new ways of 'bundling' financial services which remain fundamentally the same (Niehans, 1983, pp. 537–9). The impact of transactions costs is further analysed in section 7.4.

By reducing transactions costs, technological innovations have increased the sensitivity of holders of liquid assets to changes in the financial environment, whether expressed in terms of changing interest rate differentials or alterations in monetary regulation or control. They have thus enhanced the circumventive power of financial institutions and of corporations and contributed towards financial markets becoming more contestable. Finally, the scope for economies of scale in the application of new technology encourages structural change, which increasingly 'packages' both services and institutions, making the traditional distinctions between 'monetary' and other financial institutions difficult to sustain.

Appendix: The anatomy of British banking

Table 6.6 Liabilities and assets, mid-May, 1984

	Total liabilities/ assets	Sterling liabilities		Other currency liabilities		Sterling assets	Other currency assets
		Total	Deposits and CDs	Total	Deposits and CDs		
£b	670.1	196.8	166.1	473.3	464.5	198.3	471.8
%	100	29.4	24.8	70.6	69.3	29.6	70.4

Table 6.7 Deposits and CDs in relation to money aggregates, mid-May 1984

	Total	Sterling	Other currency	M1	£M3	PSL1	PSL2
£b	630.6	166.1	464.5	45.9	101.7	106.0	175.5
%	100	26.3	73.7	7.3	16.1	16.8	27.8

Table 6.8 Sterling deposits and CDs, mid-May 1984

	Total	UK private sector		UK monetary sector		Public sector	Overseas sector	CDs
		Sight	Time	Sight	Time			
£b	166.1	35.3	52.9	7.6	32.0	2.2	25.2	10.8
%	100	21.2	31.8	4.6	19.3	1.3	15.2	6.5

Table 6.9 Other currency deposits and CDs, mid-May 1984

		Sight and time			
	Total	UK monetary sector	Other	Overseas	CDs
£b	464.5	89.9	15.5	285.6	73.4
%	100	19.4	3.3	61.5	15.8

Table 6.10 Sterling assets: total and main categories, mid-May 1984

	Total	Currency and balances with Bank of England	Market loans				Advances				Investments
			Total	London Discount market	UK monetary sector	Bills	Total	UK private sector	UK public sector	Overseas	
£ b	198.3	2.5	57.3	4.8	41.4	3.5	106.3	93.2	2.4	10.7	13.7
%	100	1.3	28.9	2.4	20.9	1.8	53.6	47.0	1.2	5.4	6.9

Table 6.11 Other currency assets: total and main categories, mid-May 1984

		Market loans and advances				
			UK			
	Total	Total	Monetary sector and monetary sector CDs	Private and public sectors	Overseas	Investments
£ b	471.8	448.4	95.3	28.2	324.9	17.3
%	100	95.0	20.2	6.0	68.9	3.7

Table 6.12 Sterling deposits, by categories of banks, mid-May 1984 (£billion)

Banks	Total	Sight	UK monetary sector	UK private sector	Overseas	CDs
Retail (Ret.)	91.8	34.9	9.9	67.1	6.9	6.0
Accepting hses (AH)	9.3	2.4	1.8	5.6	1.1	0.7
Other British (OB)	28.0	6.0	13.7	7.9	5.1	1.0
American (Am.)	9.1	2.3	2.9	2.3	2.9	0.9
Japanese (Jap.)	6.3	0.2	3.7	0.7	1.3	0.6
Other overseas (OO)	19.5	3.0	6.8	4.3	7.1	1.3
Consortium (Con.)	2.1	0.3	0.9	0.2	0.8	0.1
Total	166.1	49.1	39.7	88.1	25.2	10.6

Table 6.13 Other currency deposits, by categories of banks, mid-May 1984 (£ billion)

Banks	Total	UK monetary sector	Overseas	CDs
Ret.	31.6	6.2	19.8	2.1
AH	13.5	4.0	7.5	0.3
OB	49.5	13.8	29.5	4.3
Am.	96.2	8.6	55.6	29.3
Jap.	127.6	30.1	72.1	24.1
OO	130.6	21.8	91.9	13.0
Con.	15.5	5.5	9.2	0.2
Total	464.5	90.0	285.6	73.3

Table 6.14 Sterling lending, by categories of banks, mid-May, 1984 (£ billion)

Banks	Total sterling assets	Market loans UK monetary sector and CDs	LDMA[b]	Overseas	Advances UK private sector	Overseas
Ret.	97.6	12.2	3.2	0.4	60.2	5.0
AH	10.6	4.9	0.2	0.3	2.6	0.8
OB	33.2	8.7	0.3	1.2	16.7	1.1
Am.	10.9	2.8	0.3	0.7	4.9	1.1
Jap.	6.7	2.4	0.2	1.4	0.9	0.8
OO	21.6	8.3	0.4	1.6	7.5	1.6
Con.	2.5	1.0	0.0	0.3	0.4	0.3
Total	183.1	41.3	4.6	5.9	93.2	10.7

[a] UK monetary sector and CDs.   [b] London Discount Market Association.

Table 6.15 Other currency lending, by categories of banks, mid-May 1984 (£ billion)

Banks	Total	Market loans and advances		
		UK monetary sector and CDs	UK private sector	Overseas
Ret.	33.7	11.9	3.2	16.7
AH	13.2	3.8	1.1	7.6
OB	51.9	9.4	3.4	35.9
Am.	94.5	10.6	7.5	74.9
Jap.	127.1	28.1	3.7	87.7
OO	130.1	29.3	7.5	89.0
Con.	16.7	2.1	0.3	13.0
Total	467.2[a]	95.2	26.7	324.8

[a] Totals here are different from those in other tables because detailed data have a 'miscellaneous' column with sterling and other currency assets placed together.
Source: *BEQB*, 24(2) June 1984, various tables.

Notes

1　BE (1971a, 1971b); for critical assessment see Grant (1977); Gowland (1978); Zawadzki (1981).
2　This situation encouraged proposals for remedies in terms of a monetary base control, with monetary base represented by an asset over whose supply the central bank would have complete control (Duck and Sheppard, 1978).
3　Details are briefly summarized in the Treasury's *Economic Progress Report*, no. 138, October 1981.
4　For details and the rationale of these changes see *Green Paper on Monetary Control*, Cmnd 7858, 1980, HMSO; also *Hansard*, 24 November 1980, col. 312.
5　Percentage ratios of unfunded PSBR to the total PSBR were 56.0 in 1972/3, 39.1 in 1973/4, 47.5 in 1974/5, 49.6 in 1975/6, 15.6 in 1976/7, −18.9 in 1977/8, 8.0 in 1978/9, 7.8 in 1979/80, 14.5 in 1980/81, −30.8 in 1981/2, 6.7 in 1982/3 and −29.2 in 1983/4 (negative signs indicate overfunding) (*BEQB*, 24(2), June 1984, table 11.3; *Financial Statistics*, June 1984, table 11.5; see also BE, 1984c).
6　These were 92.8 per cent in 1979/80, 90.9 per cent in 1980/81, 119.1 per cent in 1981/2, 86.7 per cent in 1982/3 and 84.4 per cent in 1983/4 (*BEQB*, 24(2), June 1984, table 8).
7　In the financial years shown in table 6.5, the percentage shares of total gross official sales of stocks consisting of stocks of over one year and up to five years (the first figure), and of stocks consisting of over fifteen years and undated (the second figure) were: 21.0 and 55.4; 19.3 and 37.1; 30.9 and 29.1; 36.6 and 15.6; 42.5 and 17.1.

8 One of the characteristics of modern financial change is the emergence of hybrid financial instruments. The most recent development in the realm of 'wholesale' finance is the emergence of floating rate note issues by which large banks (Lloyds, Midland) are now beginning to raise funds. The 'perpetual floater' combines the characteristics of 'wholesale' loans with long-term capital issues.

9 Below is a selection, which is not likely to be comprehensive, of some of the high-interest accounts or money funds classified by the type of institutions offering them.

Licensed deposit-takers

Adam & Co. (Adam Current, Adam High Interest Cheque Account); Aitken Hume (Monthly Income Account); Citibank Savings (Cheque Plus Account); C. P. Choularton (Money Market Cheque Account); Dartington and Co. (Money Market Account); Lombard North Central (Lombard Cheque Savings Account); Oppenheimer Money Management (Money Management Account); Tyndall & Co. (Money Account). There are a number of other LDTs which offer interest-bearing current accounts (e.g. Avco Trust, Western Trust and Savings).

Financial or unit trusts (in association with banks)

Britannia Group (Britannia High Interest Current Account; banker, Carter Allen); M & G Financial Services (High Interest Cheque Account; banker, Kleinwort Benson); Save and Prosper Group (High Interest Bank Account; Premier High Interest Bank Account; banker, Robert Fleming).

Banks

Bank of Scotland (Money Market Cheque Account); Barclays Bank (Prime Account); Charterhouse Japhet (Premium Account); Co-operative Bank (Cheque and Save Account); Midland Bank (High Interest Cheque Account); J. Henry Schroder (Schroder Special Account). Nat West's Cashwise Account, offering low interest rate, is not normally classified in the same category of accounts.

10 The term 'free banking' can be confusing. Used in the context of this section, it means that no bank charges are made. In economic history and theory, it can mean an episode in US history when the setting up of banking enterprises became liberalized, or (especially in the context of 'new monetary economics') a system under which there are no legal restrictions relating to the issue of 'money', usually meaning notes and coin. In the last sense, the Scottish monetary system was (in the nineteenth century) the closest to 'free banking' (White, 1984b); the Austrian school of monetary economics has persistently advocated it; the Americans in particular are increasingly interested in it. New work on free banking is briefly discussed in section 7.3.3.

11 The data for 1971 are not strictly comparable with those of post-1975 because of changes in the calculation of money aggregates (see section 4.1). Sources of data: *Bank of England Quarterly Bulletins*, tables 11.1; *Financial Statistics*, tables 7.1.

12 Term shares with early withdrawal facilities at the end of 1981 constituted 8.0 per cent of building society shares included in PSL2 and 38.1 per cent of all term

shares of building societies; the respective figures at the end of 1983 were 21.1 and 70.4 per cent (*BEQB*, 1984, 24(4), table 12).

13 Five societies are known to have such packages: the Alliance (205 branches) with the Bank of Scotland offers 'Banksave'; the Bristol and West (160 branches) with Standard Chartered Bank offers 'Moneylink'; Leeds Permanent (470 branches) with Yorkshire Bank supplies 'Pay and Save'; the Nottingham (49 branches) with the Bank of Scotland has devised 'Homelink'; Sussex County (33 branches) offers the full chequing and loan services of Western Trust & Savings with any of its accounts.

14 Perhaps the best-known package is the Cash Management Account developed in the USA by Merrill, Lynch, Pierce, Fenner and Smith, which combines banking and chequing account facilities with a variety of brokerage facilities giving access to money market investment funds. Most facilities may be accessed automatically through a small plastic card.

15 In spite of waves of innovations, the gap between rates which individuals earn on assets and pay on borrowing in the USA was found to be wide, giving scope for further innovations to make markets more efficient (B. Friedman, 1980, p. 58).

16 See Tobin (1983a; 1983b); Wenninger (1984) and, for an extended analysis, Hadjimichalakis (1982).

17 The number of ATMs in UK banks has been estimated at 5309 in 1983 (a rise of over 28 per cent on the 1982 total), and 6470 are expected by the end of 1984.

18 The number of credit cards issued rose from 1.4 million in 1970 to 11.0 million in 1980 and 13.4 million in 1982, and the value of transactions using credit cards rose from £1.0 billion in 1977 to £2.2 billion in 1982 (Johnston, 1984, table 5). Between 1972 and 1984 Britain's two largest cards (Access and Visa) expanded the number of cards issued by a factor of 2.8 (to 15 million), the number of outlets by a factor of 3.3 (to 433,000) and the turnover by a factor of 80 (to £8.1 billion). For possible developments in plastic card technology see Marti and Zeilinger (1982, ch. 4).

19 The reference to cost reduction is made with some degree of introspection. Statistical evidence, though not altogether absent (e.g. Revell, 1983a, ch. 4), is scarce and diffuse.

—7—

In Search of a Hypothesis

7.1 Financial evolution as a complement to real change: a Schumpeterian approach

In this chapter we shall depart from the consideration of financial innovations by exemplifications of individual innovations and their impact on the meaning and control of money and attempt some generalizations. Particular attention is paid to factors inducing innovations and to broader characteristics of the innovation process. It should be reiterated that there is no generally acceptable framework for dealing with the subject, and the 'hypotheses' discussed below are in the main rather loosely formulated propositions based, essentially, on the existing stock of knowledge. Few attempts have been made to integrate this knowledge systematically with macroeconomic theory, which until recently has remained oblivious to the existence of financial change affecting 'money'. Experiments with the traditional demand-for-money functions, including 'innovation variables', are outlined in section 7.5.

Modern macroeconomic theory tends to emphasize states of equilibrium and usually dichotomizes real and monetary relationships, particularly in the context of the long-run neutrality of money (see section 1.1). However, interdependence in the financial system involving a constant interaction between 'real' and financial sector units has been stressed in previous sections. Below, readers are reminded of the Schumpeterian school of economic thought, which highlights this aspect but gives primacy to factors stimulating real development, with money and finance playing an adaptive, but not a secondary, role.

Not infrequently, modern economists consider financial innovation to be essentially a reaction to impulses coming from the real sector. Silber (1975b, p. 54) noted that 'innovation of money responds to a stimulus in the real sector and in turn influences the potential path of real economic activity'. And 'Institutional innovation is one aspect of a dynamic economy and

181

money-market innovations occur in response to the needs of a growing economy' (Minsky, 1957, p. 187). A similar view was reiterated more recently, contending that 'in a large part, financial innovations are an adaptation to changes in technology and management outside the financial field'.[1] This is consistent with some observations of long-run economic growth patterns which point to the primacy of real development and technological innovation, with social, financial and managerial innovation being a necessary byproduct of technological change. One of the 'long chains of sequence' characterizing economic growth begins with additions to the stock of useful science, going on to technological innovations, to growth in productivity, to changes in the structure of production, to changes in other aspects of economic structure, to changes in political and social structure, and finally to conditions of life and work, which in turn affect the demand in the economy (Kuznetz, 1971, esp. p. 349).

There may also be an indirect connection between real development and monetary or financial change. Monetary innovation is sometimes seen as a way of promoting real growth by circumventing government regulations and restrictive monetary arrangements which constrain development (Cameron, 1967; Sylla, 1982, p. 25). This would be consistent with a modern view of financial evolution as a process of removing market frictions and segmentation (see section 2.1). This aspect is further considered in section 7.3.

The essence of Schumpeterian economics is the analysis of economic evolution rather than of the states of the economy. Equilibrium is important only in so far as it explains the adaptive processes, but it is the disturbance of the equilibrium and the associated change on which Schumpeter concentrates. Economic evolution is defined as 'The change in economic process brought about by innovations together with all their effects, and the response to them by economic system ...' (1964, p. 61). Fluctuations in a capitalist society are explained by technological innovations undertaken by profit-seeking entrepreneurs to secure a temporary monopolistic advantage over their rivals. The carrying out of innovations is the essence of capitalist enterprise; it leads to 'new men' organizing 'new firms' and stimulating economic expansion. Financial development constitutes an integral part of this economic evolution.

In the remainder of this section we shall concentrate on the role of banking and finance in Schumpeterian economic processes. Banks are the dominant financial intermediary, but they are not the only creators of 'money', which is regarded essentially as a means of payment and of circulation and can be supplied also by firms issuing bills of exchange and by the government issuing fiat money. Thus, many assets, generated by diverse economic units, fulfil the principal functions of money (compare section 1.2.2). Schumpeter believed '[t]hat all forms of credit, from bank note to book-credits, are essentially the same thing, and that in all these forms credit increases the means of payment ...' (1968, p. 99).

Economic fluctuations, or cycles, are 'all-permeating', having their organizational and financial complements. Expansion initiated by technical innovations is financed not by saving, but by credit creation, considered to be 'the monetary complement of innovation' (1964, p. 85). We may note that this is somewhat reminiscent of the Keynesian view, expressed after the publication of the *General Theory*, that increases in the demand for investment necessitate additional monetary accommodation. This was later interpreted in terms of the 'finance motive' in liquidity preference, stressing the interdependence between the money market and the real sector (Davidson, 1978, ch. 7; Fisher, 1978, pp 80–1). Schumpeter strongly argues that the 'logical relation' between innovation and credit creation by banks is 'fundamental to the understanding of the capitalist system' and lies 'at the bottom of all problems of money and credit'. The financing of enterprise associated with technological innovations, and the concomitant generation of means of payment, form an essential element in the Schumpeterian process of economic evolution. The rate of interest is a premium on present over future means of payment, the price paid by borrowers for a 'social permit' to acquire factors of production without a prior contribution towards the production of commodities and services. Innovation is again the basic 'cause' of the rate of interest (Schumpeter, 1964, pp. 98–9).

It is at this point that we encounter a major flaw in Schumpeterian theory. His monetary and credit system is simply assumed to exist, as it is in many other monetary theories (Wood, 1981, pp. 146–8). It is strange that Schumpeter does not explicitly consider financial innovations as an integral part of general economic evolution. The emphasis on the innovative entrepreneur contrasts with his conservative, adaptive banker.

It is, however, safe to assume that the expansion of credit and money, together with institutional changes in the banking sector, are related to expansion in the real sector, brought about by technological innovation. Such interrelation between real and financial activity is emphasized by Minsky (1969, pp. 25–26), who claims that 'Capitalism requires that financial institutions and instruments exist which permit flexibility in financing.' Financial innovation is an important constitutent of this flexibility, enabling an economy to increase its real economic activity without necessarily raising the level of some conventional 'money'.

Given the complexities of innovationary processes and the factors which account for financial expansion, the connection between the 'logical source' of credit, that is, the finance of innovation, and actual financial processes might not be apparent and might thus be overlooked. It is 'in no case easy to discern the element of innovation under the mass of induced, derivative, and adventitious phenomena that overlies it. But in the sphere of money and credit the layer is so thick, and the surface so entirely at variance with the processes below, that the first impression of the reader may well be fatal' (Schumpeter, 1964, p. 83).

Nevertheless, to understand the financial and monetary processes of changing economies, we are warned not to lose sight of *the fundamental connection between change in the real sector and its financial consequences.*

> Whenever the evolutionary process is in full swing, the bulk of bank credit outstanding at any time finances what has become current business and has lost its original contact with innovation or with the adaptive operations induced by innovations, although the history of every loan must lead back to the one or the other. [Schumpeter, 1964, p. 88]

Schumpeter, however, admits that there are occasions when credit creation loses its direct contact with technological change. After the prosperity associated with innovational activity, there might be a 'secondary wave'. Expectations of continuing prosperity, no longer justified, might nevertheless motivate further financial transactions which result in losses. 'New borrowing will no longer be confined to entrepreneurs, and "deposits" will be created to finance general expansion, each loan tending to induce another loan, each rise in price another rise' (Schumpeter, 1964, p. 212). Thus, credit creation becomes speculative and inflationary and loses for a time its relation to innovation, only to regain it in the next stage of expansion led by further innovation. We are reminded that the 'credit machine is so designed as to serve the improvement of the productive apparatus and to punish any other use' (p. 123).

A similar analysis which appeared later in Minsky's work lies in the framework of his hypothesis of financial instability (see section 6.3.3). An accelerating pace of investment is associated with 'high spirits' of both entrepreneurs and financiers. 'Euphoric investment demand, combined with rising costs in conventional financial channels, will lead, via feedbacks on the potential payoffs to financial innovations, to an expansion in the effective ability to finance activity' (Minsky, 1969, p. 227). Part of the finance for investment comes from innovative emissions of claims by the private sector (inside money). However, the 'euphoric expectations' and 'animal spirits' resulting from 'observed bonanzas' lead to a fragile financial liability structure.

As already stated, Schumpeter does not explicitly deal with financial innovation and institutional change. However, as he deals with change over time, it is legitimate to assume that institutional change is implicit in the expansion of credit and money over successive periods of business cycles. The above theory is a variant of what we called, in section 1.2.2, 'financial theories of money', enunciated at least from the time of Adam Smith, which consider that money and financial structure adapt to the 'needs of trade' and thus essentially respond to the requirements of the real sector. It therefore contradicts propositions that monetary sectors can, in a continuous way, exercise an independent influence on economic processes. On the other hand, we are reminded that a connection with the real economy can easily be severed when misguided expectations induce purely financial and speculative expansions, leading to economic crises and instability.

This fickleness of finance, or what R. Hawtrey called 'the inherent instability of credit', is often the starting point of economic fluctuations in 'monetary' theories of the trade cycle. F. A. Hayek (1966, p. 148), for instance, followed Wicksell by emphasizing the 'elasticity of the volume of circulating media' arising out of financial development. 'Elasticity of the supply of currency media, resulting from the existing monetary organization, offers a sufficient reason for the genesis and recurrence of fluctuations in the whole economy' (pp. 187–8).[2] Some modern writing is not far removed from this idea:

> The twin characteristics of financial markets – their ultimate dependence on the profit of industry and commerce and their ability to generate speculative booms on the basis of optimism without any industrial roots – are what make it inevitable that speculative booms end in crises. [Coakley and Harris, 1983, p. 77].

The danger of financial instability in Schumpeter's scheme essentially follows the momentum of real expansion. Fundamentally, his theory links financial change with technological and institutional development in the real sector – an interesting proposition worth exploring empirically. An intriguing aspect of the financial innovations since the 1970s is that they have occurred in generally depressed economic conditions, but in the environment of structural and technological change, inflation and deregulation.

7.2 The hypothesis of constraint-induced innovation

A general theory of financial innovation has been proposed by W. L. Silber (1975a, 1983), who approached the subject from the microeconomic point of view of a financial firm. It should be stated that the theory of a financial firm in economics is as unsettled as, if not more than, the general theory of the firm. Silber accepts that financial firms maximize utility subject to some balance sheet constraint. This is simply another way of saying that, fundamentally, financial firms seek to maximize profits.

Thus, the basic question which Silber poses in his search for a general theory of financial innovation is, Why do profit-maximizing financial institutions innovate? The general answer is that 'innovation of financial instruments and practices occurs in an effort to remove or lessen the financial constraints imposed on firms' (Silber, 1975a, p. 64).

More specifically, financial institutions will incur the cost of innovations when an exogenous change in constraints takes place. Two types of such changes are distinguished:

> In one case exogenous changes in constraints force a reduction in the utility of the firm and the firm innovates in an effort to return to its previous level of utility. . . . In the second case innovation is a response to an increase in the cost of adhering to a constraint. In a programming context this corresponds to an increase in the shadow price of the constraint. [Silber, 1975a, p. 66].

In such cases the firm will attempt to circumvent the constraint by altering the opportunity set which it faces.

The main externally imposed constraints are government regulations. There might, however, also be internally imposed constraints such as self-determined liquidity rules. Using the language of linear programming, Silber highlights the situation in which the rising costs (shadow prices) of adhering to existing constraints stimulate innovation. Innovation has development costs. He gives his hypothesis of constraint-induced innovation a time dimension by postulating that 'only a sustained increase in shadow prices over time will stimulate new product innovation' (1983, p. 90).

Essentially, Silber's proposition is straightforward. Optimizing firms will innovate when exogenous changes alter their constraints and reoptimization will take place having regard to the costs of developing innovations. A programming framework is suggested for the study of innovation.

Paradoxically, Silber's 'general theory' of financial innovation is both too general and too specific. It is too general in the sense that it suggests, essentially, that financial firms innovate in order to maximize profits; the stress is mainly on 'adversity innovation', that is, on innovation when an externally imposed constraint, such as a state regulation, needs to be circumvented in pursuit of the highest attainable profit. It is too specific in the sense that it applies to firms and may not be suited to the study of innovation in the macroeconomic context dealing with the emergence of new markets, new firms or new monetary standards.

Nevertheless, the analysis of innovation of financial instruments and practices by financial firms constitutes an important aspect of our overall understanding of financial innovationary processes, and Silber is a pioneer in this direction. His informal studies of particular innovations, as well as his (and Ben-Horim's) formal application of linear programming to the study of innovation by large money market institutions (see Ben-Horim and Silber, 1977), constitute useful advances in this neglected area of monetary economics.

7.3   The hypothesis of circumventive innovation

7.3.1   *Circumventive reaction: not a new phenomenon*

On many occasions in previous chapters, instances where financial innovations constituted a response to monetary regulation, which ultimately neutralized the restrictive effect of the regulations, have been stressed. In other words, financial innovation served as a device to bypass or circumvent monetary control. The origin of the expression 'circumventive innovation' is not clear. R. C. Holland (1975, p. 161) suggested that it meant an innovation which occurs'. . . when free market forces and institutions seek to bypass the monetary and regulatory controls imposed in the name of [public policy considerations]'.

The idea that economic units seek to avoid government restriction is neither new nor confined to monetary or financial matters. Indeed, today it receives considerable attention in spheres not associated with these areas. It is an aspect of broader investigations of complex interrelationships between political powers acting in the name of public interest and economic or market powers exercised in the name of individual advantage (Kane, 1977, 1981).

The notion that economic units respond to government intervention by deliberately seeking ways around it whenever such action is likely to be rewarded by increased profits is well known; it is certainly familiar to monetary economists. In deprecating the fact that, in the 1960s, banks had to incur costs in circumventing monetary regulations, Friedman felt that the government should have been aware of the ingenuity of economic actors 'in getting around government restrictions that interfere with their pursuit of self-interest' (1980b, p. 82).

It is in the nature of many forms of government economic regulations or controls that they represent at once an obstacle to the pursuit of existing profitable activity and an opportunity to profit from the discovery of a way to pursue a closely related activity lying just outside the boundary of such devices. 'On the economic front, biting controls build up sizeable rewards for those either bold enough to defy them or clever enough to devise ways around them' (Kane, 1977, p. 63).

In his study of the subject, E. J. Kane developed a framework of 'regulatory dialectic' in which the political processes of regulation and 'the economic processes of regulatee avoidance' interact by continuously adapting to each other:

> Market institutions and politically imposed constraints reshape themselves in a Hegelian manner, simultaneously resolving and renewing an endless series of conflicts between economic and political power. The approach envisions repeating stages of regulatory avoidance (or 'loophole mining') and re-regulation, with stationary equilibrium virtually impossible. [Kane, 1981, p. 355]

In the realm of money and finance, the innovator certainly does not appear to be any less ingenious in seeking profit than a typical Schumpeterian entrepreneur–innovator. Indeed, in the world of finance the capacity to adapt to changing conditions, including a deliberate avoidance of regulations and policy imposed by monetary authorities, have been observed time and again, given propitious conditions. B. Gould *et al.* (1981, p. 29) observed that 'the whole history of money is the continual invention of new kinds of money, for reasons of greater convenience or because of a shortage of officially-approved forms'.

It has been said that 'anti-regulatory' financial innovation is essentially a phenomenon of modern times, whereas in the past it was essentially a response to a shortage of medium of exchange or to financial crises (Sylla, 1982). While this represents an accurate broad generalization, we do have examples in history of circumvention not fundamentally different from that in modern times.

It is, for instance, well known that usury laws, a sort of precursor of modern interest rate ceilings, not very different from regulation Q in the USA, were circumvented by commission payments over and above allowable interest rates, or by a requirement to deposit a minimum balance with the lender before a loan could be advanced.

Classical economists were well aware of the adaptive capacity of the financial system. J. B. Say claimed that:

> Should the increase in traffic require more money to facilitate it, the want is easily supplied.... In such cases, merchants know well enough how to find substitutes for the product serving as the medium of exchange or money (by bills at sight, or after date, bank-notes, running credits, write-offs, etc., as at London and Amsterdam) and money itself soon pours in.... [in Becker and Baumol, 1952, p. 372]

Say thus believed that the quantity of circulating media would adjust itself to economic conditions indicated by a price level (compare section 1.2.2). Recently, a similar view was expressed by C. P. Kindleberger (1984, p. 181): 'Whenever the market wants more money than some aggregate fixed by the authorities, it monetizes another kind of credit.'

When, in 1797, in giving evidence to a House of Commons committee, Thornton (1939, p. 282) was asked what would have happened if in the previous twelve months the stock of Bank of England notes had been halved, his answer was: 'I cannot conceive that the mercantile world would suffer such a diminution to take place, without substituting a circulating medium of their own; and I happen to know ... that some projects of this sort were on foot, and had been in the minds of several bankers. ...'

A study of English banking in the Industrial Revolution up to the 1844 Bank Charter Act suggested that, in the realm of monetary and banking policy, the authorities 'either made the wrong decision or took no action at all' to promote stability or growth. 'Paradoxically, however, the very obstacles placed in the way of a rational banking and monetary system stimulated the private sector to introduce the financial innovations necessary for realization of the full benefits of the technical innovations in industry' (Cameron, 1967, pp. 58–9).

The remarkable adaptability and flexibility of the financial system in the face of legislation and monetary contraction was documented by J. R. T. Hughes (1960). The Bank Charter Act (1844), which introduced the rules of monetary control under the gold standard, defined 'money' in terms of Bank of England notes and restricted their issue to the movement of gold. Note issue by country banks was also restricted. Financial innovations accounted for credit expansion not in accordance with bullion movements, as was the intention of the legislator. The monetary constraint embodied in the Act was unrealistic for the growing economy of the 1850s. 'The monetary system provided its own substitute for notes in the economic expansion which followed by deposit creation and by an increase in the volume of bills of exchange created' (Hughes, 1960, p. 257). The banks subsequently developed the cheque system and the Clearing House.

Because of such developments, R. S. Sayers (1957, p. 6) compared the workings of the Act to 'clutching at a slippery eel when it sought to apply a rule of thumb to the monetary situation by regulating the use of bank notes alone'. Men soon found ways of escaping the Act's intentions, rendering it an 'empty shell' and a 'memorial to those who believed that either nature or the law had drawn a sharp line of distinction between what was money and what was not money and that an automatic machine could sufficiently govern the monetary situation'.

In the course of financial development after the Act, in general, the demand for credit was not suppressed by increases in the cost of credit, but the supply of credit readily responded to higher interest rates (Hughes, 1960, pp. 259–66). 'Credit expansion was not hindered by the contraction of the Bank's issues and all it implied so long as there were other reasons for high expectations' (p. 263).

The examples given above fit well into the framework of what was termed in chapter 1 'financial theories' of money. The financial innovations mentioned are essentially the defensive, constraint-induced phenomena discussed earlier. State intervention appears to have been an ever-present problem in financial evolution, mainly because the state was anxious to regulate the payments system and the basic form of bank intermediation, regarding them as 'public goods'. Regulation-induced innovation may thus be regarded as a particular form of financial change, of special interest to policy-makers.

Macroeconomic policy is a relatively new, post-Keynesian, phenomenon. As observed earlier, control over monetary growth is today considered necessary either as part of an activist monetary policy or as a passive rule of behaviour. In principle, it does not matter whether one wishes to control 'money' in a discretionary way or by way of a rigid procedure. In each case monetary authorities must react in terms of monetary instruments to signals received from economic, including monetary, indicators.

It was noted earlier that, both in defining money and in controlling it, monetary authorities rely on economic regularities observed in past behaviour and, in particular, on the stability of the demand function for money.

There is a widespread awareness among economists that basing a policy upon a recognized statistical relationship will bring about a policy-induced change in the relationship. This phenomenon is sometimes referred to as 'Goodhart's law', which claims that 'any observed statistical regularity will tend to collapse once pressure is placed upon it for control purposes' (Goodhart, 1984, p. 96).

In the realm of financial intermediation, Goodhart (1981, p. 129) essentially stresses the factors already discussed in connection with regulation avoidance in general. Commercial banks and other financial institutions react to market impulses not in the interest of monetary policy, but for self-interest. In pursuing their advantages, they respond creatively by innovating. Their ingenuity appears to be most prominent in getting around central bank controls.

Another, though related, approach is to regard bank regulation as a form of tax on transactions intermediated by banks. Such a discretionary levy invites evasion, which ultimately renders the regulation ineffective and distorts rather than controls the quantity of credit, unless the means for evasion are blocked (Wills, 1982).

In a more technical, though none the less fundamental way, the problem of policy-induced change is stressed by NCM (see section 1.1.1).

> Given that the structure of an econometric model consists of optimal decision rules of economic agents, and that optimal decision rules vary systematically with changes in the structure of series relevant to the decision-maker, it follows that any change in policy will systematically alter the structure of econometric models. [Lucas, 1981, p. 126]

Thus, many current econometric models are unable to forecast the consequences of policy measures which induce a reactive response by optimizing agents with rational expectations.

Although the phenomenon of monetary regulation or policy-induced change is well known, we do not have a sufficient understanding of it to be able to construct arrangements anticipating such reactions in the policy design. Indeed, the nature of the 'creative response' (see section 5.1.1) to policy constraints is only beginning to be investigated. In particular, we do not seem to know a great deal about the processes of response by financial firms to obstacles imposed on them by regulatory authorities; certainly not enough to be able to devise control methods which might counteract or forestall circumventive action. As mentioned in section 5.1, little is known, for instance, about the way in which innovative activity is organized; how it is introduced, and at what cost; what conditions the time of introduction; and what factors govern the pace of diffusion.

Below we shall review issues relating to a hypothesis that financial innovation is fundamentally a reaction to constraints imposed by monetary intervention, and that it circumvents such intervention by changing behavioural relations, thus making the established links upon which monetary authorities base their action no longer reliable. The discussion is based mainly on recent literature in the USA and the UK, but is not comprehensive. Financial intervention by regulatory authorities may take a variety of forms. Attention is concentrated to measures directly relevant to the conduct of monetary policy, giving less weight to other forms of regulation such as supervisory or prudential control.

Broadly speaking, there are two forms of monetary action by the authorities: regulations which apply continuously (but not without variations) over a period of time, and which affect the freedom of financial institutions to manage their portfolios (fixed minimum reserve ratios, restrictions on the payment of interest rates on deposits such as the American regulation Q), and measures which are part of central bank market action and which apply variably or in a discretionary way – essentially, the use of instruments of monetary control such as funding and rediscount rates on eligible securities.

7.3.2 The Radcliffe controversy

As already stated, the realization that monetary policy can be frustrated by activities in the financial system has been present in every major monetary discussion from the bullionist disputes in Britain to the present polemic surrounding the use of monetary targets. In the monetary controversy surrounding the publication of the Radcliffe Report (1959) in the UK and the work of Gurley and Shaw (1955, 1960) in the USA, particular attention was paid to the activities of non-bank financial intermediaries. These were said to frustrate monetary policy, which was then concerned principally with the control of commercial bank deposits. It was claimed that a restriction on the expansion of bank credit would drive disappointed borrowers to seek funds from non-bank intermediaries. These in turn, in order to accommodate profitable business opportunity, would seek to attract idle balances by an aggressive interest rate policy (e.g., inducing the public to switch some of its transactions balances from banks to non-banks), resulting in an increase in credit (and thus 'near-money') from the non-bank sector while bank credit (and the money supply) remained restricted (Clayton, 1962).

Thus, the basic tenet of the Radcliffe was that money was not unique in its ability to control nominal expenditure: '. . . monetary action works upon total demand by altering the liquidity position of financial institutions and of firms and people desiring to spend on real resources; the supply of money itself is not the critical factor' (Radcliffe Report, 1959, para. 397). Though a precise definition of 'liquidity' was elusive, the basic proposition was that, in order to influence nominal income, it was important to control the total credit flow and not merely additions to the stock of 'money'.

In that debate, some economists felt that it was in the nature of intermediation by financial institutions to offset monetary constraints:

> When credit conditions are tightened and the creation of new money through
> the banking system is restricted, the financial machinery of the country
> automatically begins to work in such a way as to mobilise the existing supply of
> money more effectively, thus permitting it to do most of the work that would
> have been done by newly created money had credit conditions been easier.
> [Smith, 1956, p. 601]

The implication of the above is a variable income velocity of circulation of
money or an unstable money demand. Like its predecessor of 1931, the
Macmillan Committee, the Radcliffe Committee found velocity to be unstable, stating that 'We cannot find any reason for suggesting, or any
experience in monetary history indicating, that there is any limit to the
velocity of circulation. . . .' (para. 391).

As a matter of broad generalization, it may be said that, in the debates of
the late 1950s and the early 1960s, stress was put, especially in the UK, on
the reactive generation of 'near-money' by existing non-bank financial
intermediaries, and not so much upon innovative activity and the evolution of
the financial sector. That is, *'management reaction' rather than 'creative action'*
in financial markets predominated in the explanations of circumventive behaviour
(compare section 5.1.1). The term 'financial innovation' was only rarely used
until the mid-1970s. Nevertheless, there were studies, at that time, stressing
institutional change and actually utilizing the term in this context. Indeed,
some of them were remarkably sagacious in anticipating the present debate
on financial innovation.

Financial intermediation was seen by Gurley and Shaw (G–S) as an integral
part of economic growth process, being both a determined and a determining
variable in that process. Financial innovation was said to occur in response to
'matching' problems between preferences of surplus or deficit units and the
services offered by the financial sector. But it might also arise from other
causes. For instance, 'any rise in interest rates brought about perhaps by a
combination of restrictive monetary policy and accumulating debt creates the
opportunity for nonbank intermediaries to offer more expensive attractions'
(G–S, 1955, p. 532). 'Monetary control limits the supply of one financial
asset, money. With a sophisticated financial structure providing financial
assets, other than money and bonds, in increasing proportion to both, control
over money alone is a decreasingly efficient means of regulating flows of
loanable funds and spending on goods and services' (p. 537).

Emphasis on institutional change came from H. P. Minsky (1957, p. 185),
who asserted that evolutionary changes in financial institutions are, in
general, the result of profit-seeking activities which are most likely to occur
during periods of high interest rates and monetary restriction, and that 'such
developments in the money market tend to counteract a tight money policy'.
Only in a stable institutional framework would anti-inflationary monetary
action be effective. The author considered two financial innovations which

threatened monetary policy through offsetting increases in the velocity of circulation of money: the early rise of the federal funds market, and RPs between government bond houses and non-financial corporations (see section 5.3.1(b)). These two innovations, then on a small scale, received prominent attention in the discussions on circumventive innovations in the mid-1970s and the 1980s.

In the UK, the stress on institutional changes came after the peak of the Radcliffe debate had passed. It related to financial changes which began to emerge in the 1960s. P. Einzig (1971), for instance, viewed the development of parallel money markets as, in a large measure, a result of continuous monetary control applying only to clearing banks.

Two conflicting interpretations of the Radcliffe proposition emerged. The first, associated with Sayers (1960) and touched upon in section 1.2.2, totally rejected the usefulness of the money supply–money demand paradigm. The alternative squeezed the Radcliffe theory, with considerable loss of vital information, into the traditional mould of that paradigm, in the name of integrating the Radcliffe thesis with the main corpus of economic analysis. This was first suggested by G–S (1960, pp. 163, 212–18) and became generally accepted, especially in the USA. The Radcliffe proposition was thus analysed in terms of a change in the slope and intercept of the demand-for-money schedule.

However, within this analytical framework, economists often reached contradictory results. The more general interpretation was to comply with the basic principle that the availability of substitutes renders the demand for a product more price-elastic. Patinkin (1961) analysed the creation of a new financial instrument in terms of a leftward shift of the demand for money (as some balances previously held in the form of money are converted into the holding of the substitute), M_{d0} to M_{d1} in figure 7.1(a), and a change in the slope from M_{d1} to M_{d2}, making the money demand more interest-elastic. In terms of the *IS–LM* model (see appendix to chapter 1), this would decrease the monetary multiplier and increase the expenditure multiplier, thus rendering monetary policy less effective.

Some economists, however, claimed that the introduction of a new financial asset might have a different effect on different holders of money, causing them to experience different shifts and changes in elasticity. Those with relatively inelastic demands might have a dominant influence on the overall demand for money (Marty, 1961, pp. 59–60). The ultimate effect would be for M_d to become less interest-elastic. With the aid of figure 7.1(b), the analysis follows the same path as in figure 7.1(a), but after the shift to M_{d1} the slope of M_d decreases as for M_{d2}.

A different process of thought led L. S. R. Ritter (1962) to a similar conclusion: M_d would become less elastic with respect to long-term interest rate changes because new financial instruments would be complements rather than substitutes for 'money', but substitutes for long-term assets. Thus,

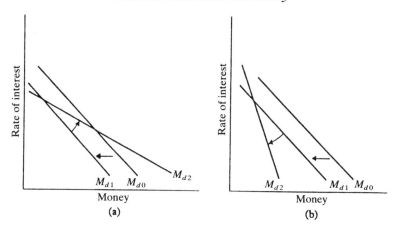

Figure 7.1 Money substitutes and the demand for money: alternative hypotheses.

changes in interest rates might involve substitutions between long-term securities and new interest-bearing assets, but not with money holdings (compare the views of Friedman and Schwartz (F–S), in section 1.3.2). The implications of the latter interpretation conflict with those of the previous one. *LM* would become less interest-elastic, suggesting an enhanced stabilization property of monetary policy.

We may recall that, subsequently, many empirical studies revealed that the interest elasticity of the demand for money was not rising, while money substitutes increased. Cagan and Schwartz (1975), having analysed the US data for the 1921–71 period, found that the elasticity was indeed falling rather than rising. A similar study for the UK (Mills and Wood, 1977) for the period 1922–74 found substantial variations in the interest elasticity of money, but 'despite much financial innovation during the data period, the elasticity displayed no marked secular trend' (p. 32). Both studies claimed to have decisively rejected the Radcliffe hypothesis. Their conclusions must, however, be reviewed in the light of the latest debate on financial innovation and doubts about the robustness of the studies of money demand at that time.

Thus, the Radcliffe debate fizzled out in a confused state when the monetarist counter-revolution focused attention, once again, on the money stock (section 1.3.2). To reiterate, the Radcliffe Committee advocated a 'financial theory of money' (section 1.2.2) and was sceptical about the usefulness of the money supply paradigm for purposes of macroeconomic analysis. It stressed the interrelations in the financial sector:

The ease with which money can be raised depends on the one hand upon the composition of the spender's assets and on his borrowing power and on the other hand upon the methods, moods and resources of financial institutions and other firms which are prepared (on terms) to finance other people's spending. [Radcliffe Report, 1959, para. 389]

Immediate access to money did not play a critical role in decision-taking.

7.3.3 *Regulation, currency competition and the financial structure*

In both the UK and the USA, one practical impact of the Radcliffe debates was the gradual extension of monetary control to embrace a wider set of financial intermediaries and not just commercial banks. This was done partly in the interest of more effective control (viz. less circumvention by intermediaries which remain unconstrained) and partly on the grounds of equity. Thus, we now have less discrimination between institutions, though discrimination still exists. In the UK, however, many traditional financial and monetary controls have now been removed, leaving the authorities effectively with only interest rates to influence monetary growth (section 6.1.1). It is of some significance that, even in this relatively regulation-free environment, financial innovations continue to frustrate monetary policy (BE, 1983a, 1983b).

It is also of some significance that, in the present monetary debate, the hypothesis of circumventive innovation is most strongly advanced in the USA, emphasizing, in particular, the circumvention of regulations applying in a continuous way (see section 5.3.1). We have already observed that, in the USA, regulations in the financial sphere contrasted with free enterprise elsewhere. Even in the 1980s, to indicate the extent of fragmentation attributable to the regulatory regime, the USA is said to have some of the best banks in the world but the world's worst banking system, where the 13 largest banks own $225 billion of domestic deposits (15.6 per cent of the total) and there are 1,934 insured commercial banks with assets of less than $10 million (Wallich, 1984, p. 25).[3]

It is interesting to observe that some influential schools of libertarian economics (the Currency school of the nineteenth century, present 'monetarists'), while stressing the entrepreneurial force of free, self-interested economic agents in the real economy, advocate strong monetary control (restriction), thereby underestimating the ingenuity of agents to overcome monetary obstacles; and that, while emphasizing the self-regulating properties of the real market, they deny such properties as far as the quantity of money is concerned. Those factions of libertarian economics which challenged such inconsistent positions remained ignored until recently. Hayek for some time has maintained that market forces are the best regulators of monetary relations, and he strenuously opposed the state monopoly of money. 'The past instability of the market economy is the consequence of the exclusion of the most important regulator of the market mechanism, money, from itself being regulated by the market forces' (Hayek, 1976, p. 47).

Much attention is now devoted to the dusting-down of some nineteenth-century British 'free banking' debates (White, 1984b) and the Austrian theories of 'free banking'. New versions of 'competitive money', 'competitive currency' or 'free-market money' theories have begun to proliferate. 'Currency competition is free if the users of money are free to choose the currency which suits them best and if private entrepreneurs are free to produce as much of their own money as they wish' (Vaubel, 1977, p. 437). Hayek's analysis of currency competition has been extended and advanced particularly by Vaubel (1977, 1984), who demonstrated that the forces of free competition in the issue of money, far from leading to inflation, prevent inflationary impluses mainly by checking the expansionary proclivities of the government and permitting users to manage their portfolios more effectively. The author's analysis, however, points to the 'money industry' being subject to declining costs. Ultimately, currency competition destroys itself through large economies of scale in the use of money. The financial industry tends towards a union and must be nationalized. Thus, the salutary effects of free currency competition are not infinite.

It should be made clear that the proponents of free money are not necessarily against some form of monetary constitution, and do not necessarily object to the institution of legal tender. They are, however, against the state or central bank limiting currency competition by regulation (that is, against 'enforced tender') and managing money in a discretionary way. Such a power offers governments the incentive to create money in order to finance public expenditure, leading to inflation (Bernholz, 1983, pp. 397–411).

Considerable interest in 'free money' is now reflected in the American literature. S. I. Greenbaum and C. F. Heywood (1971) are usually identified with the 'regulation theory of financial innovation' (e.g. Silber, 1975b, p. 64). In fact, the two authors considered a more general explanation of a diversified financial structure rather than circumventory processes. Technology and regulation were seen as the dominant influences on the evolution of the structure of firms in the financial sector. Technological progress, together with the rise of wealth and the desire to avoid risk, helped to explain growth in the financial industry and an increasing menu of financial assets. These factors alone could not, however, explain the high degree of diversification in the structure of the industry. In the absence of regulations, there would be fewer firms and less specialization in the financial sector.

Regulators imposed restrictions for the sake of 'stability' (serving the interests of the public, management, and the owners of industry or the regulators). 'Regulatory agencies seek stability by pinning, with varying degrees of rigidity, variables that are otherwise market-determined' (Greenbaum and Haywood, 1971, p. 585). If existing interests continued to be protected, and if technological change created new opportunity, new financial institutions would develop and in time would become candidates for protection in exchange for a restriction of their activities. However, the objective of the regulators to secure 'stability' might misfire during a period of economic difficulty: 'a policy that encourages specialized financial institutions runs the risk of instability or substantially increased intervention when interest-rate movements become erratic' (p. 586). The main point is that the structure of the financial industry is critically affected by regulations, and would be quite different if it were shaped by free market forces alone.

This trend of thought has been taken a step further by the 'new monetary economics' first mentioned in section 2.1. Though the school does not represent an entirely uniform theory (White, 1984a), it does stress that our orthodox monetary theories were hitherto unwittingly based on regularities and phenomena justified by the existence of binding monetary regulation, not totally or effectively circumvented. Thus, the quantity theory is, in some quarters, seen as 'nothing more than an artifact of government regulation. An economy organized along free-market principles could function without money at all' (Hall, 1982, p. 1552). Elsewhere (Fama, 1980, 1983), government monetary and financial regulations are seen as a critical factor explaining the nature of money and the demand for it in fiduciary monetary standards such as those which have operated in the last century in the UK and the USA. Monetary systems were founded on regulations which created artificially the demand for central bank reserves (high-powered money) in which prices were denominated. Regulations are the key foundation of control over the money supply. They stabilize the demand for money through monetary constraints (e.g. reserve requirements) which are further buttressed by yet more regulations prohibiting non-bank financial institutions from undertaking banking transactions and controlling their portfolios. Money and the constructs of the traditional monetary economics are thus essentially the products of regulations, and inefficient regulations at that.

The concept of the 'legal restrictions theory of the demand for money' has also been used (Wallace, 1983) to explain the coexistence of alternative default-free assets on which yields at any point of time differ significantly. Under a *laissez-faire system*, the demand for zero-return government currency would be reduced (possibly to zero) and the private sector would supply notes with returns reflecting supply costs where high-denomination paper might merit a return similar to a quantity discount.

Free market economies would have had an entirely different (more efficient) financial system (settlements and intermediation) which could function without money. 'Central bank intermediation matters only in the presence of binding legal restrictions' (Wallace, 1983, p. 6).

7.3.4 *Circumventive processess*

The above regulatory theories of financial structure and money demand are not inconsistent with the hypothesis of circumventive innovation, but they stress a different aspect of the influence of regulations on financial activity. Interest in them is motivated by an anticipation of completely regulation-free banking or a search for a criterion of theoretical efficiency with which to evaluate present monetary arrangements. However, economies are still far removed from idealized *laissez-faire* monetary arrangements. Some economists lend support to the view that regulations, and indeed government monetary policy in general, create situations which induce financial firms to innovate and discover ways of avoiding the official constraints, and thereby frustrating the objectives of intervention. Strong support for such a hypothesis comes from the work of E. J. Kane (1977, 1981, 1983) and D. D. Hester (1981).

In his analysis of financial innovation, Kane concentrates on the general processes through which US regulations concerning financial institutions, principally banks, have been eroded by the regulatees 'blowing round' the restrictive measures imposed on them.

The regulations which impede the realization of these objectives, seen in terms of the growth of total assets and a diversification of activities (compare section 6.2.2), include restrictions on branching in different geographical areas, on mergers or entry into different lines of business, and, most of all, on price (interest rate) competition for deposits. Such regulations originated primarily for prudential motives (safety and soundness of banking), but they tended to evolve and later embraced other regulations, brought about for different reasons, including those protecting politically strong sectors.

The circumvention of financial control is discussed in the framework of the 'regulatory dialectic', mentioned earlier, in which the invisible hand of the market interacts with the visible hand of the regulatory authorities in a cyclical fashion. Thus, 'a new regulation kicks off an immediate search for feasible avoidance or circumvention activities' (Kane, 1981, p. 358). Circumvention results typically in the generation of 'substitute' or 'formally different' products not subject to regulation. Regulatory agencies then tend to react and in time to re-regulate, thus disturbing again the opportunities facing regulatees and starting a new cycle.

The above interaction is subject to time lags. The adaptive efficiency of regulatees has been better, owing essentially to accelerating technological advancement and the greater alertness of financial institutions to uncertainties caused by inflation and other environmental changes. On the other hand, regulatory agencies are constrained in their re-regulating reactions chiefly by bureaucratic and political impediments and uncertainties. 'The political system is far more forgiving of excessive delay than it is of hasty and ill-considered action' (Kane, 1981, p. 361). Thus, 'avoidance lags tend to be shorter than regulatory lags' (Kane, 1983, p. 97).

As a result of the slower state response in the dialectic process, considerable deregulation has been achieved. Indeed, the Monetary Control Act of 1980, referred to earlier, in effect, formally brought innovatory financial practices within the law, and in some cases permitted the extension of their use (e.g. the NOW accounts discussed in section 5.3.2).

Strong though qualified support for the hypothesis of circumventive innovation comes from Hester (1981, p. 141), who, having reviewed seven financial innovations which occurred in the US economy mainly after 1960, concluded that 'each of the innovations is itself a response to conditions that existed in money and capital markets on some date. Indeed, it can be claimed that each innovation was induced by monetary policy decisions that were taken before that date.' However, the notion that innovation is induced by monetary actions needs to be qualified by considering the underlying conditions and the environment in which circumventory processes would develop. Before elaborating these, some preliminary points should be made.

Hester selected for his investigations innovations which are usually considered to be of prime importance to the conduct of monetary policy (with the possible exception of financial futures markets). These include negotiable CDs, Eurobranching, RPs, MMMFs and one-bank holding companies. He demonstrated effectively that recent US monetary history could be characterized by successive phases of monetary restraint and innovative activity, and that the Federal Reserve authorities had failed to counter innovations successfully in the interest of the effectiveness of monetary policy. Finally, innovations were judged to have been on the whole beneficial, essentially because they overcame restrictions on the efficient operations of money and capital markets. Innovations occurred normally when a combination of forces was at work. The most important of these were high and variable interest rates, changes in the regulatory regime and ambiguities in regulations, and technical progress in information processing.

High and variable interest rates, usually, but not necessarily induced by monetary policy, were seen as the most important cause of innovations. It seems that innovations began to occur, or to increase their rate of diffusion, when interest rates reached a certain threshold level. In the USA interest rate ceilings on deposits imposed under regulation Q played an important part in providing such a threshold.

We have seen in section 5.3 that when, in 1966, regulation Q became binding at or below market rates, a wave of financial innovations was observed. The innovations included some not elaborated earlier, such as the 'congeneric transformation of banks' into one-bank holding company organizations, capable of avoiding monetary restrictions imposed on banks. Episodes of high interest rates in later years (1969, 1973, 1974) were, in a similar way, associated with innovatory activity, weakening monetary policy.

Hester identified two waves of innovationary activity in the USA (1966–9) and 1973–5), induced by restrictive monetary policy and high interest rates, combined with other underlying economic conditions. These resulted in making the accepted linkages between monetary aggregates unreliable, manifesting themselves in a rise in the velocity of the circulation of money (usually M1).

The overriding conclusion is that 'financial institutions innovate whenever customer relationships are jeopardized by slow monetary growth' (Hester, 1981, p. 183). This condition occurs predominantly during restrictive monetary policies based either on market actions manifested in high interest rates or on restrictive regulatory measures. In the process of their diffusion, innovations alter relations between macroeconomic variables and result in a significant weakening of the ability of monetary policy to achieve its aims.

An interesting hypothesis relevant to the evaluation of the nexus between regulation and institutional change was advanced by Wojnilower (1980) on the basis of an analysis of the last 30 years of US financial history. He stated that credit shortages at the peaks of trade cycles were mainly responsible for financial innovation and regulatory change. This contrasts with previous propositions, where high interest rates were highlighted as a vital, ubiquitous ingredient of circumventive innovation – or indeed its principal stimulus.

Wojnilower denied that the demand for credit was interest-elastic. 'The growth of credit is therefore essentially supply-determined' (1980, p. 277). Reductions in credit and aggregate demand occur only because of interruptions in the credit supply, a 'credit crunch'. Such interruptions can arise from a variety of causes, such as regulatory obstacles (e.g. ceilings on interest rates) or a loss of confidence consequent upon the failure of a major business institution or market. For example, this occurred in 1966, when regulation Q became effective unexpectedly (because on previous occasions, when market interest rates approached the ceiling, the ceiling was lifted), undermining the liability management of banks (particularly those using CDs) and forcing financial institutions to cut their advances. 'Lending to all but the most established and necessitous customers was halted abruptly (Wojnilower, 1980, p. 287). The 1970 'credit crunch' followed the failure of Penn Central Transportation Company. 'It prompted an instant toughening of perceived borrowing capacity by business firms' (p. 293).

Following such credit bottlenecks, both the authorities ('to avoid the consequent recessions') and the private markets ('to protect future earnings') deliberately undertook measures which were designed to prevent a future interruption in the flow of credit. Thus, financial innovation, often prompted by regulatory inadequacies, is seen as a product of restricted *credit availability* rather than the high cost of credit stressed in the studies mentioned above. The results of such financial innovations were, in general, 'increases in credit, interest rates, and inflation. . . .' (p. 278).

7.3.5   *Aberrant behaviour*

To what extent can monetary authorities enforce their intended restrictive action, or react effectively to circumvention by private financial institutions? One strategy might be for the authorities to take steps in order to prevent financial innovation from taking place. They could re-regulate, though this would in time encourage further avoiding or evasive innovation (Kane's dialectic process). They could relax market action to allow monetary expansion – but this would undoubtedly defeat the original objectives of controlling inflation. Preferably, they could design a monetary strategy which would take into account the circumventory propensities of financial institutions. Such a design would have to be based on a sound knowledge of innovationary processes in the private financial sector, which so far it is doubtful that we possess.

There can be a number of difficulties standing in the way of designing a monetary strategy based on the control of the quantity of money which would incorporate arrangements anticipating financial innovations or counteracting their effects. Financial innovations are, in general, difficult to detect, and are not easily predictable.

Innovations tend to remain unnoticed for some time. They start on a small scale – 'grow from small seeds' – and at first escape notice. Their potential for circumvention is not appreciated until after diffusion has taken place through wider adoption and imitation (Hester, 1981). We may note that a similar point was made by Minsky as early as 1957, when he observed that financial changes 'often centre around some technical detail of money-market behaviour, and, as they usually start in a small scale, their significance for monetary policy is generally ignored at the time they first occur' (p. 171).

Innovating institutions hardly volunteer information on their new activity and might not be helpful in the initial stages of authorities' attempts to monitor developments. 'Secrecy, deception, and incomplete information are ever-present barriers to a monetary authority seeking to apply monetary controls to an economy in transition' (Hester, 1981, pp. 170–1).

The authorities might also fail to appreciate the threat posed by a particular innovation and hence might be slow to initiate measurement and monitoring. 'The standard requirement for an innovation to be taken seriously is empirical evidence of its occurrence' (Hester, 1981, p. 171). Furthermore, where the appearance of an innovation had not been overlooked by the authorities, there might still be a delay in taking action because of the uncertainty as to the direction and magnitude of its effect on monetary policy – a minimum number of observation points would normally be needed, for instance, to work out its impact on the demand for a targeted money (Freedman, 1983, pp. 104–5). In the UK it seems that, even after three years, it is not clear what behavioural characteristics M2 possesses; it was introduced to take account of innovations making M1 and £M3 less reliable (section 4.2).

Thus, a considerable time might elapse between the appearance or identification of an innovation and a possible reaction to it by the authorities. From the point of view of an indicative definition of money, the inclusion of a new financial instrument either into the domain of monetary assets or into a redefined or new monetary aggregate is likely to take place after considerable, though unknown, delay.

Financial innovations are therefore not easily predictable and are difficult to monitor, and their impact on monetary policy is difficult to forecast. Furthermore, they tend to be irreversible in the sense that they do not disappear when the underlying innovation-inducing symptoms recede. Thus, accounts or cash management devices inspired by high interest rates, and Eurocurrency arrangements made to avoid national restrictions, do not fade away when interest rates fall or restrictions are withdrawn. They add to the stock of financial knowledge and experience, and their continuation makes the financial system more flexible and conducive to new circumventing arrangements.

In conclusion, there is considerable evidence of interaction between monetary control measures and financial innovation. Monetary regulations are highlighted as key factors inducing avoiding behaviour, yet they appear to be only one of the necessary conditions for innovation to take place. From the evidence available so far, we cannot deduce that creative financial response is inevitably and exclusively a reaction to monetary restriction. Innovation continues to occur and to affect monetary control even in countries relatively free from continuous monetary restrictions. The overwhelming impression, however, is that we have not yet researched the subject sufficiently to be confident about the nature of circumventive innovation – especially the conditions necessary for its 'take-off', the rate of diffusion, the factors governing diffusion, and the extent to which it lends itself to anticipation or counteraction by the authorities. Perhaps one of the most intriguing and puzzling aspects is reversibility.

What is clear is that, in the realm of monetary relations, a mechanical sliding up and down a traditional money demand curve is a gross oversimplification. Rising interest rates are an important catalyst of innovative activity and appear to contribute to irreversible supply-side changes. At this stage we recognize that financial innovation does widely occur, is difficult to detect in the early stages of development, is rather unpredictable, and has been an important factor in re-regulatory and deregulatory processes. Furthermore, it does change established monetary relationships, making monetary control unreliable if not ineffective. Hester (1981) conjectured that

a monetary authority that wants to achieve a target level of economic activity probably should reduce the growth rate of monetary aggregates or increase interest rates when it perceives that innovations are occurring. However, its action might be self-defeating. There is no assurance that its objective can be achieved more than temporarily; it may just spawn another round of innovations. [Hester, 1981, p. 142]

7.4 The hypothesis of transactions cost

7.4.1 *Financial innovations and transactions costs*

On a number of occasions, the importance of transactions costs has been mentioned (see sections 1.4, 5.3.4, 6.4). The purpose of this section is to consider a hypothesis that the dominant factor in financial innovation is the reduction of transactions costs. There are two aspects of this proposition: (1) that the reduction of transactions costs is seen as the prime motive for financial innovation, and (2) that financial innovation is essentially a response to the potential for cost reduction offered primarily by technical progress. Perhaps the best-known protagonist of the former, more general, view is J. R. Hicks. More recently, J. Niehans has emphasized the latter aspect, claiming that: 'The primary (though not the only) motor of financial innovations is the gradual decline in transactions costs' (1982, p.27). Thus, financial evolution is interpreted as a reflection of technical progress which reduces the costs, though it is admitted that we do not have a full analytical understanding of this process.

As already stated, transactions costs are not easy to define and are even more difficult to measure. They are frequently described as the costs of 'going to a bank' or as broker's fees, which include a variety of costs such as direct charges for buying and selling financial assets (brokerage) and the cost of transferring the title to ownership between contracting parties. Baumol's (1952, p. 546) 'broker's fee' encompasses all non-interest-rate costs of borrowing and making cash withdrawals, including 'opportunity losses' arising from having to dispose of an asset at the time when cash is needed. Important components of transactions costs are those whose roots are ultimately found in uncertainty, namely search and information (gathering and processing) costs. These may range from the costs of using information technology, indispensable in liability or cash management, to reading the financial pages.

Although in their empirical work economists neglected transactions costs, largely because of the difficulties of definition and measurement, they frequently highlighted them in the *theory* of the demand for money (see section 1.4). When, in 1935, Hicks first turned to monetary economics and began to consider its basic principles, he identified what he thought to be the 'central issue in the pure theory of money', namely why, when interest rates were positive, people would hold money rather than lend it or use it to pay off old debts (Hicks, 1967, p. 66).

Issues raised by this question troubled Keynes too, and are still being considered in the incessant debate on the demand for money. Hicks felt at the time that the answer would have to be given in terms of 'frictions' (rather than uncertainty, as proposed by Keynes), and he criticized economists for neglecting frictions in economic theory.

The friction singled out as being the most obvious and important was the cost of transferring assets from one form to another. 'This is of exactly the same character as the cost of transfer which acts as a certain impediment to change in all parts of the economic system. . . .' Such transactions costs were also considered in the context of the impact on the demand for money of such factors as the risk of investments, the expected net yield on assets, the income and wealth of investors, and the supply of money substitutes. Holding money was seen as a way of avoiding risk for low-income units at a given transfer cost, but it also inhibited a wide diversification of portfolios as a way of avoiding risk by large-income groups.

Transactions costs were clearly preceived as an important determinant of the demand for money; their reduction would reduce the demand, but would also have wider repercussions. Hicks anticipated a number of developments in monetary theory and, in conclusion, reflected that high transactions costs make economic units 'insensitive' to changes in anticipations and hence contribute to the stability of capitalism. Decreases in these costs in the course of the development of capitalism are 'likely to be a direct cause of increasing fluctuations' (Hicks, 1967, p. 81).

In his later work on money, Hicks frequently returned to the theme of transactions costs in monetary theory and policy and inspired current investigations into the Walrasian system with money (see section 3.1.1). The *raison d'être* for money was indeed conceived in terms of lowering transactions costs (1967, pp. 4–16), and the motive for doing this was no different from the motive to reduce other costs: 'one way of looking at monetary evolution is to regard it as the development of ever more sophisticated ways of reducing transaction costs'. Thus, the generation of different media serving as money, the development of new, better organized markets, the genesis of such devices as the cheque system and the clearing system, and the evolution of liquidity management (1967, pp. 31–6) are all linked by the drive to lower transactions costs.

While not contradicting the above approach, and recognizing that both currency and 'bank money' owe their existence to transactions costs, Niehans (1982) focused on the impact of modern information technology on transactions costs and on financial innovation. Indeed, as observed in section 6.4.3, to Niehans (1983), only technological change reflected in the reduction of transactions costs constitutes true innovation. New ways of bundling and unbundling financial services amount merely to 'adaptive innovation'. The basic point is that 'the financial evolution of recent decades can, to a considerable extent, be interpreted as a response to declining transactions costs. Today, both the theory of bank money creation and policy-makers are still groping for a fuller analytical understanding of this evolution' (Niehans, 1982, p. 17).

7.4.2   Decline in the demand for traditional money

Under the influence of the Keynesian liquidity preference theory, the transactions demand is frequently distinguished from the asset demand for money, the former being often presented on the basis of inventory models originally suggested by Baumol (1952), and the latter following Tobin's (1958) mean–variance model of portfolio balance.

Confining our analysis to the traditional concept of money as a non-interest-bearing means of transactions (base or possibly M1), it can be intuitively concluded that falling transactions costs would imply holding less money as a reserve or for transactions purposes. This, indeed, is consistent with both deterministic and probabilistic transactions money demand models.[4]

Niehans (1978, 1982) offers a less restrictive model for the analysis of the demand for money by combining elements of Baumol's inventory-theoretic model (stressing transactions costs) with Tobin's mean–variance model (stressing uncertainty about interest rates), deriving a complex expression for the investment opportunity locus analogous to that of Tobin (1958):[5]

$$E\left(\pi\right) = \frac{E(i)}{\sigma_i}\,\sigma_\pi - 4cn + 4cn\,\sqrt{1 - \frac{\sigma_\pi}{\sigma_i}}$$

where $E(\pi)$ is the expected mean return on portfolio, consisting of money and a security (consol); the price of the security in conditions of uncertainty fluctuates randomly, resulting in the distribution of interest rate i with $E(i)$ the mean and σ_i the standard deviation; σ_π is portfolio risk, which, for a given σ_i, is determined by the proportion of the portfolio held by securities (viz. the proportion times σ_i); c represents transactions costs, which in this model are proportional to the values invested; and n is the number of income periods, assuming that annual income is received regularly in n equal instalments. The above expression may be approximated in figure 7.2 by schedule OP_1 in the same mean–variance space as the familiar Tobin model; the main difference between this investment opportunity locus and that of Tobin is that the latter is a straight line; whereas the former has decreasing the latter has constant marginal returns as money content α falls and security content $(1-\alpha)$ of the portfolio rises in figure 7.2.

The optimum portfolio which would maximize the investor's utility would depend on the investor's preference with respect to expected return and risk. An investor who is risk-neutral (or is acting in the absence of uncertainty) would choose the portfolio with maximum return at point A. However, a risk-averter with the standard upward-sloping indifference curve, such as I_1, would select a portfolio to the left of A. Given I_1 curve, investor's utility would be maximized at B when it would consist of α_1 money and $(1-\alpha_1)$ securities $(0 \leqslant \alpha \leqslant 1)$.

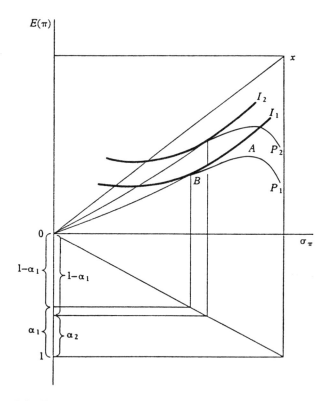

Figure 7.2   Demand for money, with uncertainty and transactions costs.

A fall in transactions costs c would lead to a rise in the opportunity locus to OP_2 as shown in figure 7.2 and to a new utility-maximizing portfolio consisting of less cash and more securities $(\alpha_1 > \alpha_2)$. A rise to a new indifference curve (assuming no income effect) indicates increased welfare for the investor. As transactions costs fall, the opportunity locus to the left of its maximum becomes steeper and to the right flatter, both drifting towards line OX. The share of money in the portfolio would decline. If transactions costs were to fall to zero $(c = 0)$, then the opportunity locus would become a straight line, as indicated by the first component of the equation above, and it would be indistinguishable from the opportunity line in Tobin's mean–variance model. This would indicate that money would be held only as an asset. One would then have to reflect on the extent to which a non-interest-bearing asset would be held if relatively safe interest-earning assets were available and could be acquired without paying transfer costs.

Could technological change and financial innovation reduce transaction costs to a negligible level or eliminate them completely? A response to this must be rather speculative.

The effect of the vanishing demand for money on monetary theory and policy would be quite profound. Briefly, as 'money' fades away, the traditional concepts would become obsolete. For instance, to survive, the quantity theory would have to be rewritten; the place of money would have to be taken by exogenous government debt. 'The quantity theory relates not so much to money as to the whole array of financial assets exogenously supplied by the government' (Niehans, 1982, p. 9). In the context of the monetarist macroeconomic system, the neutrality principle, mentioned in section 1.1.1, would still operate, but the array of government assets would take the place of money. In a cashless world, government bonds become claims to future streams of commodities or other assets and not to future streams of money (White, 1984a, p. 710). Thus, government activity would determine, instead of money, the exogenous debt and interest rate structure, and therefore the price level. In the long run, real variables would be neutral with respect to the whole debt (Niehans, 1982, p. 23).

With regard to monetary policy, banks would not hold many reserves and would adjust mainly to the structure of interest rates. Central bank policy would be based not on the control of any monetary target, but on the maturity transformation of assets and on its effect on the structure of interest rates. This conclusion is almost identical to that of the Radcliffe Committee, reached (by a different process of thought) not long before the monetarist influence began to gather momentum in the 1960s. Hicks also predicted a tendency towards a 'credit economy', defined as 'one that contains no money that does not bear interest; so that the key instrument of monetary control must be the rate of interest or interest rates' (1982, p. 230).

7.4.3 *Other effects*

We have considered the growing obsolescence of money when transactions costs are falling. In such a situation, the demand for interest-bearing money substitutes rises and differences between 'money' and 'non-money' assets become fuzzy, but the spectrum of instruments used for making payments increases (BIS, 1983, p. 59).

Decreasing transactions costs, brought about mainly by technological progress (section 6.4), permit effective liability management. As financial and non-financial units become more sensitive to investment opportunities, and are better able to take advantage of them owing to falling transactions costs, defensive innovations become part of the competitive reaction, which includes making financial markets more contestable (Kane, 1983, p. 99) (compare section 6.4). This increases the 'competitive aggressiveness' of economic agents (BE, 1983b, p. 374) and enhances their circumventive capacity, encouraging financial innovations designed to bypass officially imposed restrictions.

With high transactions costs, the enforcement of regulations is relatively easy as regulations and optimal financial management are related by the same costs. However, with declining transactions costs, 'such regulative measures will increasingly be evaded by structural shifts in the financial industry, the regulated sector shrinking while the free sector expands'. The Eurocurrency market is offered as a good example of this (Niehans, 1982, 1983). By using technological advances to drive the costs down, imperfections created by domestic policy measures were overcome by the setting up of a new innovative, and near-perfect, financial market using interest-bearing money. The current progress in computing and information technology in finance is expected to extend similar effects at the domestic level.

The explanation of financial innovation exclusively in terms of a response to declining transactions costs, whether induced by technological change or in any other way such as competition, is probably an oversimplification. It forms, however, a useful hypothesis deserving of further investigations.

The characteristic feature of our attempts to probe into the innovation-inducing factors is that *a combination of circumstances seems necessary for financial innovation to occur.* It is unlikely that a simple hypothesis will suffice to explain innovation-generating influences and processes. Indeed, no simple hypothesis is likely to be sufficient to explain monetary and financial behaviour and how the financial system reacts to change or manages change. *Financial innovation is essentially a manifestation of interdependent influences, and the process of financial innovation seems complex and as yet not fully understood.* It seems to require what J. S. Fjorde (BE, 1983b, p. 376) called 'an integrated study', a multi-disciplinary approach, not often attempted by modern economists.

7.5 Empirical studies and financial innovation

7.5.1 *The need for microeconomic enquiries*

Most studies of financial innovations are confined to a general, descriptive treatment of innovative processes with reference to monetary theory or policy. Those who have probed the subject agree that financial innovation deserves much more investigation and that new research programmes in this area should be encouraged. Certainly there is a great need for more statistical studies of a microeconomic nature into financial innovatory stimuli and processes (see section 5.1).

It is in the macroeconomic context that financial innovation has recently received most attention. A notable exception is a pioneering study by M.

Ben-Horim and W. L. Silber (1977). This follows Silber's hypothesis of constraint-induced innovation, mentioned earlier.

Banks, or financial firms in general, are assumed to be profit-maximizers reacting to profit opportunities by innovating. This proposition was investigated with the help of a linear programming model of the portfolio behaviour of a financial firm. Using historic data, the model was solved period by period and the shadow price of the constraints was derived as a byproduct of optimization. The hypothesis was that the time series of the shadow prices should rise (signifying a rising cost of adhering to constraints) prior to the introduction of financial innovation and then drop after the introduction.

The study was reasonably successful in identifying the pressure to innovate (high shadow prices) prior to the introductin of CDs in the USA. Such an approach can clearly be attempted to predict the likely timing of innovations or an increase in the rate of diffusion of innovation by firms. Its use might be more appropriate to the innovation of financial instruments by institutions than to the creation of new institutions or markets. The need for detailed data might be a factor discouraging its more widespread utilization.

Further support for the hypothesis of constraint-induced innovation is offered in a study which is basically a check-list of 'exogenous causes' of 38 financial innovations in the USA during the 1970–82 period (Silber, 1983). The main potential causes of the innovations are given as: inflation, volatility of interest rates, technology, regulative changes, internationalization. The study, however, is more of a plea for further investigations of the innovations identified than a coherent and completed empirical work.

The main empirical effort involving financial innovations was made in the context of the demand-for-money studies. Its catalyst was the instability of the function first observed in the 1970s. The vast majority of the studies are American and refer to the frequent overprediction of money demanded by the standard demand-for-money functions in the 1970s.[6] The objective was to clarify the 'missing money' phenomenon, and financial innovations were among the most plausible potential explanations.

It may be observed that, just as in the case of the Gurley–Shaw and Radcliffe debate, economists almost instinctively turned to the demand-for-money paradigm when faced with the possibility of financial change causing monetary instability. There was, once again, a strong presumption that an intrinsically stable demand for money exists, but that it needs to be respecified.

A wide-ranging debate followed the identification of the instability of conventionally specified demand-for-money functions. It is assumed that readers are familiar with the main strands of this debate and thus no attempt is made here at a comprehensive summary, particularly as this has been well accomplished elsewhere (Judd and Scadding (J–S), 1982).

Attention is given mainly to financial innovation, though clearly it is difficult to separate a specific issue such as this from more general matters dealing, for instance, with the specification or selection of data. It should also be remembered that, in view of the rich variety of specifications and data used, almost any generalization involves a risk of omission or commission.

7.5.2   *Financial innovations and the instability of the money demand*

The breakdown of the standard demand-for-money relationship in the 1970s has already been mentioned (section 1.4). In an extensive study of the behaviour of US money aggregates, T. D. Simpson and R. D. Porter (1980) set out, among other things, to 'convince the skeptic that in the last six years something new has happened to the money demand relationship' (p. 172). In spite of their evidence, together with other studies corroborating it, some sceptics continue to defend the conventional theory of demand-for-money stability. R. W. Hafer and S. E. Hein presented empirical evidence arguing that the traditional short-run equation for money demand M1 in 1974 was only subject to a downward (intercept, not slope) shift, and concluded (1982, p. 16) that 'the economic relationships inherent in the conventional money demand functions are more stable than previous investigations have suggested'. Hein (1982) also argued that the causes of observed instability in the 1980s were money supply shocks rather than demand shifts. The underlying money demand relationship (for M1) remained stable during the period of significant financial innovations. This followed a trend of reasoning similar to that of Artis and Lewis (1976) in the UK. Indeed, a set of propositions variously labelled as 'disequilibrium', 'buffer stock' or 'shock absorber' theories of money appeared in an attempt to account for the instability in monetary relationships by emphasizing *temporary* off-demand-curve holdings of money following money 'supply shocks' produced by, for instance, deregulation or credit reforms (White, 1981; Laidler, 1983).

Willing holders of windfall acquisitions of money fail to dispose of the undesired (above-demand) balances quickly owing to some market stickiness or uncertainty, with the consequence that temporary disequilibria on the money market led by money supply increases persist for a time. In some cases it is stressed that interest rates fail to provide the usual equilibrating mechanism, and it is changes in nominal income which gradually absorb the excess money balances. The processes by which the new 'money' is created and acquired by agents are rarely specified, and it is difficult to understand why, in present financial markets, which are increasingly sensitive to market impulses, disequilibria should persist in the holding of assets comprising 'money'. However, though sceptics remain and continue to confirm their faith in the existence of a stable demand-for-money relationship, today most economists agree that the traditional money demand equations are no longer reliable.

From the analysis of financial innovations, we inferred that both a shift and a change in the slope of the demand schedule for money would be expected following some creative financial changes. The debate on the instability, and in particular on the 'missing money' episode (see sections 1.4, 3.2.2), concentrated on the 'shift' in demand (assuming the exclusion of an important variable), but the instability observed in many traditional demand-for-money functions concerned both the intercept and a change in other parameters (J–S, 1982, pp. 995–6).

Advances in econometric methodology (time series analysis, noted in section 3.2.2)), could perhaps, to some degree, explain episodes of instability. It is therefore of some interest to observe that in the USA, where much of the debate on the influence of financial innovation took place, the new econometric methods were not widely adopted. Thus, bearing in mind the contentious meaning attaching to the term 'stability' in the context of the money demand, the view widely accepted was that the traditional demand functions had become unstable and unreliable. Referring to the demand for M1 in the USA, Boughton (1981a, p. 591) concluded that: 'Rather than experiencing a single shift, or even a series of shifts, the function appears to be inherently unstable throughout the 1970s. Demand functions for different aggregates in different countries experienced different degrees of "instability".'

From our point of view, the important issue is the extent to which financial innovation was responsible for the instability. In general, much blame was attributed to two factors which, in an interdependent, financially sophisticated economy, are inherently interconnected: (1) monetary strategy based on attempts to confine monetary growth, and (2) financial innovations, doubtless including the circumventive innovations discussed above. Boughton (1981a, pp. 592–3) summarized it nicely for the USA: 'By attempting more closely to control monetary growth, the Federal Reserve may have altered the underlying demand relationship. The institutional changes affecting M1 certainly contributed to the problem as well.'

In their review of the demand-for-money studies, J–S (1982) were rather cautious in attributing instability in the demand for money to financial innovation. On the basis of studies incorporating innovation-related variables (to be discussed below), they at first found the 'innovation hypothesis as still lacking conclusive confirmation' (p. 1001). However, following the survey of other hypotheses, they admitted that financial innovations were the 'most likely cause' of the instability after 1973. Their caution was motivated by a number of factors (pp. 1001–5), of which three deserve explicit mention. (1) The robustness of some results from equations allowing for financial innovation was suspect, in the sense that the equations performed well in one period but deteriorated in another. (2) It was difficult to explain why household demand-for-money functions shifted by almost the same amount as business demand-for-money functions, on which corporate cash management was expected to have had a strong impact. (3) Some evidence suggested that, in other advanced economies (with the exception of Canada) which experienced both inflation and high interest rates, no instability of the demand for narrowly defined money had been observed.

While not wishing to dispute the first point, it should be stated that the second caveat was based mainly on H. T. Farr *et al.* (1978). Other evidence on the instability of business demand for money (attributable mainly to cash management) as opposed to household demand is available. For periods before 1973, household demand was shown to be stable for most 'definitions' of money, whereas the demand of firms for M1 was unstable (Wilbratte, 1975). For periods after 1973, this was corroborated by Goldfeld (1976, pp. 713–16), who indeed suspected the business sector of being the prime cause of the overall money demand puzzle (p. 725). Innovations affecting households occurred mainly after the mid-1970s (see section 5.3), and there is evidence of their causing some instability (J–S, 1982, p. 1003).

The caveat referring to the demand stability in other advanced countries also invites a comment. Boughton's (1981a) work, included in J–S (1982), concluded that there was instability in M1 in Canada and in M1 and M2 in France, 'a gradual evolution of the coefficients, rather than a specific shift' of M1, and instability of M2 in 1977 in Japan, and instability of £M3 in the UK. Of the five industrial countries, apart from the USA, in no country was there clear-cut evidence of stability of M1, though there was no instability to compare with that of M1 in the USA. It should also be remembered that financial innovation in the USA is further advanced than in other countries (BIS, 1983). More recent studies in the UK indicate that M1 too has deviated from the predicted path (Allen, 1983, pp. 97–103).

Evidence of instability of the traditional demand functions for money elicited quite widespread reaction in terms of attempts to remodel the function to take into account the new monetary developments and thus 'solve' the money puzzle. Readers should, however, recall the methodological difficulties involved in the study of the demand functions when the definition of money is not clear. Financial innovations made it more difficult to provide an indicative definition of money. The 'empirical' quest (see section 3.2) for the definition was, however, still available and was soon utilized.

Two basic approaches were attempted: (1) to 'redefine' the dependent variable by including new money substitutes (e.g. RPs and MMMFs) in the 'definition' of money and (2) to respecify the demand-for-money equation by incorporating one or more 'innovation variables' among the arguments on the right-hand side of the equation.

The first approach in this context is essentially the method of 'defining' money by the criterion of its demand stability (see section 3.2.2). It was utilized in the 'redefinition' of the aggregates in the USA. Not suprisingly, the addition of new liquid assets to narrow aggregates resulted in some improvement in the stability of the demand function, though the statistical significance of the results was questioned (Berkman, 1980b, pp. 147–9). The usefulness of the 'redefining' approach as opposed to the 'respecifying' approach was also questioned by J–S (1982, p. 1001). In a study of the performance of the 'redefined' aggregates in the USA, Berkman (1980a, p. 96) concluded that: 'One unambiguous result these statistical exercises provide is that money demand equations and reduced-form regressions have no power to discriminate among alternative aggregate definitions.'

The more favoured approach was based on the respecification on the right-hand side of the demand equation. Previously we referred to studies (see p. 71) which tried to account for technical change by the inclusion of a time trend in the demand equation. Such a variable hardly conveys an explicit measure of financial innovation, and assumes that technical changes occur uniformly rather than spasmodically. Though financial innovation is a continuing phenomenon, it does not behave in a regular way and indeed is an unpredictable process.

The procedure based on the inclusion of a more explicit innovation variable, or its proxy, was generally judged to be more successful in improving the stability of the demand for money function and its forecasting performance. Studies concentrated on the impact made by financial innovation on corporate cash management or the reduction of transactions costs.[7] The theoretical framework most frequently used was the transactions theory of money demand mentioned in section 7.4. The key difficulty was to find an appropriate proxy for the above variables, as direct measures do not as yet exist.

In attempting to capture the impact of improved cash management, it was thought that a simple surrogate for the relevant financial innovations might be previous-peak variables for interest rates or income or both (Goldfeld, 1976, p. 699; J–S, 1982, pp. 1000–1). Most stress was put on previous peaks of interest rates. The incentive for economizing on liquid resources or for investing in cash management techniques comes essentially from higher interest rates in relation to costs. The new management methods, once adopted, are not normally reversed when interest rates decline (see section 7.3.5). The variables mentioned above have also been used as indicators of the reduction of transactions costs in general.

Using the previous peaks of interest rate variables conveys a 'threshold effect' (see p. 199), whereby the peaking of interest rates draws attention to new opportunities in managing liquidity better. On the other hand, new technology is diffused along some logistic-curve path and might take time to be assimilated. To represent such behaviour, a 'ratchet variable' was developed to smooth somewhat the effect of past peaks (Simpson and Porter, 1980, pp. 179–81). Ratchet variables also seem more plausible than past-peak data as proxies for reductions in transactions costs. Equations using various interest rate ratchet variables provided an 'encouraging' improvement in the standard specification of the demand for money in the 1970s and early 1980s, though problems with the measurement of financial innovations were readily admitted by researchers (e.g. Simpson and Porter, 1980, p. 185). Some of these will be mentioned later.

Innovation variables designed to convey changes in the payments and transactions system were incorporated into the demand functions for non-interest-bearing monetary assets (currency in circulation with the public, M0, non-interest-bearing sight deposits and NIBM1 – see section 4.2) in the UK (Johnston, 1984). Research procedure was based on the general-to-specific econometric methodology outlined in section 3.2.2, and innovation variables were: the number of bank current accounts per head of population; the number of building society share accounts per head of population; the number of ATMs and cash dispensers; and the sum of credit cards issued by Access, American Express and Barclaycard. Such variables were to help to explain the impact on the demand for non-interest-bearing 'money' of cash management in the personal sector and the resulting shift to more attractive interest-bearing accounts. The variables did significantly help to explain the behaviour of non-interest-bearing assets, in particular currency and M0. All 'money' variables were found to be responsive to interest rate changes, non-interest-bearing sight deposits and NIBM1 more so than the other two measures (Johnston, 1984, p. 46).

Though the experiments on the inclusion of innovation variables in the demand-for-money equations met with some success, the design and interpretation of these variables are not clear. Financial innovations, without doubt, contributed significantly to the instability in traditional monetary relationships. They do, however, present a complex set of interactions between economic units, about which we do not yet know very much, and which change the very nature of 'monetary' relationships and perhaps other macroeconomic relationships. It is difficult to imagine how the important interplay between financial innovations and regulation (see section 7.3) can be captured by a simple variable, or how a change in regulation would affect the predictive power of demand functions for various aggregates.

Demand-for-money functions have done a useful job in signalling that changes in the traditional relationships have taken place, and they are indeed capable of reflecting structural changes occurring in the financial system. They can be modified to deal with the impact of some financial innovations, though they are unlikely to take into account their process especially as this process is so unpredictable. 'It is unfortunate that the bulk of the evidence on financial innovations is so indirect, relying as it does on fitting regression equations specified to reflect various implications of theories about financial innovation' (J–S, 1982, p. 1002).

There is now considerable unease about econometric work based essentially on the traditional approaches to monetary theory. Lieberman (1980, p. 44) warned that the technological changes in money markets 'make explorations of even the best-fitting money demand equations hazardous'.

Concluding their work on the impact of financial innovation, mainly corporate cash management, on the demand for money, Porter *et al.* (1979) warned that:

given the unpredictable timing and size of the shifts in M1 demand, it is likely that even the best adjustment will be off the mark. In such an environment, it is more important than ever that policy-makers supplement information on monetary aggregates with data on near money and financial assets, interest rates, and direct indicators of current and future developments in the economy. [Porter *et al.*, 1979, pp. 227–8]

In the UK, Goodhart (1984, p. 180), mindful of the possibility that a swing in monetary growth may reflect a shift in the pace of monetary innovation and not a 'real' development, commented that the recent financial changes imply 'that monetary aggregates should be interpreted and analysed with scrupulous care – on judgemental, institutional and empirical basis, rather than just mechanically extrapolated from previously fitted equations'. The Governor of the Bank of England recently suggested that: 'The real world is a place of ever-changing complexity and untidyness, a difficult reality that contrasts with the predictability and order of economic models' (BE, 1984b, p. 477).

The usefulness of economic or econometric models cannot be denied. It is however doubtful whether, at this time, we possess sufficient understanding of financial innovation, which does appear rather 'untidy', to be confident about utilizing the traditional modelling in their study. In time, new models and techniques will probably be developed, though doubt will always remain about the information content of money aggregates in a changing financial environment.

Notes

1 A comment by A. G. Hart in Wachtel (1982, p. 90).
2 Currently such theories are being re-examined by the NCM school (see e.g. Lucas, 1981).
3 The situation is further complicated by the existence of five federal supervisory authorities (Comptroller of the Currency, Federal Reserve Board, Federal Deposit Insurance Corporation, Federal Home Loan Bank Board, National Credit Union Administration) and 50 state bank regulators.
4 Baumol's model is as follows:

$$M = (bY/2i)^{1/2}$$

where b represents transactions costs, Y the value of transactions and i the interest rate on an alternative to holding money (e.g. a security). An example of a probabilistic model has been given in chapter 5, n. 8, with t standing for transactions costs. As b or t falls, M decreases. When they are zero no money is held. There has been considerable development from the above model. For a survey see D. Fisher (1978, ch. 5).
5 The derivation and the mathematical properties of the model can be found in Niehans (1978, pp. 43–55).

6 These are usually taken to be the Goldfeld (1973, 1976) specifications, but compare section 3.2.2.

7 With reference to the equation given in chapter 5, n. 8, the innovation variables were expected to lower t and σ^2 (that is, the variance of cash flow). The lower value of σ^2 would indicate less uncertainty in receipts and outflows of cash brought about by better cash management methods.

—8—

Concluding Observations: The Post-money Economy

8.1 The main issues

Both monetary theory and monetary policy have, in recent years, been dominated by a currency theory of money, which, though denying the direct relevance of the money supply to real development, emphasizes the importance of controlling it in the interest of price stability, necessary for effective decision-making by economic agents. A targeting of the money supply has been the practical reflection of this philosophy (chapter 1).

Such an approach is rather atavistic, having its roots in financial systems where banks could be associated with the performance of both payments and intermediation functions. In sophisticated financial systems, removed from metallic money standards, the situation is different.

We have argued (chapters 1–2) that the payments and transactions functions attributed to money are, in a sophisticated capitalist economy, performed by the financial system together with other functions of intermediation and asset transmutation. A modern society is essentially a post-money society. It is a credit or *financial economy*, in which it is difficult to identify an 'asset' called 'money' performing the functions ascribed, in the past, to a more primitive commodity money or legal tender. It is even more unreasonable to expect such an 'asset' to sustain the theoretical prerequisites of intermediate targeting, that is, the predictable behaviour of 'money' in relation to control instruments and in relation to the ultimate macroeconomic variables. This is so essentially because financial evolution is related to the capacity of the creative private sector to innovate, thereby generating financial assets, services and markets in response to incentives to overcome market imperfections and uncertainty.

The search for 'money' thus seems rather quixotic; monetary theory does not point to any clear indicative definition and often focuses on the demand for money as if what constitutes money were self-evident; definitions based on empirical or statistical efficiency present serious methodological problems

217

in the absence of a strong theoretical foundation; measures of 'moneyness', such as the monetary-quantity indices, seem intellectually most promising, though their application in the identification of an optimal money quantity implies the need to take into account all financial assets, and their adoption for policy purposes may be difficult, owing to control problems, and improbable, for it would involve the culture shock of relating to 'statistical' money (chapter 3). Thus, we continue to grope for a collection of 'monetary' assets to target and control and, in spite of ingenious and technically complex endeavours to find it, in practice we resort to rather arbitrary bundles: M (and L or PSL) (chapters 3 and 4).

M. Friedman sometimes refers to the quantity theory as an 'empirical generalization', which is associated with the methodology of positive economics. The object is to identify some reliable statistical relationships helpful in organizing knowledge and in designing policy. The search for such relationships has been particularly persistent in the context of the demand for money. Rarely have such varied data purporting to proxy the same concept – 'money' – been subjected to such persistent torture, with such ingenious and innovative devices, in the hope that it would confess the secrets of some golden rule which, by controlling something 'small' (money), would bring about the stability of something 'large' (nominal income) in order to lay the foundation of free market prosperity. So far, 'nature' has not confessed (compare Leamer, 1983, pp. 36–9). It seems that our expectations of econometric procedures have been rather unrealistic, especially in attempting to resolve conceptual issues (such as what is money). We have sometimes succumbed to the temptation of easy access to powerful statistical packages and used them as sufficient substitutes for conceptualization and definitional issues.

Money cannot be understood without understanding the behaviour of the financial system from which it emanates. The nature of financial evolution, and in particular the capacity for creative response which is involved in financial innovation, are particularly germane to the understanding of the problems of defining, measuring and controlling 'money'. The main conclusion which emerges is that in macroeconomics, mainly because of the failure of money targeting, we now take notice of the symptoms of financial innovation without fully understanding its microeconomic processes (chapters 5–7).

8.2   Financial innovation

Our analysis of recent financial innovations suggests that it is useful to look on them as 'swarms' or 'clusters' of distinctive but interrelated devices embraced by phenomena of 'liability management' in the financial sector (section 6.3), corporate 'cash management' in the non-financial sector (section 5.3.4) and the Eurocurrency system in the overseas sector (section

5.2). All are rather amorphous, but by no means unconnected, bundles of financial interrelations capable of responding, in a creative and novel way, to the challenges of market frictions and uncertainty, exhibiting characteristics lethal to the effectiveness of monetary action founded on a 'currency theory' of money (section 1.2.1).

Financial innovation is neither a new phenomenon nor just an emphemeral phenomenon. Although, given our existing, imperfect knowledge, it is difficult to be precise about the processes inducing innovation, there is much evidence to suggest that financial innovation is a demand-induced activity, often arising from some financial adversity, and calculated to overcome a constraint imposed by monetary control. But it is doubtful whether it would occur without the underlying demand from the 'real' sector for financial services (payments, intermediation, asset transmutation). Changes in the financial surpluses or deficits of non-financial units (sections 2.2, 2.3) might well have an important bearing on financial innovation. We have thus stressed the 'real' connection following a modified Schumpeterian theory of economic evolution (section 7.1), and the influence of corporate cash management (section 5.3.4).

The hypothesis of constraint-induced innovation offers a reasonable, general explanation of financial innovation (section 7.2). One aspect of it, which was stressed in the text, was the circumventive innovation triggered by monetary intervention (section 7.3). It is not clear whether a creative monetary response is more likely to be induced by quantity constraints (credit crunches) or price constraints (high interest rates). Often, both occur simultaneously, particularly at a time of restrictive monetary action. Recent financial innovations appear to be associated with interest rates reaching some threshold level, though they should not be considered in isolation from other factors promoting creative change.

Financial innovation also occurs in environments where monetary regulation is not oppressive. Increased foreign and domestic competition, technological change, uncertainty caused by variable prices, interest rates and exchange rate changes can all give some impetus to financial innovation. On the other hand, these factors might be related to some previous financial intervention. Cause and effect are difficult to separate.

Like technological innovation, financial innovation can reduce costs. In this realm, the nexus between financial and technological change is particularly intriguing. The extent to which financial innovations stimulate technological innovations in finance or are a response to falling transactions costs made possible by technological advances is not clear. In the last three decades, however, technological innovations have been a ubiquitous ingredient in the creation of novel financial instruments, processes and markets (section 6.4).

Falling transactions costs, arising from the interaction between technological and financial change, have made both financial and 'real' economic units more sensitive to profit opportunities, better able to take advantage of them, and less inhibited about stepping over the customary business boundaries. The financial markets have become more contestable and more competitive. The traditional distinctions between banks and other financial institutions have become even more blurred now than at the time of the Radcliffe Report (1959) when this was first highlighted. Indeed, many large corporate treasuries in non-financial enterprises now discharge quasi-banking services with the help of cash management packages supplied often by banks. Technological innovations and reduced transactions costs contribute to the symbiosis of transactions and investment characteristics within the same asset, making the traditional differentiation between monetary and savings assets increasingly tenuous.

Thus, the factors inducing financial innovation are complex and need further investigation. It seems that no simple explanation is likely to be satisfactory and that an interdisciplinary, 'integrated' approach to the phenomenon might be most rewarding (see section 7.4.3).

8.3   Circumventive innovation

Much attention has been devoted to circumventive innovation designed to overcome restrictive regulations and monetary action. Monetary history is full of examples of endeavours to define and then regulate (hence restrain) the money supply, which were followed by a creative response in the private financial sector. An interesting feature of the historical experience is that during periods of the ascendancy of the free trade philosophy (both in the nineteenth century and now), advocates of *laissez-faire* in general often insist on the need to control money (however defined). The ingenuity of the private and self-interested entrepreneur is thus limited to his enterprise in the real sector, and apparently is not considered to be transferable to the problem of overcoming the constraints imposed by monetary control. Information supplied in Part III of the book has proved this to be an incorrect judgement.

In recent decades, financial innovations have been responsible for altering the relationships between monetary aggregates and, in terms of the traditional demand-for-money analysis, the parameters of the conventional demand functions. It is doubtful whether either a redefinition of the money supply or a respecification of the demand-for-money function would be successful (section 7.5.2). The salvation of the orthodox monetary strategy might lie in a policy design which anticipates and compensates for financial innovation, or in a policy which successfully prevents a slippage caused by innovations eroding distinctions between 'money' and 'near money' (Mayer, 1982, pp. 29, 32–3). A number of characteristics of the financial innovation process cast serious doubts as to the possibility of either of such arrangements.

It should be reiterated that the phenomenon of financial innovation is not new and certainly is not unique to the 1970s. It is a continuing, but unpredictable and often spasmodic, process; a phenomenon which, like technological innovations, frequently occurs in 'swarms' or 'epidemics'. It usually starts unobtrusively, ignored by monetary authorities until conditions for imitation and diffusion occur. Precisely what conditions trigger these is not known. Furthermore, little firm information on diffusion processes is available, though it seems that the imitation and diffusion of innovations can be quicker in the financial system than in the industrial sphere because of lower set-up costs.

It may take time before monetary authorities are able to react to financial innovations. The collection of data, the availability of sufficient observations to provide reasonably convincing evidence of the impact of innovations on monetary policy, and the formulation of a strategy of response might be prolonged. Thus, the identification and incorporation of new 'monetary' assets in a money aggregate or a reaction to novel financial processes could only happen after a considerable time lag. The response cycle of private financial agents to monetary constraints such as regulations is considered shorter than that of monetary authorities to circumventive action.

An important feature of circumventive innovations is that they involve a learning process which attempts to make financial units impervious to future intervention by the authorities. The innovative procedures endeavour to insulate financial institutions from future restrictive actions by ensuring an uninterrupted flow of funds even in conditions of financial stringency (sections 5.3.1(a), 6.3.1).

Furthermore, financial innovations seem irreversible. Markets such as the Eurodollar market, processes such as cash management and instruments such as CDs or RPs do not disappear after the conditions giving rise to such innovations are removed. They remain, adding to the flexibility and conductivity of the financial markets and enriching their structure. Movement up and down a theoretical demand-for-money curve in response to supply changes also seems too simplistic. High interest rates are an important element of innovation-inducing conditions which can irreversibly alter the supply side of 'money'.

Thus, circumventive financial innovation has proved to be, to use a Schumpeterian phrase, a *process of 'creative destruction' of monies narrowly defined for purposes of macroeconomic control*, and a process which has significantly affected our financial structure. The transmission mechanism of a restriction on a money supply contains an often forgotten element of innovation, a shift in behaviour, which alters or distorts financial flows, institutions and practices often before the transmission process reaches the ultimate goal. *And the capacity for financial innovation, and thus circumvention, is today much greater than in the past.* It would, therefore, be implausible for a constraint upon the stock of money, selected out of many financial assets, to bring about the 'concertina effect' in the financial system proposed by a quantity-theoretical framework. Thus, what might start as a restrictive or containing policy would end by restructuring financial flows and financial technology in an unpredictable way (sections 6.1, 7.3). A redefinition of 'money' to take account of the slippage would become Sisyphean labour.

The Eurocurrency market, liability management, cash management by corporations and individuals and the rising content of interest-bearing assets in monetary aggregates have *decreased the capacity of the authorities to influence monetary conditions by changing the general level of interest rates.* Empirical evidence in the early 1970s showing a decline in the interest elasticity of the demand for money was generally interpreted as supporting the monetarist proposition of the uniqueness of money and the effectiveness of monetary policy. More recent interpretation is essentially in terms of the effect of financial innovations on the parameters of the money demand (section 7.5.2). The low interest elasticity of the demand for money, and hence the interest inelasticity of *LM*, are now generally attributable, in large measure, to financial innovations making it difficult for the authorities to change relative interest rates by influencing general market rates.

8.4   The money confusion

Given the above analysis of financial behaviour, the difficulties of policies which are inspired by the quantity theory tradition, and hence demand the identification of 'money' for macroeconomic control purposes, are understandable. Money, when subjected to official restraint, has proved to be even more contumacious today than in the past (section 7.3.1). Examples of the resulting confusion related to the question of what constitutes the indicative definition of money abound and have been given in the text.

In the USA, the original targeted 'money', M1, was redefined, succeeded by M1A and M1B to become again M1, in order to be 'suspended' as a reliable target and an indicator of domestic monetary conditions. In the UK, since the late 1970s £M3 has been the money target, but by now it has been buttressed by other M's and PSL's, some targeted, some not, and 'announced' in a way not likely to inspire uniform expectations or indicate a clear 'monetary' strategy. In the context of the 1983 budget, (H. M. Treasury, 1983, p. 7) it was suggested that: 'the interpretation of monetary conditions will continue to take account of all the available evidence, including the exchange rate, structural changes in financial markets, saving behaviour and the level and structure of interest rates. Policy decisions will be aimed at maintaining monetary conditions that will keep inflation on a downward trend' (compare section 4.2). It is difficult to disagree with the wisdom of this statement, for it implies the need to embrace the total behaviour of the financial sector in the analysis of 'monetary' conditions. However, it implies a 'flow-of-funds' analysis of market conditions rather than simply the monetarist strategy of controlling 'the supply of money' to the exclusion of all else.

Perhaps the most serious confusion not elaborated in the text refers to the behaviour of the money market. 'My problem is to know what money is', confessed H. Kaufman (1980, pp. 66–8), a well-known, non-academic financial economist in the USA. He went on to urge the central bank to abandon 'monetary' control and concentrate on influencing the credit system. Another non-academic economist testified in support of Goodhart's law (section 7.3.1) that 'to all except perhaps the most indigent of economic actors, the money stock – in contrast to oil and credit, is a meaningless abstraction' (Wojnilower, 1980, p. 324). To a British professional economist (Bootle, 1984, p. 16), the concept of the 'the money supply' is a 'meaningless anachronism' – a legacy of gold.

Yet financial markets became, on the whole, conditioned by the monetarist philosophy. Nevertheless, they developed their own brand of behaviour: careful, devout, obsessive 'money watching', often inspiring almost a reflex action translating current information on deviations of actual aggregates from targets into information on the future of interest rates or exchange rates (Tobin, 1980, p. 50). For example, money markets normally expect a change (rise) in interest rates when the money supply is off its target path (above a limit). Instant responses have been noted to announcements of even short-term monetary data, which, as central banks widely warn, contain a high noise content (Lombra, 1980, pp. 278–9).

In recent years, the US money market has avidly watched the announcements of changes in the money supply, M1, which became unreliable, even in the long-term, and compared them with the expected outcomes prepared by expert analysts. A typical reaction was vividly described by D. Lipsey of the *Sunday Times* (21 August 1983). When the Federal Reserve declared a large fall in M1 when a large rise had been forecast, the initial anticipations of an increase in interest rates and of a subsequent inflow of foreign currencies were abandoned. Instead, a lower dollar exchange rate began to be predicted, causing the selling of dollars. 'There is about this everyday tale of market folks both a lower and a higher lunacy. The lower lunacy is that in logic it resembles spotting a starling, declaring it to be a swallow, and on that basis prophesying the imminent arrival of summer.' The higher lunacy refers to a contrast with the behaviour predicted by the theory underlying money targets – a lower money supply should eventually lead to less inflation and a stronger currency. 'But now, the markets are doing precisely the reverse. When US money supply grows fast, the dealers expect higher interest rates and pile into dollars. When it grows slowly, they expect lower rates and bail out.' Not infrequently, money-watching, instead of reassuring economic agents of a stabler economic climate, has turned into a source of independent financial disturbance.

8.5 Financial fragility and economic efficiency

There are two issues related to financial innovations which have only been touched upon in the text: the stability or fragility of the financial system, and the extent to which financial innovations contribute to the overall efficiency of the economy. These are serious problems deserving of greater attention, but their elaboration is beyond the scope of this book.

As the deposit base of the financial system increasingly moves from more stable retail deposits to more sophisticated wholesale inter-bank transactions, the system becomes potentially more volatile (section 6.3.3). Progressive deregulation also poses problems. It is not always an outcome of a deliberate policy, but an enforced reaction to the push of financial change. 'Central banks and official regulation cannot effectively stand in the path of change for long and must eventually adapt to it' (BE, 1983a, p. 362). Today's pace of deregulation is related to the pace of innovatory activity. Deregulation in turn creates difficulties for monetary authorities. For instance, the Federal Reserve's introduction of reserve base control in 1979 ('conversion to monetarism') was 'largely an accidental byproduct of financial deregulation' (Hale, 1983, p. 30).

Economists such as Hicks have repeatedly stressed the threat of instability emanating from frictionless economic systems (section 7.4.1) and considered a developed financial system to be very sensitive and therefore unstable (e.g. Hicks, 1967, pp. 59–60; 158–9). 'A monetary system – a sophisticated monetary system with much "fluidity" – is inherently unstable; it needs to have frictions. . . .' Regulations constituting such frictions might be a nuisance, but, together with the lender of last resort, they are necessary for stabilization purposes. In view of the instability and 'casino instincts' of financial markets, dangers are perceived in complete deregulation in the USA. Some 'legally institutionalized fuses in the credit process' are deemed necessary in the interest of stability (Wojnilower, 1980, p. 326).

Pursuing his theory of interaction between the government and the financial world, Kane (1983, p. 100) encouraged the incorporation of the dialectic of economic and political responses into policy. 'Until a concept of regulation-induced innovation begins to play a major role in policy-makers' analysis of the effects of alternative forms of innovation-induced re-regulation, the possibility of financial instability remains a serious threat.' However, financial innovation, thus far experienced, has been unpredictable, and the capacity of the authorities to react to avoidance has so far been rather less than that of the financial markets to circumvent monetary measures. Some see the 'regulation *v.* deregulation' issue as a conflict between private benefits and social costs or between micro- and macro-optimality (Mayer, 1982).

The dilemma of the need for 'fuses' and the growing ability of financial units to bypass them has been partly responsible for a revival of interest in alternative monetary systems (section 7.3.3). Some new theories regard state regulations as essentially enhancing the demand for legal currency and state-issued claims and contend that traditional central bank action can be effective only in the presence of binding regulations. On the other hand, 'free money' or 'free banking' theories question the traditional libertarian philosophy espousing *laissez-faire* in all spheres except money and urge free competition as being sufficient to prevent an over-issue of private monies. Studies of the 'new monetary economics' have been described as 'at a minimum entertaining and mind-stretching', but leaving doubts (Fischer, 1982, p. 15). Though far from becoming 'free banking' economies in a theoretical sense, both the USA and the UK have been moving quickly into uncharted areas of relatively free competition. The dilemma of finding an institutional arrangement which would restrain when necessary and support when appropriate is today even greater than it has been in the past.

When considering very similar issues, that is, a reconciliation of stability and competition, Bagehot stated that 'Money will not manage itself and Lombard Street has a great deal of money to manage' (1973, p. 10). This did not constitute a plea for central bank or other public control, but an attack on the laxity of private financial firms in managing their affairs. Perhaps, in approaching the issue of stability in a deregulated world of finance, greater stress should be placed upon stringent self-regulation. It is clear that the standard role of the central bank as the lender of last resort concerned essentially with the management of liquidity must be reviewed.

Liquidity crises are closely linked with problems of financial institutions which become insolvent because of imprudent management. With reference to the 1825 crisis, a newspaper passed a comment which is still valid today: 'Credit, like the honour of a female, is of too delicate a nature to be treated with laxity – the slightest hint may inflict an injury which no subsequent effort can repair' (Mathias, 1969, p. 361). A solvency crisis can easily set off a liquidity crisis, 'because even a rumour of insolvency can lead to a run, and, if not checked, the liquidity crisis could spread even more quickly than the solvent crisis that caused it' (Guttentag and Herring, 1983, p. 4). The central bank must thus intervene in cases of insolvency. This raises the issue of 'moral hazard' in institutions which lend imprudently, knowing of the possibility of being bailed out by the central bank.

In exercising its supportive role, the central bank might have to insist on appropriate self-regulation, business practices and arrangements in all financial firms, and in this way prevent financial crises, panics and instability. The episode of the rescue of Johnson Matthey Bankers in 1984 suggests that the task is daunting. Nevertheless, the concept of 'parental', microeconomic central bank 'control', in addition to the bank's market operations, might form the basis of a revised function of the 'lender of last resort', applicable in a substantially deregulated environment (section 6.3.3). Whether such an approach would result in restraint when such is needed and support when it is deserved remains an interesting question. It would extend considerably the central bank's scope and depth of analysis of the financial world, and there are indications that the Bank of England is already involved in such work (Wilson Committee, 1979, vol. 4, pp. 96–9; BE 1982e).

The extent to which financial innovations increase the allocative efficiency in the economy is even more difficult to assess. The standard approach is to suggest that, analogously with technological innovations, financial innovations increase productivity and welfare by removing market obstacles and increasing choice (e.g. Hester, 1981, p. 194; Silber, 1983, p. 94). Falling transactions costs, especially when brought about by technological advances, increase wealth-holders' welfare (section 7.4.2).

The issue is, however, more complex than that, particularly when we deal with circumventive innovations where expenditure is incurred to overcome control. Resources are needed for circumventive innovation, which contributes to creating a complex layering of financial strata. The efficiency of this phenomenon is a *terra incognita* of the financial world, and this inevitably raises questions of private versus social costs (Mayer, 1982).

Not all regard financial evolution as necessarily indicating greater social efficiency. If the efficiency of financial sophistication were to be judged by its impact on real development, that is the extent to which financial expansion translates the generation of savings into productive real investment rather than accumulations of financial assets, then recent financial changes have not always resulted in visible improvements (Tobin, 1984). The fundamental problem with the subject is the absence of a generally accepted analytical framework and measures of financial efficiency (Bain, 1981, ch. 15; Revell, 1983b).

8.6   Alternative approaches

The book has focused narrowly on the nexus between the reactively changing financial environment, the traditional concept, and the definition and measurement of money and its control. References to a comprehensive macroeconomic scheme have, of necessity, been rather tenuous and fragmentary, concentrating on the impact of financial change on *LM*. It was argued that financial innovations made the conventional money demand, and thus *LM*, unstable, possibly very interest-inelastic, and subject to unpredictable shifts and tilts.

There are indications that recent financial changes have also altered the interest sensitivity of the demand for real expenditure (BIS, 1983, pp. 34, 61; BE, 1983a, p. 362; 1983b, p. 366; Wenninger, 1984). More widespread use of variable interest rates suggests that it is not only prospective or marginal borrowers that are affected by changes in the rates, but all borrowers. Thus, the interest sensitivity of real expenditure is likely to have increased (parameters c and v in equations (A1.16) and (A1.17), thus changing the relative value of multipliers a_1 and a_2 – see the appendix to chapter 1). Falling transactions costs, which are likely to be widely dispersed throughout the economy, and deregulation might also have an impact on the parameters of the *IS* function. However, all such effects are uncertain and unpredictable (Wenninger, 1984).

If, on the other hand, as is now widely thought, the *LM* function has become highly interest-inelastic – nearly vertical according to some (Tobin, 1983a) – then changes in *IS* would have an impact principally on interest rates and not on nominal income, whereas monetary disturbances would have a greater effect than real changes on nominal income. However, the stability of the whole model would be in question.

The above effects have been discussed mainly in the framework of a simple, conventional *IS–LM* model. It was argued that *modern monetary analysis must take place with reference to the whole financial sector*. The adequacy of the *LM* analysis encapsulating the traditional money supply–money demand paradigm has been questioned.

It is not the intention to present a definite alternative. However, in order to progress it is important, as Keynes pointed out in the Preface to the *General Theory* (1973, p. xxiii), to 'escape from habitual modes of thought and expression'. Essentially, the book is intended to suggest and encourage such an escape rather than provide answers, which can only come from new research programmes. We must move away from the view that in sophisticated financial economies we can identify money whose control is sufficient to yield predictable macroeconomic results and create a stable economic climate.

Monetary theory needs to be transformed into a financial theory, taking into account credit flow relationships or incorporating a multi-asset financial sector protrayed in a flow-of-funds approach (section 2.4). The balance sheet analysis of the financial sector, rather than the analysis of an isolated 'monetary' sector, offers a more sensible alternative. Progress with such extended analysis would necessitate considerable enquiry and a greater insight into the behaviour of the financial system. The demand-for-money function is not able fully to convey such behaviour. Even when constantly redesigned and made more sophisticated, it cannot continue to be treated as a substitute for a knowledge of our complex financial and institutional relationships. The incorporation of 'innovation variables' (section 7.5.2) in the demand-for-money functions might improve the performance of standard equations, but it does not offer a satisfactory answer to the understanding or modelling of financial change. A transformation of current orthodoxy, emphasizing the critical importance of the money stock, into a more comprehensive financial theory, embracing an interaction between the real and financial sectors, is necessary.

Today's economies are still removed from, but nevertheless tending towards, what Hicks termed the 'credit economy', where all financial assets bear interest rates (section 7.4.2). B. Friedman (1982, 1983) recently urged the rehabilitation of credit as a subject worthy of attention, pointing out that credit–income relationships in the USA and other developed economies were found to be at least as regular and stable as money–income relationships, and suggesting the targeting of both credit and money. One attractive feature of credit as the target is that it might pose fewer definitional problems and be less ambiguous as an indicator of tightness or ease in the money market. However, the targeting of both money and credit would beg even more questions of definition than the targeting of money alone. Furthermore, predictions from any isolated past financial regularity must be treated with caution, especially if they are to serve as a basis for policy.

Control of all financial aggregates is sometimes seen as an answer to the difficulty of defining a unique aggregate reflecting 'the money supply' (Gowland, 1982, pp. 6–7). It is hard to find a theoretical justification for a multiple money supply control, except possibly in terms of a higher yield of information to assess monetary conditions. On this basis, even wider disaggregation might be justified, provided that no single total is considered to have unique attributes of 'money'. Indeed, the publication of components of 'monetary aggregates' without aggregation might well be a logical outcome of such an approach (Berkman, 1980a, pp. 82–3; Pierce, 1980, pp. 259–60). All aggregates, and in particular broad aggregates, can internalize financial changes and result in a loss of useful information. Indeed, when financial innovations occur, the loss of information from aggregates might be so high that it would make the aggregate misleading as an information variable (compare section 6.1.2).

Therefore, a re-examination of the Radcliffe–Hicks–Yale position concerning monetary management, but in today's conditions of deregulation, competition and international financial integration, might provide an alternative research programme to the demand for money. This approach stresses the importance of the total debt structure and total credit flow, and not merely a 'money supply'. With the possibility of a highly interest-inelastic LM, a policy aimed primarily at influencing the level and structure of interest rates should be reconsidered. Interest rates are observable and do not raise as many definitional issues as money aggregates.

At the same time, there is a need to develop a new and well understood function of the lender of last resort to the whole financial sector, essentially as a means of bringing discipline and stability, which money targeting alone cannot achieve. The central bank still exercises the crucial function of being the custodian of money which everyone understands – that is, the currency into which all financial claims are convertible. However, in view of the flexibility of the financial sector and its relative independence from the traditional influences of monetary authorities, issues of solvency as well as liquidity must be embraced in the function. Concentration on an effective performance of such a function might indeed result in better financial discipline than the pursuit of policies based on targeting elusive and arbitrary monetary aggregates, frequently transmitting unclear, if not misleading, signals.

It is indeed difficult to understand the persistence with policies of intermediate targeting of selected 'money' quantities, particularly in view of official announcements that, in effect, all financial developments are relevant to policy analysis (see above). In such a situation, if a definite expression of policy is desirable, it might well be preferable directly to set a target for an ultimate variable such as real economic activity (as measured by GNP).

The Governor of the Bank of England (BE, 1984b), while still supporting the use of targets as a 'backbone' of policy, admitted that, because of the variability of short-run monetary relationships, monetary targets are operated pragmatically, providing only a first approximation of monetary conditions:

> The existence of targets places the onus on the authorities to explain why they are *ignoring the signals* given by diverging monetary growth, or why they are making *course corrections by changing target indicators or target ranges*. They act as *a trip-wire*, preventing the authorities, consciously or unconsciously, from ignoring danger signals.... [BE, 1984b, p. 476; my italics]

The difficulty with the 'trip-wire' concept of targets is that the mere placement of the trip-wire generates signals which can be variously interpreted. More importantly, the trip-wire itself, rather than the matter which it has been designed to guard, has become the prime focus of attention. *There is a danger that obsessive concentration on growth rates of some elusive and outdated money stock, in the context of the currently fashionable two-stage targeting strategy, excessively diverts our concern from more important issues such as appropriate policies fostering overall financial stability and real economic activity.*

Modern financially sophisticated economies, with a high potential for innovative reactions, need *financial rather than monetary strategies* for disciplined development, and attention must be paid not merely to selected 'monetary' assets, but to the overall flow of services supplied by the financial system, and in particular to the way in which this flow helps to generate real wealth, which often receives secondary consideration.

Bibliography

BE in the text refers to Bank of England and *BEQB* to *Bank of England Quarterly Bulletin*.

Allen, W. A. (1983) 'Recent developments in monetary control in the UK'. In L. H. Meyer (ed), *Improving Money Stock Control*. Hingham, Mass.: Kluwer-Nijhoff, pp. 97–123.

Andrew, A. P. (1899) 'What ought to be called money'. *Quarterly Journal of Economics*, 13, 219–27.

Arrow, K. S. and Hahn, F. H. (1971) *General Competitive Analysis*. San Francisco: Holden Day.

Artis, M. J. and Lewis, M. K. (1976) 'The demand for money in the UK, 1963–73'. *Manchester School*, 44, 147–81.

Artis, M. J. and Lewis, M. K. (1981) *Monetary Control in the UK*. Oxford: Philip Allan.

Backus, D. K. *et al.* (1980) 'A model of US financial and non-financial economic behaviour'. *Journal of Money, Credit, and Banking*, 12(2), 259–93.

Bagehot, W. (1973) *Lombard Street* (1st edn, 1873). Homewood, Ill.: R. D. Irwin.

Bailey, R. W., Driscoll, M. J., Ford, J. L. and Mullineux, A. W. (1982) 'The information content of monetary aggregates in the UK'. *Economic Letters*, 9, 61–7.

Bain, A. D. (1981) *The Economics of the Financial System*. Oxford: Martin Robertson.

Bank of England (1970) 'The stock of money'. *BEQB*, 11(2), 189–93.

Bank of England (1971a) 'Competition and credit control'. *BEQB*, 11(3), 189–93.

Bank of England (1971b) 'Competition and credit control'. *BEQB*, 11(4), 477–81.

Bank of England (1972) 'Sterling certificates of deposit'. *BEQB*, 12(4), 487–95.

Bank of England (1973) 'Does money really matter?' (Governor's speech). *BEQB*, 13(2) 193–202.

Bank of England (1977) 'DCE and the money supply'. *BEQB*, 17(1), 39–42.

Bank of England (1978) 'Reflections on the conduct of monetary policy' (Governor's speech). *BEQB*, 18(1), 31–7.

230

Bank of England (1979) 'Component of private sector liquidity'. *BEQB*, 19(3), 278–82.

Bank of England (1981) 'Monetary control provisions'. *BEQB*, 21(3), 347–9.

Bank of England (1982a) 'Transactions balances – a new monetary aggregate'. *BEQB*, 22(2), 224–5.

Bank of England (1982b) 'Recent changes in the use of cash'. *BEQB*, 22(4), 519–29.

Bank of England (1982c) 'Composition of monetary and liquidity aggregates'. *BEQB*, 22(4), 530–7.

Bank of England (1982d) 'Bill of Exchange'. *BEQB*, 22(4), 514–18.

Bank of England (1982e) 'The role of the banking supervisor'. *BEQB*, 22(4), 547–52.

Bank of England (1982f) 'The role of the Bank of England in the money market'. *BEQB*, 22(1), 86–94.

Bank of England (1982g) 'Banks and industry'. *BEQB*, 22(4), 506–10.

Bank of England (1983a) 'The nature and implications of financial innovation'. *BEQB*, 23(3), 358–62.

Bank of England (1983b) 'Competition, innovation and regulation in British banking.' *BEQB*, 23(3), 363–76.

Bank of England (1983c) 'External flows and broad money'. *BEQB*, 23(4), 525–9.

Bank of England (1983d) 'A note on recent innovations in capital markets'. *BEQB*, 23(2), 182–3.

Bank of England (1984a) 'Insurance in a changing financial services industry' (Governor's speech). *BEQB*, 24(2), 195–9.

Bank of England (1984b) 'Some aspects of UK monetary policy'. *BEQB*, 24(4), 474–81.

Bank of England (1984c) 'Funding the public sector borrowing: 1952–83'. *BEQB*, 24(4), 482–92.

Bank of England (1984d) 'Changes to monetary aggregates'. *BEQB*, 24(1), 78–83.

Barnett, W. A. (1980a) 'Economic monetary aggregates'. *Journal of Econometrics*, 14, 11–48.

Barnett, W. A. (1980b) 'Economic monetary aggregates – reply'. *Journal of Econometrics*, 14, 57–9.

Barnett, W. A. (1982) 'The optimal level of monetary aggregation'. *Journal of Money, Credit, and Banking*, 12(2), 687–720.

Barnett, W., Offenbacher, E. and Spindt, P. (1981) 'New concepts of aggregated money'. *Journal of Finance*, 36(2), 497–505.

Barnett, W. A. and Spindt, P. A. (1982) *Divisia Monetary Aggregates*, Staff Studies 116. Washington DC: Board of Governors of the Federal Reserve System.

Barth, J. R., Kraft, A. and Kraft J. (1977) 'The "moneyness" of financial assets'. *Applied Economics*, 9, 51–61.

Baumol, W. J. (1952) 'The transactions demand for cash'. *Quarterly Journal of Economics*, 67, 545–56.

Baumol, W. J. (1982) 'Contestable markets'. *American Economic Review*, 72(1), 1–15.

Becker, G. S. and Baumol, W. J. (1952) 'The classical monetary theory'. *Economica*, 19, 355–75.

Bell, G. (1973) *The Euro-dollar Market and International Financial System*. London: Macmillan.

Ben-Horim, M. and Silber, W. L. (1977) 'Financial innovation: a linear programming approach'. *Journal of Banking and Finance*, 1, 277–96.

Berkman, N. G. (1980a) 'Abandoning monetary aggregates', In *Federal Reserve Bank of Boston* (1980), pp. 76–100.

Berkman, N. G. (1980b) 'The new monetary aggregates'. *Journal of Money, Credit, and Banking*, 12(2), 135–54.

Bernholz, P. (1983) 'Inflation and monetary constitutions in historical perspective'. *Kyklos*, 36(3), 397–419.

BIS (Bank for International Settlements) (1983) *Fifty-third Annual Report, 1982/3*, 13 June, section III.

Blanden, M. (1983) 'A good start in LIFFE'. *The Banker*, April, 105–13.

Bootle, R. (1984) 'Origins of the monetarist fallacy'. *Lloyds Bank Review*, 153, 16–36.

Bordo, M. D. and Jonung, L. (1981) 'The long-run behaviour of the income velocity of money in five advanced countries, 1870–1975'. *Economic Inquiry*, 19, 96–116.

Boughton, J. M. (1979) 'The demand for money in major OECD countries'. *OECD Economic Outlook*, Occasional Studies, January, 35–57.

Boughton, J. M. (1981a) 'Recent instability of the demand for money: an international perspective'. *Southern Economic Journal*, 47(3), 579–97.

Boughton, J. M. (1981b) 'Money and its substitutes'. *Journal of Monetary Economics*, 8, 375–86.

Bronfenbrenner, M. (1980) 'Davidson on Keynes on money'. *Journal of Post Keynesian Economics*, 2(3), 308–13.

Brunner, K. and Meltzer, A. H. (1963) 'Predicting velocity'. *Journal of Finance*, 18, 319–54.

Brunner, K. and Meltzer, A. H. (1971) 'The uses of money'. *American Economic Review*, 61, 784–805.

Brunner, K. and Meltzer, A. H. (1972) 'Friedman's monetary theory'. *Journal of Political Economy*, 80(5), 837–51.

Bryant, R. C. (1980) *Money and Monetary Policy in Interdependent Nations*. Washington DC: Brookings Institution.

Bryant, R. C. (1983) *Controlling Money*. Washington DC: Brookings Institution.

Cagan, P. (1982) 'The choice among monetary aggregates as targets and guides for monetary policy'. *Journal of Money, Credit, and Banking*, 14(4), Part 2, 661–85.

Cagan, P. and Schwartz, A. J. (1975) 'Has the growth of money substitutes hindered monetary policy?' *Journal of Money, Credit, and Banking*, 7(2), 137–59.

Caldwell, B. (1982) *Beyond Positivism*. London: Allen and Unwin.

Cameron R. (ed.) (1967) *Banking in the Early Stages of Industrialisation*. Oxford: University Press.

Carrington, J. C. and Edwards, G. T. (1981) *Reversing Economic Decline*. London: Macmillan.

Casson, M. (1981) *Unemployment: A Disequilibrium Approach*. Oxford: Martin Robertson.

Chesher, A. D., Sheppard, D. K. and Whitwell, J. L. (1975) 'Have British banks been imprudent?' *The Banker*, January, 31–9.

Chetty, V. K. (1969) 'On measuring the nearness of near-money'. *American Economic Review*, 59(3), 270–81.

Chrystal, K. A. (1983) *Controversies in Macroeconomics*, 2nd ed. Oxford: Philip Allan.

Clausen, A. W. (1980) 'The changing character of financial markets'. In Feldstein (1980), pp. 86–94.

Clayton, G. (1962) 'British financial intermediaries in theory and practice'. *Economic Journal*, 72, 869–86.

Clayton, G. Gilbert, J. C. and Sedgwick, R. (eds) (1971) *Monetary Theory and Monetary Policy in the 1970's*. Oxford: University Press.

Clower, R. W. (1964) 'Monetary history and positive economics'. *Journal of Economic History*, 24, 364–80.

Clower, R. W. (1968) 'Comment: the optimal growth rate of money. *Journal of Political Economy*, 76(4), Part II, 876–80.

Clower, R. W. (1971) 'Theoretical foundations of monetary policy'. In Clayton *et al.* (1971), pp. 15–28.

Coakley, J. and Harris, L. (1983) *The City of Capital*. Oxford: Basil Blackwell.

Coghlan, R. T. (1978) 'A transactions demand for money'. *BEQB*, 18(1), 48–60.

Coghlan, R. T. (1980) *The Theory of Money and Finance*. London: Macmillan.

Coghlan, R. T. and Sykes, C. (1980) 'Managing the money supply'. *Lloyds Bank Review*, 135, 1–13.

Cooley, T. F. and LeRoy, S. F. (1981) 'Identification and estimation of money demand'. *American Economic Review*, 71(5), 825–44.

Cooley, T. F. and Prescott, E. C. (1973) 'Systematic (non-random) variation models varying parameter regression'. *Annals of Economic and Social Measurement*, 2(4), 463–73.

Courakis, A. S. (1978) 'Series correlation and a Bank of England study of the demand for money'. *Economic Journal*, 88, 537–48.

Courakis, A. S. (1981) 'Monetary targets'. In A. S. Courakis (ed.), *Inflation, Depression and Economic Policy*, London: Mansell, 1981, pp. 259–357.

Cramp, A. B. (1962) 'Two views on money'. *Lloyds Bank Review*, 65, 1–15.

Crowther Committee on Consumer Credit (1971) *Report*, Cmnd 4596. London: HMSO.

Dale, R. (1984) *The Regulation of International Banking*. Cambridge: Woodhead-Faulkner.

Davidson, P. (1978) *Money in the Real World*, 2nd edn. London: Macmillan.

Davidson, P. (1980) 'The dual-faceted nature of the Keynesian revolution'. *Journal of Post Keynesian Economics*, 2(3), 291–307.

Davidson, P. (1982) *International Money and the Real World*. London: Macmillan.

Davies, G. and Davies, J. (1984) 'The revolution in monopoly theory'. *Lloyds Bank Review*, 153, 38–52.

Davies, S. (1979) *The Diffusion of Process Innovation*. Cambridge: University Press.

Dennis, G. E. J. (1981) *Monetary Economics*. London: Longman.

Dennis, G. E. J. (1982) 'Monetary policy and debt management'. In D. T. Llewellyn *et al.* (eds), *The Framework of UK Monetary Policy*. London: Heinemann, pp. 244–93.

DePrano, M. and Mayer, T. (1965) 'Tests of the relative importance of autonomous expenditures and money'. *American Economic Review*, 55, 729–52.

Desai, M. (1981) *Testing Monetarism*. London: F. Pinter.

Donovan, D. J. (1978) 'Modeling the demand for liquid assets: an application to Canada'. *IMF Staff Papers*, 25, 676–704.

Dooley, M. P., Kaufman, H. M. and Lombra, R. E. (eds) (1979) *The Political Economy of Policy-making*. Beverly Hills: Sage Publications.

Dornbusch, R. and Fischer, S. (1981) *Macroeconomics*, 2nd edn. New York: McGraw-Hill.

Driscoll, M. J. and Ford J. L. (1980) 'The stability of the demand for money function and the predictability of the effects of monetary policy'. *Economic Journal*, 90, 867–84.

Duck, N. W. and Sheppard, D. K. (1978) 'A proposal for the control of the UK money supply'. *Economic Journal*, 88, 1–17.

Dufey, G. and Giddy, I. H. (1978) *The International Money Market*. Englewood Cliffs, NJ: Prentice-Hall.

Edwards, F. R. (1972) 'More on substitutability between money and near-monies'. *Journal of Money, Credit, and Banking*, 4(3), 551–71.

Einzig, P. (1971) *Parallel Money Markets*, Vol. 1. London: Macmillan.

Ellis, J. G. (1981) 'Eurobanks and the inter-bank market'. *BEQB*, 21(3), 351–64.

Ewis, N. A. and Fisher, D. (1984) 'The translog utility function and the demand for money in the US'. *Journal of Money, Credit, and Banking*, 16(1), 34–51.

Fama, E. F. (1980) 'Banking in the theory of finance'. *Journal of Monetary Economics*, 6, 39–57.

Fama, E. F. (1983) 'Financial intermediation and price level control'. *Journal of Monetary Economics*, 12, 7–28.

Farr, II. T., Porter, R. D. and Pruitt, M. (1978) *Improving the Monetary Aggregates*. Washington DC: Board of Governors, Federal Reserve System, November, pp. 91–116.

Federal Reserve Bank of Boston (1980) *Controlling Monetary Aggregates*. Conference Series no. 23, October.

Feige, E. L. (1964) *The Demand for Liquid Assets*. Englewood Cliffs, NJ: Prentice-Hall.

Feige, E. L. and Pearce, D. K. (1977) 'The substitutability of money and near-monies'. *Journal of Economic Literature*, 15(2), 439–69.

Feldstein, M. (ed.) (1980) *The American Economy in Transition*. Chicago: University Press.

Ferris, J. S. (1981) 'A transactions theory of trade credit use'. *Quarterly Journal of Economics*, 96, 243–70.

Fetter, F. W. (1965) *The Development of British Monetary Orthodoxy*. Cambridge, Mass.: Harvard University Press.

Fitzgerald, M. D. (1983) 'Innovations in financial futures'. *The Banker*, April, 95–103.

Fischer, S. (1982) 'A framework for monetary and banking analysis'. Conference Papers. Supplement to *Economic Journal*, 93, 1–16.

Fisher, D. (1978) *Monetary Theory and the Demand for Money*. London: Martin Robertson.

Foot, M. D. K. (1981) *Monetary Targets*. In Griffiths and Wood (1981), pp. 13–40.

Foot, M. D. K., Goodhart, C. and Hotson, A. C. (1979) 'Monetary base control'. *BEQB*, 19(2), 149–59.

Frankel, J. A. and Mussa, M. L. (1981) Monetary and fiscal policies in an open economy'. *American Economic Review*, Papers, 21(2), 253–8.

Freeman, C. (1982)   *The Economics of Innovation*. London: F. Pinter.

Freedman, C. (1983)   'Financial innovation in Canada'. *American Economic Review*, Papers, 73(2), 101–6.

Friedman, B. (1980)   'Postwar changes in the American financial markets'. In Feldstein (1980), pp. 9–78.

Friedman, B. (1982)   'The roles of money and credit in macroeconomic analysis'. In J. Tobin (ed.), *Macroeconomics, Prices and Quantities*. Oxford: Basil Blackwell, pp. 161–99.

Friedman, B. (1983)   'Monetary policy with a credit aggregate target'. In K. Brunner, A. H. Meltzer (eds), *Money, Monetary Policy and Financial Institutions*, Carnegie–Rochester Conference Series on Public Policy, 18, pp. 117–47.

Friedman, M. (1948)   'A monetary and fiscal framework for economic stability. *American Economic Review*, 38(3), 245–64.

Friedman, M. (1956)   'The quantity theory of money – a restatement'. In M. Friedman (ed.), *Studies in the Quantity Theory of Money*, Chicago: University Press, pp. 3–21.

Friedman, M. (1968a)   'Money: Quantity Theory'. *International Encyclopaedia of the Social Sciences*; reprinted in Walters (1973), pp. 36–66.

Friedman, M. (1968b)   'The role of monetary policy'. *American Economic Review*, 58, 1–17; reprinted in R. L. Teigen (ed.), *Readings in Money, National Income and Stabilisation Policy*, 4th edn. Homewood, Ill.: R. D. Irwin, 1978, pp. 365–79.

Friedman, M. (1970)   'A theoretical framework for monetary analysis'. *Journal of Political Economy*, 78(2), 193–238.

Friedman, M. (1973)   *Money and Economic Development*. New York: Praeger.

Friedman, M. (1974)   *The Monetary Correction*, Occasional Paper no. 41. London: Institute of Economic Affairs.

Friedman, M. (1980a)   'Factors affecting the level of interest rates'. In T. M. Havrilesky and J. T. Boorman (eds), *Current Issues in Monetary Theory and Policy*, 2nd edn. Arlington Heights, Va.: A. H. M. Publishing Corp., pp. 378–94.

Friedman, M. (1980b)   'The changing character of financial markets'. In Feldstein (1980), pp. 78–86.

Friedman, M. (1981a) 'Memorandum'. In House of Commons (1981)   Treasury and Civil Service Committee, *Memoranda on Monetary Policy*, HMSO, pp. 55–61.

Friedman, M. (1981b)   'A memorandum to the FED'. *Wall Street Journal*, 3 January, p. 6.

Friedman, M. (1982)   'Monetary Policy'. *Journal of Money, Credit, and Banking*, 14(1), 98–118.

Friedman, M. and Meiselman, D. I. (1963)   'The relative stability of monetary velocity and the investment multiplier in the US, 1897–1958'. In Commission on Money and Credit, *Stabilisation Policies*. Englewood Cliffs, NJ: Prentice-Hall, pp. 165–223.

Friedman, M. and Meiselman, D. I. (1965)   'Reply to Ando and Modigliani and De Prano and Mayer'. *American Economic Review*, 55(4), 753–85.

Friedman, M. and Schwartz, A. J. (1963a)   *A Monetary History of the United States*. Princeton: University Press.

Friedman, M. and Schwartz, A. J. (1963b)   'Money and business cycles'. *Review of Economics and Statistics*, 45; reprinted in Walters (1973), pp. 105–65.

Friedman, M. and Schwartz, A. J. (1970) *Monetary Statistics in the United States*. New York: National Bureau of Economic Research.

Friedman, M. and Schwartz, A. J. (1982) *Monetary Trends in the US and the UK*. Chicago: University Press.

Frost, T. (1982) 'Effects on wholesale banking'. In Institute of Bankers, *The Banks and Technology in the 1980's*, London, pp. 43–60.

Gaines, T. C. (1967) 'Financial innovation and the efficiency of Federal Reserve policy'. In G. Horwich, (ed.), *Monetary Process and Policy*. Homewood, Ill.: R. D. Irwin, pp. 99–118.

Goldfeld, S. M. (1973) 'The demand for money revisited'. *Brookings Papers on Economic Activity*, 3, 577–638.

Goldfeld, S. M. (1976) 'The case of the missing money'. *Brookings Papers on Economic Activity*, 3, 683–730.

Goldfeld, S. M. (1982) 'Comment on the optimal level of monetary aggregation'. *Journal of Money, Credit, and Banking*, 14(4), 716–20.

Goldsmith, R. W. (1969) *Financial Structure and Development*. New Haven, Conn.: Yale University Press.

Goldsmith, R. W. (1982) Comment. In Kindleberger and Laffargue (1982), pp. 41–3.

Goodfriend, M. (1985) 'Reinterpreting Money Demand Regressions'. In C. Brunner, A. H. Meltzer (eds), *Understanding Monetary Regimes*. Carnegie-Rochester Conference Series on Public Policy, 22, pp. 207–241.

Goodhart, C. A. E. (1975) *Money, Information and Uncertainty*. London: Macmillan.

Goodhart, C. A. E. (1979) 'Money in an open economy'. In Ormrod (1979), pp. 143–67.

Goodhart, C. A. E. (1981) 'Comment'. In B. Griffiths and G. E. Wood (eds), *Monetary Targets*. New York: St Martin's Press, pp. 129–31.

Goodhart, C. A. E. (1984) *Monetary Theory and Practice*. London: Macmillan.

Gould, B., Mills, J. and Stewart, S. (1981) *Monetarism or Prosperity*. London: Macmillan.

Gowland, D. (1978) *Monetary Policy and Credit Control*. London: Croom Helm.

Gowland, D. (1982) *Controlling the Money Supply*. London: Croom Helm.

Grant, A. T. K. (1977) *Economic Uncertainty and Financial Structure*. London: Macmillan.

Graziani, A. (1984) 'The debate on Keynes' finance motive'. *Monte Dei Paschi di Siena*, Economic Notes, 1, 5–34.

Greenbaum, S. I. and Heywood, C. F. (1971) 'Secular change in the financial services industry'. *Journal of Money, Credit, and Banking*, 3(2), 571–89.

Griffiths, B. (1970) *Competition in Banking*, Hobart Paper 51. London: Institute of Economic Affairs.

Griffiths, B. (1972) 'The welfare cost of the UK clearing banks cartel'. *Journal of Money, Credit, and Banking*, 4(2), 227–44.

Griffiths, B. and Wood, G. E. (eds) (1981) *Monetary Targets*. New York: St Martin's Press.

Griffiths, B. and Wood, G. E. (eds) (1984) *Monetarism in the UK*. London: Macmillan.

Gurley, J. G. and Shaw, E. S. (1955) 'Financial aspects of economic development'. *American Economic Review*, 45(4), 515–38.

Gurley, J. G. and Shaw, E. S. (1960) *Money in a Theory of Finance*. Washington: Brookings Institution.

Guttentag, J. and Herring, R. (1983) *The Lender-of-Last-Resort Function in an International Context. Essays in International Finance*, no. 151. Princeton: University Press.

Hadjimichalakis, M. G. (1982) *Monetary Policy and Modern Money Markets*. New York: Lexington Books.

Hafer, R. W. and Hein, S. E. (1982) 'The shift in money demand'. *Federal Reserve Bank of St Louis Review*, 64(2), 11–16.

Hale, D. D. (1983) 'What financial deregulation is doing to the US economy'. *The Banker*, October, 27–33.

Hall, M. (1983) *Monetary Policy Since 1971*. London: Macmillan.

Hall, R. E. (1982) 'Monetary trends in the US and the UK: a review from the perspective of new developments in monetary economics'. *Journal of Economic Literature*, 20(4), 1552–6.

Hamburger, M. J. (1977) 'The demand for money in an open economy'. *Journal of Monetary Economics*, 3, 25–40.

Havrilesky, T. M. and Boorman, J. T. (1978) *Monetary Macroeconomics*. Arlington Heights, Va.: AHM Publishing Corp.

Hayek, F. A. (1966) *Monetary Theory of the Trade Cycle* (1st edn 1933). New York: A. M. Kelly.

Hayek, F. A. (1976) *Denationalisation of Money*, Hobart Paper 70. London: Institute of Economic Affairs.

Hein, S. E. (1982) 'Short-run money growth volatility'. *Federal Reserve Bank of St Louis Review*, 64(6), 27–36.

Helm, D. (ed) (1984) *The Economics of John Hicks*. Oxford: Basil Blackwell.

Hendershott, P. S. (1977) *Understanding Capital Markets*. Vol. I, *A Flow-of-funds Financial Model*. New York: Lexington Books.

Hendry, D. F. (1979) 'Predictive failure and econometric modelling in macroeconomics'. In Ormrod (1979), pp. 217–42.

Hendry, D. F. (1983) 'Econometric modelling: the consumption function in retrospect'. *Scottish Journal of Political Economy*, 30(3), 193–220.

Hendry, D. F. and Ericsson, N. R. (1983) 'Assertion without empirical basis'. In Bank of England Panel of Academic Consultants, *Monetary Trends in the UK*, Panel Paper no. 22, pp. 45–101.

Hendry, D. F. and Mizon, G. E. (1978) 'Serial correlation as a convenient simplification, not a nuisance'. *Economic Journal*, 88, 549–63.

Hendry, D. F. and Richard, J-F. (1981) 'The econometric analysis of time series'. *International Statistical Review*, 51(2), 111–63.

Hester, D. D. (1981) 'Innovations and monetary control'. *Brookings Papers on Economic Activity*, 1, 141–89.

Hester, D. D. (1982) 'On the adequacy of policy instruments and information when the meaning of money is changing'. *American Economic Review*, Papers, 72(2), 40–4.

Hetzel, R. L. (1984) 'Estimating money demand functions'. *Journal of Money, Credit, and Banking*, 16(2), 185–93.

Hewson, J. and Sakakibara, E. (1975a) *The Eurocurrency Markets and Their Implications*. New York: Lexington Books.

Hewson, J. and Sakakibara, E. (1975b) 'The effect of US controls on US commercial bank borrowing in the Eurodollar market'. *Journal of Finance*, 30(4), 1101–10.

Hicks, J. R. (1937) 'Mr Keynes and the classics'. *Econometrica*, 5(2); reprinted in Hicks (1967), pp. 126–42.

Hicks, J. R. (1950) *A Contribution to the Theory of the Trade Cycle*. Oxford: Clarendon Press.

Hicks, J. R. (1965) *Capital and Growth*. Oxford: Clarendon Press.

Hicks, J. R. (1967) *Critical Essays in Monetary Theory*. Oxford: Clarendon Press.

Hicks, J. R. (1977) *Economic Perspectives*. Oxford: Clarendon Press.

Hicks, J. R. (1980–1) 'IS–LM – an explanation'. *Journal of Post Keynesian Economics*, 3(2), reprinted in Helm (1984), pp. 216–29.

Hicks, J. R. (1982) 'The credit economy'. In Helm (1984), pp. 230–9.

H. M. Treasury (1979) 'Some problems in the development of the Treasury model'. In Ormrod (1979), pp. 53–85.

H. M. Treasury (1983) *Financial Statement and Budget Report 1983/4*. March, HC 216, HMSO.

H. M. Treasury (1984) *Building Societies: A New Framework*. Cmnd 9316. London: HMSO.

Holland, R. C. (1975) 'Speculation on future innovation'. In Silber (1975), pp. 159–63.

House of Commons (1981) *Third Report for the Treasury and Civil Service Committee: Monetary Policy* (3 vols). Vol. 1, *Report*. London: HMSO.

Hughes, J. R. T. (1960) *Fluctuations in Trade, Industry and Finance*. Oxford: University Press.

Hulett, D. T. (1971) 'More on the empirical definition of money'. *American Economic Review*, 61, 462–8.

Humphrey, T. M. (1982) 'The real bills doctrine'. *Federal Reserve Bank of Richmond Economic Review*, September/October, 3–13.

Johnson, H. G. (1962) 'Monetary theory and policy'. *American Economic Review*, 52(3), 336–84.

Johnson, H. G. (1971) 'The Keynesian revolution and the monetarist counter-revolution. *American Economic Review*, Papers, 61(2), 1–14.

Johnson, H. G. (ed.) (1972) *Readings in British Monetary Economics*. Oxford: Clarendon Press.

Johnston, R. B. (1983) *The Economics of the Euro-Market*. London: Macmillan.

Johnston, R. B. (1984) *The Demand for Non-Interest-Bearing Money in the United Kingdom*, Government Economic Service Working Paper No. 66, February. London: HMSO.

Jonung, L. (1978) 'The long-run demand for money'. *Scandinavian Journal of Economics*, 80, 216–30.

Judd, J. P. and Scadding, J. L. (1982) 'The search for a stable money demand function'. *Journal of Economic Literature*, 20(3), 993–1023.

Judge, G. (1983) 'The stability of behavioural relationships and their empirical estimates'. *British Journal of Economic Issues*, 5(12), 1–14.

Kaldor, N. (1981) 'Fallacies of monetarism'. *Kredit und Kapital*, 4, 451–62.

Kamien, M. I. and Schwartz, N. I. (1982) *Market Structure and Innovation*. Cambridge: University Press.

Kane, E. J. (1977) 'Good intentions and unintended evil'. *Journal of Money, Credit, and Banking*, 9(1), 55–69.

Kane, E. J. (1979) 'The three faces of commercial bank liability management'. In Dooley *et al.* (1979), pp. 149–74.

Kane, E. J. (1981) 'Accelerating inflation, technological innovations, and the decreasing effectiveness of banking regulation'. *Journal of Finance*, 36(2), 355–67.

Kane, E. J. (1983) 'Policy implications of structural changes in financial markets'. *American Economic Review*, Papers, 73(2), 96–100.

Kaufman, G. G. (1969) 'More on an empirical definition of money'. *American Economic Review*, 59(1), 78–87.

Kaufman, H. (1980) Discussion. In Federal Reserve Bank of Boston (1980), 66–8.

Keynes, J. M. (1971) *A Treatise on Money*, 2 vols. (1st edn 1930). London: Macmillan.

Keynes, J. M. (1973) *The General Theory of Employment, Interest and Money* (1st edn 1936). London: Macmillan.

Khan, M. S. (1974) 'The stability of the demand for money function in the US 1901–1965'. *Journal of Political Economy*, 82(6), 1205–19.

Kindleberger, C. P. (1978) *Manias, Panics and Crashes*. London: Macmillan.

Kindleberger, C. P. (1984) Review of Wachtel (1982). *Economic Journal*, 94, 181–2.

Kindleberger, C. P. and Laffargue, J. P. (eds) (1982) *Financial Crises*. Cambridge: University Press.

Klein, B. (1974) 'Competitive interest payments on bank deposits and the long-run demand for money'. *American Economic Review*, 64, 931–49.

Klovland, J. T. (1983) 'The demand for money in secular perspective'. *European Economic Review*, 21, 193–218.

Knapp, G. F. (1924) *The State Theory of Money* (1st edn 1905). London: Macmillan.

Koot, R. S. (1975) 'A factor-analytic approach to an empirical definition of money'. *Journal of Finance*, 30(4), 1081–9.

Koot, R. S. (1977) 'On the St Louis equation and an alternative definition of the money supply'. *Journal of Finance*, 32(3), 917–20.

Kuznets, S. (1971) *Economic Growth of Nations*. Cambridge, Mass.: Harvard University Press/Belknap Press.

Laidler, D. (1969) 'The definition of money'. *Journal of Money, Credit, and Banking*, 1(3), 508–30.

Laidler, D. (1971) 'The influence of money on economic activity'. In Clayton *et al.* (1971), pp. 75–135.

Laidler, D. (1977) *The Demand for Money*, 2nd edn. New York: Dun-Donnelley.

Laidler, D. (1980) 'The demand for money in the United States – yet again'. In K. Brunner and A. H. Meltzer (eds), *On the State of Macroeconomics*, Carnegie–Rochester Conference Series, 12, pp. 219–71.

Laidler, D. (1981) 'Monetarism: an interpretation and an assessment'. *Economic Journal*, 91, 1–28.

Laidler, D. (1983) 'The "buffer stock" notion in monetary economics'. Supplement to *Economic Journal*, 94, 17–34.

Laumas, G. S. (1968) 'The degree of moneyness of savings deposits'. *American Economic Review*, 58, 501–3.

Laumas, G. S. and Mehra, Y. P. (1976) 'The stability of the demand for money'. *Review of Economics and Statistics*, 58, 463–8.

Laumas, G. S. and Mehra, Y. P. (1977) 'The stability of the demand for money function, 1900–1974'. *Journal of Finance*, 32(3), 911–16.

Lavington, F. (1934)   *The English Capital Market*, 3rd edn (1st edn 1922). London: Macmillan.

Lawrence, E. C. and Elliehausen, G. E. (1981) 'The impact of federal interest rate regulation on the small saver'. *Journal of Finance*, 36(3), 677–84.

Leamer, E. E. (1983) 'Let's take the con out of econometrics'. *American Economic Review*, 73(1), 31–43.

Lee, T. H. (1966) 'Substitutability of non-bank intermediary liabilities for money'. *Journal of Finance*, 21(3), 441–57.

Lerner, A. P. (1947) 'Money as a creature of the state'. *American Economic Review*, Papers, 37(2), 312–17.

Lieberman, C. (1977) 'Transactions demand for money and technological change'. *Review of Economics and Statistics*, 59, 307–17.

Lieberman, C. (1979) 'A transactions *v.* asset demand approach to the empirical definition of money'. *Economic Inquiry*, 17(2), 240–51.

Lieberman, C. (1980) 'Demand for money revisited'. *Journal of Money, Credit, and Banking*, 12(1), 43–57.

Llewellyn, R. T. (1980)   *International Financial Integration*. London: Macmillan.

Lombra, R. E. (1980) 'Monetary control: consensus or confusion'. In Federal Reserve Bank of Boston (1980), 270–305.

Lombra, R. E. (1982)   Conference comment. *Journal of Finance*, Papers, 37, 393.

Lombra, R. E. and Kaufman, H. M. (1978) 'Commercial banks and the federal funds market'. *Economic Inquiry*, 16(4), 549–62.

Lucas, R. E. (1981)   *Studies in Business Cycle Theory*. Oxford: Basil Blackwell.

McClam, W. D. (1982) 'Financial fragility and instability'. In Kindelberger and Laffargue (1982), 256–91.

McCloskey, D. N. (1983) 'The rhetoric of economics'. *Journal of Economic Literature*, 21(2), 481–517.

McKenzie, G. W. (1976)   *The Economics of the Eurocurrency System*. London: Macmillan.

McKenzie, G. W. (1981) 'Regulating the Euro-markets'. *Journal of Banking and Finance*, 5(1), 109–34.

McKenzie, G. W. and Thomas, S. (1983) 'Liquidity credit creation and international banking'. *Journal of Banking and Finance*, 7(4), 467–80.

McKinnon, R. I. (1973)   *Money and Capital in Economic Development*. Washington DC: Brookings Institution.

Maisel, S. J. (ed.) (1981)   *Risk and Capital Adequacy in Commercial Banks*. Chicago: University Press.

Marti, J. and Zeilinger, A. (1982)   *Micros and Money*. London: Policy Studies Institute.

Marty, A. L. (1961) 'Gurley and Shaw on money in the theory of finance'. *Journal of Political Economy*, 69(1), 56–62.

Mason, W. E. (1976) 'The empirical definition of money: a critique'. *Economic Inquiry*, 14(4), 525–38.

Mathias, P. (1969)   *The First Industrial Nation*. London: Macmillan.

Mayer, T. (1975) 'The structure of monetarism'. *Kredit und Kapital*, 8, 191–218; 293–316.

Mayer, T. (1982) 'Financial innovation – the conflict between micro and macro optimality'. *American Economic Review*, 72(2), Papers, 29–34.

Meigs, A. J. (1975) 'Recent innovations: do they require a new framework for monetary analysis?' In Silber (1975), pp. 177–96.

Meltzer, A. H. (1963) 'Demand for money: the evidence from time series'. *Journal of Political Economy*, 71, 219–46.

Meltzer, A. H. (1969a) 'Controlling money'. *Federal Reserve Bank of St Louis Review*, 51, 16–24.

Meltzer, A. H. (1969b) 'Money, intermediation and growth'. *Journal of Economic Literature*, 7(1), 27–56.

Miles, M. A. (1978) 'Currency substitution, flexible exchange rates, and monetary interdependence'. *American Economic Review*, 68(3), 428–36.

Miller, M. H. and Orr, D. (1966) 'A model of the demand for money by firms'. *Quarterly Journal of Economics*, 80(3), 413–42.

Mills, T. C. (1983) 'Composite monetary indicators for the UK'. *Bank of England Discussion Paper*, Technical Series, no. 3.

Mills, T. C. and Wood, G. E. (1977) 'Money substitutes and monetary policy in the UK, 1922–1974'. *European Economic Review*, 10, 19–36.

Minford, P. and Peel, D. (1983) *Rational Expectations and the New Macroeconomics*. Oxford: Martin Robertson.

Minsky, H. P. (1957) 'Central banking and money market changes'. *Quarterly Journal of Economics*, 71(2), 171–87.

Minsky, H. P. (1969) 'Private sector asset management and the effectiveness of monetary policy'. *Journal of Finance*, 34(2), 223–38.

Minsky, H. P. (1977) 'A theory of systemic fragility'. In E. I. Altman and A. W. Sametz (eds), *Financial Crises*. New York: John Wiley, pp. 138–52.

Minsky, H. P. (1978) 'The financial instability hypothesis'. *Thames Papers in Political Economy*, Autumn.

Minsky, H. P. (1982) 'The financial instability hypothesis'. In Kindleberger and Laffargue (1982), pp. 13–39.

Mints, L. W. (1945) *A History of Banking Theory*. Chicago: University Press.

Mises, L. von (1953) *Theory of Money and Credit* (1st edn 1912). London: Jonathan Cape.

Mises, L. von (1978) *On the Manipulation of Money and Credit*, trans. P. L. Greaves. New York: Free Market Books.

Mitchell, W. C. (1927) *Business Cycles*. Washington DC: National Bureau of Economic Research.

Modigliani, F. and Papademos, L. (1980) 'The structure of financial markets and the monetary mechanism'. In Federal Reserve Bank of Boston (1980), pp. 111–55.

Monetary Policy Report to Congress (1983) *Federal Reserve Bulletin*, 69, 127–39.

Monetary Policy Report to Congress (1984) *Federal Reserve Bulletin*, 70, 69–89.

Monopolies Commission (1968) *Barclays, Lloyds, Martins: Report on the Proposed Merger*. London: HMSO.

Moore, B. J. (1968) *An Introduction to the Theory of Finance*. New York: Free Press.

Moore, B. J. (1983) 'Unpacking the post-Keynesian black box'. *Journal of Post Keynesian Economics*, 5(4), 537–56.

Morgan, E. V. and Harrington, R. L. (1973) 'Reserve assets and the money supply'. *Manchester School*, 41(1), 73–86.

Moroney, J. R. and Wilbratte, B. J. (1976) 'Money and money substitutes'. *Journal of Money, Credit, and Banking*, 8(1), 181–98.

Mundell, R. A. (1963) 'Capital mobility and stabilisation policy under fixed and flexible exchange rates'. *Canadian Journal of Economics and Political Science*, 39, 475–85.

National Prices and Incomes Board (1967) *Bank Charges*. London: NPIB.

Nicholas, T. (1982) 'Effects on retail banking'. In Institute of Bankers, *The Banks and Technology in the 1980s*, London, pp. 19–41.

Niehans, J. (1978) *The Theory of Money*. Baltimore: Johns Hopkins University Press.

Niehans, J. (1982) 'Innovation in monetary policy'. *Journal of Banking and Finance*, 6, 9–28.

Niehans, J. (1983) 'Financial regulation, multinational banking and monetary policy'. *Journal of Banking and Finance*, 7(4), 537–51.

OECD (1979) *Monetary Targets and Inflation Control*, Monetary Studies Series. Paris: OECD.

Ormrod, P. (ed.) (1979) *Modelling the Economy*. London: Heinemann.

Ostroy, J. M. (1973) 'The informational efficiency of monetary exchange'. *American Economic Review*, 64(4), 597–610.

Papademos, L. and Modigliani, F. (1983) 'Inflation, financial and fiscal structure, and the monetary mechanism'. *European Economic Review*, 21, 203–50.

Parkin, M. (1978) 'A comparison of alternative techniques of monetary control under rational expectations'. *Manchester School*, 46(3), 252–87.

Parkin, M. and Bade, R. (1982) *Modern Macroeconomics*. Oxford: Philip Allan.

Patinkin, D. (1961) 'Financial intermediaries and the logical structure of monetary theory'. *American Economic Review*, 51(1), 95–116.

Phillips, P. H. (1983) *Building Society Finance*, Wokingham: Van Nostrand Reinhold.

Pierce, J. L. (1980) 'Making reserve targets work'. In Federal Reserve Bank of Boston (1980), pp. 241–3.

Pierce, J. L. (1982) 'How regulations affect monetary control'. *Journal of Money, Credit, and Banking*, 14(4), Part 2, 775–95.

Pierce, J. L. (1984) 'Did financial innovations hurt the great monetarist experiment?'. *American Economic Review*, 74(2), 392–6.

Podolski, T. M. (1973) *Socialist Banking and Monetary Control*. Cambridge: University Press.

Poole, W. (1970) 'Opimal choice of monetary policy instruments in a simple stochastic macro model'. *Quarterly Journal of Economics*, 84, 197–216.

Porter, R. D., Simpson, T. D. and Manskopf, E. (1979) 'Financial innovation and monetary aggregates'. *Brookings Papers on Economic Activity*, 1, 213–29.

Radcliffe Report (1959) *Committee on the Working of the Monetary System*, Cmnd 827. London: HMSO.

Radecki, J. L. and Wenninger, J. (1983) 'Shifts in money demand'. *Federal Reserve Bank of New York Quarterly Review*, Summer, 1–11.

Redlich, F. (1947) *The Molding of American Banking*, Part I. New York: Hafner.

Reid, M. (1982) *The Secondary Banking Crisis, 1973–5*. London: Macmillan.

Reisman, D. A. (1971) 'H. Thornton and classical monetary economics'. *Oxford Economic Papers*, 23(1), 70–89.

Revell, J. R. S. (1972) 'A secondary banking system'. In Johnson (1972), pp. 422–31.

Revell, J. R. S. (1973) *The British Financial System*. London: Macmillan.

Revell, J. R. S. (1983a) *Banking and Electronic Fund Transfers*. Paris: OECD.

Revell, J. R. S. (1983b) 'Efficiency in the financial sector'. In D. Shepherd *et al.* (eds), *Microeconomic Efficiency and Macroeconomic Performance*. Oxford: Philip Allan, pp. 137–70.

Ritter, L. S. (1962) 'The structure of financial markets, income velocity, and the effectiveness of monetary policy'. *Schweizerische Zeitschrift fur Volkvirtschaft und Statistik*, 98(3), 276–89.

Ritter, L. S. (1963) 'The role of money in Keynesian theory'. In D. Carson (ed.), *Banking and Monetary Studies*. Homewood, Ill.: R. D. Irwin, pp. 134–50.

Robbins, L. (1958) *Robert Torrens and the Evolution of Classical Economics*. London: Macmillan.

Robinson, S. W. (1972) *Multinational Banking*. Leiden: A. W. Sijthoff.

Rohlwink, A. (1984) 'How asset and liability management improves performance'. *The Banker*, March, 41–5.

Rosenberg, N. (1982) *Inside the Black Box: Technology and Economics*. Cambridge: University Press.

Sargent, J. R. (1981) 'Problems of monetary targeting in the UK'. In Griffiths and Wood (1981), pp. 95–120.

Sargent, T. J. and Wallace, N. (1982) 'The real-bills doctrine versus the quantity theory.' *Journal of Political Economy*, 90(6), 1212–36.

Sayers, R. S. (1957) *Central Banking after Bagehot*. Oxford: Clarendon Press.

Sayers, R. S. (1960) 'Monetary thought and monetary policy in England'. *Economic Journal*, 70, 710–24.

Schmookler, J. (1966) *Invention and Economic Growth*. Cambridge, Mass.: Harvard University Press.

Schumpeter, J. A. (1947) 'The creative response in economic history'. *Journal of Economic History*, 7, 149–59.

Schumpeter, J. A. (1963) *History of Economic Analysis* (1st edn 1954). London: Allen and Unwin.

Schumpeter, J. A. (1964) *Business Cycles* (1st edn 1939). New York: McGraw-Hill.

Schumpeter, J. A. (1968) *The Theory of Economic Development* (1st edn 1934). Cambridge, Mass.: Harvard University Press.

Scitovsky, T. (1969) *Money and the Balance of Payments*. London: Unwin University Books.

Select Committee on Nationalized Industries (1969) Bank of England, HC 258. London: HMSO.

Shackle, G. L. S. (1972) *Epistemics and Economics*. Cambridge: University Press.

Shackle, G. L. S. (1974) *Keynesian Kaleidics*. Edinburgh: University Press.

Shaw, E. S. (1973) *Financial Deepening in Economic Development*. Oxford: University Press.

Sheppard, D. K. (1971) *The Growth and Role of UK Financial Institutions*. London: Methuen.

Silber, W. L. (ed.) (1975a) *Financial Innovation*. Farnborough, Hants: Lexington Books/D.C. Heath.

Silber, W. L. (1975b) 'Towards a theory of financial innovations'. In Silber (1975a), pp. 53–85.

Silber, W. L. (1983) 'The process of financial innovation'. *American Economic Review*, Papers, 73(2), 89–95.

Simons, H. C. (1936) 'Rules versus authorities in monetary policy'. *Journal of Political Economy*, 44(1), 1–30.

Simpson, T. D. (1980) 'The redefined monetary aggregates'. *Federal Reserve Bulletin*, February, 97–114.

Simpson, T. D. and Porter, R. D. (1980) 'Some issues involving the definition and interpretation of the monetary aggregates'. In Federal Reserve Bank of Boston (1980), pp. 161–234.

Slovin, M. B. and Sushka, M. E. (1975) 'The structural shift in the demand for money'. *Journal of Finance*, 30(3), 721–31.

Smith, W. L. (1956) 'On the effectiveness of monetary policy'. *American Economic Review*, 46(4), 588–606.

Spanos, A. (1984) 'Liquidity as latent variable'. *Oxford Bulletin of Economics and Statistics*, 46(2), 125–43.

Startz, R. (1979) 'Implicit interest on demand deposits'. *Journal of Political Economy*, 37, 1190–1291.

Stoneman, P. (1983) *The Economic Analysis of Technological Change*. Oxford: University Press.

Sumner, T. T. (1980) 'The operation of monetary targets'. In K. Brunner, A. H. Meltzer (eds), *Monetary Institutions and the Policy Process*, Carnegie–Rochester Conference Series on Public Policy, 13, pp. 91–130.

Sylla, R. (1982) 'Monetary innovation and crises in American economic history'. In Wachtel (1982), pp. 23–40.

Tatom, J. A. (1982) 'Recent financial innovations' *Federal Reserve Bank of St Louis Review*, 64(4), 23–35.

Tavlas, G. S. (1977) 'Chicago schools old and new on the efficacy of monetary policy'. *Banca Nazionale del Lavoro Quarterly Review*, 120, 51–73.

Temin, P. (1976) *Did Monetary Forces Cause the Great Depression?* New York: W. W. Norton.

Thirlwall, A. (1974) *Inflation, Saving and Growth in Developing Economies*. London: Macmillan.

Thompson, W. N. (1984) 'Money in UK macro models'. In D. Demery *et al.* (eds), *Macroeconomics*. Harlow: Longman, pp. 100–68.

Thornton, H. (1939) *An Enquiry into the Nature and Effects of the Paper Credit of Great Britain* (1st edn 1902). London: Allen and Unwin.

Timberlake, R. H. (1983) 'Methodological considerations in demand for money construction'. *Kredit und Kapital*, 3, 381–93.

Timberlake, R. H. and Fortson, J. (1967) 'Time deposits in the definition of money'. *American Economic Review*, 57(1), 190–4.

Tobin, J. (1958) 'Liquidity preference as behaviour towards risk'. *Review of Economic Studies*, 25, 65–86.

Tobin, J. (1965) 'Monetary interpretation of history'. *American Economic Review*, 55(3), 464–85.

Tobin, J. (1980) 'Stabilisation policy ten years after'. *Brookings Papers on Economic Activity*, 1, 18–71.

Tobin, J. (1981) 'The monetarist counter-revolution to-day'. *Economic Journal*, 91, 29–42.

Tobin, J. (1982) 'Money and finance in the macroeconomic process'. *Journal of Money, Credit, and Banking*, 14(2), 171–203.

Tobin, J. (1983a) 'Financial structure and monetary rules'. *Kredit und Kapital*, 2, 155–71.

Tobin, J. (1983b) 'Monetary policy: rules, targets, shocks'. *Journal of Money, Credit, and Banking*, 15(4), 506–18.

Tobin, J. (1984) 'On the efficiency of the financial system'. *Lloyds Bank Review*, 153, 1–15.

Vaubel, R. (1977) 'Free currency competition'. *Weltwirkschaftliches Archiv*, 113, 435–61.

Vaubel, R. (1984) 'The government's money monopoly: externalities or natural monopoly? *Kyklos*, 37(1), 27–58.

Viner, J. (1955) *Studies in the Theory of International Trade*. London: Allen and Unwin.

Volker, P. A. (1984) 'Report to a House of Representatives Committee'. *Federal Reserve Bulletin*, 70, 312–18.

Wachtel, P. (ed.) (1982) *Crises in the Economic and Financial Structure*. New York: Lexington Books.

Wallace, N. (1983) 'A legal restrictions theory of the demand for "money" and the role of monetary policy'. *Federal Reserve Bank of Minneapolis Quarterly Review*, Winter, 1–7.

Wallich, H. C. (1982) *Monetary Policy and Practice*. New York: Lexington Books.

Wallich, H. C. (1984) 'US deregulation'. *The Banker*, May, 25–8.

Walters, A. A. (ed.) (1973) *Money and Banking*. Harmondsworth: Penguin.

Weintraub, S. (1981) 'Monetarism's muddles'. *Kredit und Kapital*, 4, 464–95.

Wenninger, J. (1984) 'Financial innovation – a complex problem even in a simple framework'. *Federal Reserve Bank of New York Quarterly Review*, Summer, 1–8.

White, L. H. (1984a) 'Competitive payments systems and the unit of account'. *American Economic Review*, 74(4), 699–712.

White, L. H. (1984b) *Free Banking in Britain*. Cambridge: University Press.

White, W. H. (1981) 'The case for and against "disequilibrium" money'. *IMF Staff Papers*, 28(3), 534–72.

Wicksell, K. (1936) *Interest and Prices* (1st edn 1898). London: Macmillan.

Wilbratte, B. J. (1975) 'Some essential differences in the demand for money by households and by firms'. *Journal of Finance*, 30(4), 1091–9.

Wills, H. R. (1982) 'The simple economics of bank regulation'. *Economica*, 49, 249–59.

Wilson Committee (1979) *Secondary Stage Evidence*, Vols. 3 and 4. London: HMSO.

Wilson Committee (1980) *Appendices*, Cmnd 7937. London: HMSO.

Wilson Report (1980) 'Committee to Review the Functioning of Financial Institutions'. *Report*, Cmnd 7937. London: HMSO.

Wojnilower, A. M. (1980) 'The central role of credit crunches in recent financial history'. *Brookings Papers in Economic Activity*, 2, 277–326.

Wood, J. H. (1981) 'Financial intermediaries and monetary control'. *Journal of Monetary Economics*, 8, 145–63.

Zawadzki, K. F. (1981) *Competition and Credit Control*. Oxford: Basil Blackwell.

Index

Numbers with decimal points refer to sections, figures or tables; other numbers are page or chapter numbers.

247